Approaches to Teaching the Works of Gertrude Stein

Approaches to Teaching the Works of Gertrude Stein

Edited by

Logan Esdale

and

Deborah M. Mix

The Modern Language Association of America
New York 2018

Library of Congress Cataloging-in-Publication Data

Names: Esdale, Logan editor. | Mix, Deborah M. editor.
Title: Approaches to teaching the works of Gertrude Stein / edited by Logan Esdale and Deborah M. Mix.
Description: New York : The Modern Language Association of America, 2018. | Series: Approaches to teaching world literature | Includes bibliographical references and index.
Identifiers: LCCN 2018009931 | ISBN 9781603293433 (cloth : alk. paper) | ISBN 9781603293440 (pbk. : alk. paper)
Subjects: LCSH: Stein, Gertrude, 1874–1946—Study and teaching.
Classification: LCC PS3537.T323 Z5475 2018 | DDC 818/.5209—dc23
LC record available at https://lccn.loc.gov/2018009931

Approaches to Teaching World Literature 152
ISSN 1059-1133

Cover illustration of the paperback and electronic editions: *Newspaper and Fruit Dish*, by Juan Gris (1916), oil on canvas, gift of Collection Société Anonyme. Photo credit: Yale University Art Gallery.

Second printing 2018

Published by The Modern Language Association of America
85 Broad Street, suite 500, New York, New York 10004-2434
www.mla.org

CONTENTS

ACKNOWLEDGMENTS

We are grateful to the teachers who introduced us to Stein, the colleagues who encouraged this project, and the students who continue to help us read her work in new ways. The contributors to this volume have been wonderful and patient collaborators, and we're delighted to share their ideas. The Modern Language Association editorial staff and the anonymous readers have made the volume better along the way.

We want to hail our own teachers: Peter Quartermain, who assigned Ulla Dydo's *A Stein Reader* in a course on twentieth-century American poetry when Logan was an undergraduate at the University of British Columbia, and Charles Bernstein and the other faculty members in the Poetics Program in the University at Buffalo, State University of New York, who offered a Stein-based lingua franca when Logan was a doctoral student. Patrick O'Donnell, Robert Lamb, Siobhan Somerville, and Nancy Peterson shaped Deborah's approaches to Stein in myriad ways.

It seems we are always working some Stein into our syllabi, realizing how rousing her texts can be—and how many roles they can play—in the classroom. Thank you to the students who have persevered when they've wanted to give up, who have shared their frustrations and their insights, and who, in Logan's classes, have made so many brilliant poems with the words in *Tender Buttons*.

Logan sends particular salutations to his colleagues at Chapman University—Martin Nakell, Rebecca Goodman, and Joanna Levin—and at California State University, Long Beach—George Hart, Bill Mohr, and Eileen Klink—for their support. Deborah is grateful to friends and colleagues at Ball State University, including Adam Beach, Patrick Collier, and Emily Rutter, and at other institutions, especially Linda Kinnahan and Elizabeth Savage. Heartfelt thanks to our families: Lara Odell and Ida Esdale; and Timothy, Sadie, and Georgia Berg, for their love and support.

Finally, we want to thank each other.

Part One

MATERIALS

Family Life and Education

Born on 3 February 1874, Gertrude Stein was the youngest of five children, and one of two daughters, in a German Jewish immigrant family.[1] She was born in Allegheny, Pennsylvania, a suburb of Pittsburgh, where her father, Daniel, and his brother Solomon had a clothing and textiles store. She grew up in relatively affluent circumstances and was doted on as the baby of the family. The Steins lived in Europe from 1875 to 1879, in Vienna and then Paris—so English was a third language for Gertrude, along with German and French—before settling in Oakland, California, in 1880, where Daniel invested in real estate, stocks, and streetcar companies. (Solomon's family had gone to New York.) Gertrude was especially close to her brother Leo, two years her elder. She was also attached to her oldest brother, Michael, but little interested in her middle brother, Simon, or her sister, Bertha. After the death of her mother, Amelia (in 1888), and her father (in 1891), Michael became the head of the family, managing the investments and dispensing income.[2] In 1892 Gertrude and Bertha moved to Baltimore to be with their mother's family, and Gertrude set her sights on following her brothers to college: Michael had studied at the University of California, Berkeley, and at Johns Hopkins University, and Leo transferred from Berkeley to Harvard University in 1892.

Although Gertrude did not graduate high school, she was admitted in 1893 as a special student to the Harvard Annex, the women's college affiliated with Harvard (known as Radcliffe College by 1894), where, after belatedly completing a Latin requirement, she graduated magna cum laude in 1898. As an undergraduate she was active socially as a member of the Philosophy Club and the Idler's Club (drama), and she worked under the direction of Hugo Münsterberg, who called her an "ideal student" (Mellow 32), in the Harvard Psychological Laboratory. She also came to the attention of William James, who involved her in his experiments on automatic writing.[3] Despite her skepticism about automatic writing itself, she recalled James as having left "the really lasting impression of her Radcliffe life" (*Autobiography* 78). In particular, his ideas about consciousness and perception are often cited as a significant influence on her notion of the "continuous present," the principle that the act of perception requires "beginning again and again," as she puts it in "Composition as Explanation" (499); in the same essay she describes the "Melanctha" story in *Three Lives* as enacting this vision through "a constant recurring and beginning . . . in the direction of being in the present" (498).

In 1897 Stein returned to Baltimore and enrolled in medical school at Johns Hopkins. She was more interested in research than in tending to the sick, and by the program's final year (1900–01) she was reconsidering her commitment to medicine and not performing well. The faculty did not pass her, and although she continued some brain research for another year, assisting Llewellys Barker, and could make up course work for reevaluation, her medical career came to a close without a degree. Stein would later say that she left the program because "she was so bored she could not remember the things that of course the dullest medical student could not forget" (*Autobiography* 82). Her biographers, however, have described how she found herself in conflict with some of the faculty members, particularly the men responsible for teaching seminars in obstetrics and gynecology (Wagner-Martin 44; Wineapple 141). Her study of those subjects and her friendships with college-educated women, as well as encounters with Baltimore's immigrant and African American communities, would help shape her presentation of gendered and racial identities in texts such as *Three Lives*. At a time when few women attended college or received medical training, Stein was a trailblazer, though she would largely refuse to accept the mantle of feminist foremother. Recalling in *The Autobiography of Alice B. Toklas* a conversation with an equal-rights activist, she explained (under the Toklas mask), "Not . . . that she at all minds the cause of women or any other cause but it does not happen to be her business" (83).

What exactly her business was then was uncertain; by 1902 it was evident that at twenty-eight years old she would not become a doctor. She had been of two minds for the last decade: she admired certain professors and enjoyed access to university resources and student communities, but she could be careless about the requirements for the completion of her studies; within the institutions she found peers who shared her intellectual curiosity, but she also rebelled against training for a profession. Since her undergraduate days, though, her studies in psychology, zoology, and neurology had complemented her predilection for analyzing friends and sorting their behavior and thinking into types. Indeed, if she had a business then, it was studying the character of American women and men—their lives, their families, and where they were from. Unlike her New York relatives, the Solomon Stein family, Gertrude wanted not only to consume culture but also to create it. She identified with California's prudent, straight-talking pioneers and sun-baked, beckoning hills; Baltimore was her second home.[4] Out of these places and family dynamics and her aptitude for character study would come her first writing: her Hortense Sänger stories (written in 1895; set in San Francisco–Oakland and Baltimore), *Q. E. D.* (written in 1903; set in Baltimore, New York, and Europe), "Fernhurst" (written in 1904–05; set in Bryn Mawr), *Three Lives* (written in 1905–06; set in Baltimore), and *The Making of Americans* (written in 1903–11; set in New York, Baltimore, and Oakland).[5] More than culture or ideas or a job, she was interested in people—not in their sickness but in all the varieties of their normality.

Transatlantic Stein

By 1902 Stein was embarking on a number of transitions: she began the move from America to Europe; she was in love with May Bookstaver, a Bryn

Mawr graduate in 1898, and coming out as lesbian; and she was becoming a writer. Leo had moved to Italy in 1900, and in May 1902 Gertrude joined him there; by late summer they were in England, first in Fernhurst, a countryside village, and then in London, where she stayed until February 1903. She was reading voraciously—biographies, novels, memoirs, letter collections—and from this self-assigned reading program "she hoped to emerge a writer" (Wineapple 177). While the desire to be near Bookstaver would take her back to New York in 1903 and again in 1904, that period of almost a year in Europe (1902–03) seems to have proved to her that except for Bookstaver she had little reason to return. When that relationship (begun in 1900) came to an end (in 1903–04), and 27 rue de Fleurus, albeit a rental, had the feel of home—Leo was settled in by April 1903, and Michael, his wife Sarah, and their son Allan moved to Paris in December—the decision to live abroad was finalized. Stein would return to America only once more in her life, thirty years later. She remained abroad, but, as she said in 1944, "I have lived in France the best and longest part of my life and I love France and the French but after all I am an American" (*Wars* 132). This patriotic sentiment appears in *Wars I Have Seen* (1943–44), her third memoir after *The Autobiography of Alice B. Toklas* (1932) and *Everybody's Autobiography* (1936–37), which all remember growing up and being in America.

With Leo leading the way, the Steins began collecting art by Cézanne, Gauguin, Renoir, Vallotton, Manguin, Degas, Toulouse-Lautrec, Manet, Bonnard, Matisse, and Picasso. Gertrude and Leo were not rich—in these early Paris years they had a monthly income of around $150 each, or around $3,600 annually together (Mellow 26)—but by practicing some frugality they could afford to employ a servant and to buy the work of artists whose careers were just beginning or were not yet acclaimed.[6] As enthusiasts they had an open door to visitors wanting to see modern art, and by 1906 "[s]o many people clamored after a look that Gertrude and Leo concluded they had better organize one night a week—they chose Saturday" (Wineapple 242). This Saturday salon (and that of Michael and Sarah, who lived close by, at 58 rue Madame) would continue until 1914, except during summer holidays in Florence.[7] In these years, as visitors studied their art collection, Stein studied the visitors, their habits and modes of self-expression. The most important visitor arrived in 1907: Alice Toklas. They met at Michael and Sarah's, and, basically, "until Gertrude's death thirty-nine years later, they were never apart. They never travelled without each other, or entertained separately, or worked on independent projects" (Souhami 12).[8] While they did not publicly discuss their lesbian identities—because doing so probably would have threatened Stein's career—their relationship was quite openly known at the time. Stein sometimes relegated Toklas to "wifely" duties and assumed a dominant role in social gatherings, but she did not hide Toklas or their status as a couple. In the next section we offer a detailed narrative on Toklas and her role in Stein's life and career. To the end of this section, when Toklas is not referred to by name, her presence should be implied.

In the years after 1906, though Stein's American friends knew that she was writing, it was the family art collection that led to her first transatlantic renown. By the 1913 Armory Show in New York, her two identities—collector and writer—were both receiving public attention. *Three Lives* (1909) attracted positive reviews, and in 1912 some of her prose-poetry portraits (of Matisse, Picasso, and Mabel Dodge) had been published "to acclaim as well as to controversy" (Wagner-Martin 110). To time with the Armory Show, Dodge published "Speculations; or, Post-impressionism in Prose," which reinforced the link between Stein and modern art.[9] Although a good deal of the attention Stein received then, and especially after *Tender Buttons* was published a year later, was in the form of caricature, and she has ever since been read in a context with painters, by 1913 she was established as a writer and authority on modernism.[10] The war was about to shatter international arts communities, and just before it did, the Stein household also came apart: by spring 1914 they had split up their collection, and Leo had moved to Italy. (In the next section, on Toklas, we say more about the Gertrude-Leo split.) The heyday of the salon had passed, but Stein had had her first experience of fame.

In 1908–10 Stein started leaving American settings and fiction behind to write prose-poetry portraits, not just of people but also of things, culminating in *Tender Buttons* (1912). Writing portraits was one way she came to know her Paris environment; as she did them, she was looking and listening more than remembering.[11] "It really takes a war to make you know a country, I had known only Paris until 1914 and then I learned to know France," she reflected in 1939, as another war was beginning (*Paris* 72). For more than a year (1915–16) she was on the island of Mallorca, still writing intensively. But starting in March 1917, Stein and Toklas drove a Ford supply truck in southern France (Perpignan and Nîmes) for the American Fund for French Wounded, and, after armistice in November 1918, they did relief work (February to June 1919) in German-speaking Alsace, because "[w]e both spoke German" (Toklas, *What* 101). This crisis put Stein's polyglot and medical school backgrounds into action. America entered the war shortly after she did, and she enjoyed meeting doughboys.[12] She liked that they considered her only as a fellow American. After the war, however, she became a mentor to some (e.g., Ernest Hemingway) and collaborated with others (e.g., Virgil Thomson), and while not everyone would have liked Janet Flanner's assessment in the mid 1920s that "[n]o American writer is taken more seriously than Miss Stein by the Paris modernists," it was hard to disagree (qtd. in Wagner-Martin 180).[13] If Stein's fame as a writer had earlier been dependent on her art collection, now it was dependent on her personality and image: on the one hand, little magazines such as *The Little Review* and *Transition* were publishing her writing; on the other, her new (as of 1 January 1927), closely cropped haircut, given to her by Toklas, could appear equally noteworthy (Holbrook and Dilworth 24).

The affinity Stein felt for France went beyond Paris. In 1922–23 she and Toklas stayed in Saint-Rémy and then Nice; subsequently, from 1924 to 1928 they spent the summer and fall at a hotel in the small town of Belley, and then its close neighbors: a rented house in Bilignin (1929–43) and a rented house near Culoz (1943–44). The women loved their garden and the cuisine, the landscape and the people in it, many of them farmers. Much of what Stein wrote in the last two decades of her career was written in the country, not in Paris. Although friends visited her in Bilignin, this move took her away from the American tourists and expatriates in Paris and the international community in general; instead of the Eiffel Tower, she had a view of the Alps. When Thomson got to know her in the late 1920s, he found that she "read and spoke French comfortably" (*Virgil Thomson* 185), and that ability allowed her to fit in with the locals. The rural lifestyle must have sharpened her fluency. This context explains, in part, her turn to the French language, working in particular with Thomson, Georges Hugnet, and Bernard Faÿ on translation projects in the late 1920s and early 1930s.[14] As she grew closer to the people of France, she wanted them to be able to read her work.

Stein never stopped writing portraits, and around 1913, after fiction and then poetry, she began writing plays.[15] She uses fragments of common, conversational language and puts voices in dialogue, voices to be performed.[16] In 1932, she added memoir to her list of genres with *The Autobiography of Alice B. Toklas*, and when it came out the next year, her audience burgeoned: her earlier experiences with fame—as cubist poet and Paris monument—now appeared minor in comparison. The *Autobiography* describes the lives of Stein and Toklas, the international Paris arts scene, and World War I, but it is also an annotated bibliography, contextualizing much of her work title by title. In her follow-up, *Everybody's Autobiography*, she reflects on success. Some things did not change—an audience divided in its opinion, for instance: "I can be accepted more than I was but I can be refused almost as often" (47). Success led to a return home, via an American lecture tour (largely organized by Toklas) from October 1934 to May 1935.[17] This return was exciting: "I used to say that was long ago in between I never had thought of going, I used to say that I would not go to America until I was a real lion a real celebrity at that time of course I did not really think I was going to be one. But now we were coming and I was going to be one" (173). The experience of being lionized was, however, equally disconcerting, and much of what she wrote after 1933 addresses the tension between publicity and creativity and is self-conscious toward readers.[18]

In January 1938 Stein and Toklas left 27 rue de Fleurus and rented 5 rue Christine, but over the next eight years they would spend only a little more than two of them at this new Paris address. After the move they were soon in Bilignin, and besides the winter of 1938–39 in Paris and an overnight visit there in September 1939, they were in Bilignin and Culoz until December 1944; the war began while they were there, and that was where they stayed. For the last year and a half of Stein's life, she and Toklas lived in Paris. Stein died on 27 July 1946 following an operation for abdominal cancer; she was 72.

These war years (1939–44) have been a major focus of attention in the last two decades. Stein has always been controversial: first, from *Three Lives* on, she turned literary conventions and grammar rules upside down to both acclaim and derision. More recently, critics have contrasted her progressive aesthetics with her conservative politics, examining her representation of African American characters in "Melanctha," for instance, or her criticism of Roosevelt's New Deal.[19] And then there is Stein and Toklas's survival during World War II. Albeit through food shortage and little contact with the outside world, this Jewish lesbian couple managed to avoid Nazi removal; their lives were at risk. (Culoz was liberated in August 1944.) This survival must have entailed some complicated interactions and perhaps some willful ignorance. We strongly encourage reading widely on this subject and searching out the facts.[20] We can offer here only a brief summary.

From June 1940 to November 1942 the Belley area was in the unoccupied southern zone, where Vichy nominally had control,[21] and the death toll for Jews in France as a whole (25% deported, never to return) was not as high as in other parts of Europe (Poznanski 462, 475). Stein and Toklas received protection from the villagers of Belley. A farmer with whom Stein discussed her decision to stay and not leave for Switzerland or America said, inclusively, "Here in this little corner we are *en famille*" (Stein, *How Writing* 121). As Joan Retallack has pointed out, "She and Toklas were protected by goodwill; anyone [in Belley] could have turned them in, but no one did" (*Selections* 67).[22] They were also protected by Bernard Faÿ, but in this relationship trouble lies. A French professor of American history—his books include *The American Experiment* (1929), *George Washington: Republican Aristocrat* (1931), and *Roosevelt and His America* (1933)—Faÿ had been a close friend since the late 1920s. He had promoted Stein's writing and advised her on legal matters and her American lecture tour; she had dedicated *Lectures in America* to him. In August 1940, he was appointed by Philippe Pétain's Vichy government to be the director of France's national library, the Bibliothèque Nationale, and adviser to Pétain himself. Exactly what protection Faÿ was able to extend to Stein and Toklas in Bilignin remains unknown. The controversy explored by Janet Malcolm's *Two Lives* (2007) and Barbara Will's *Unlikely Collaboration* (2011), for instance, concerns the Stein-Faÿ friendship and his suggestion, apparently, that she translate into English a book of Pétain's, *Paroles aux français: Messages et écrits, 1934–1941*, a task she started but did not complete.[23] (Faÿ would be arrested in 1944 for collaboration with the Nazis and found guilty in 1946, in part for his role in the persecution of Freemasons.) In the end, Faÿ did help save Stein and Toklas's art collection in Paris, but their survival over the last year and a half, when the Belley area was under German control, was probably due in large part to village safeguarding.

Grateful for America's role in her liberation, Stein was an emphatic patriot after the war. The two major texts of her brief postwar period are *Brewsie and Willie*, based on conversations with American GIs, and the opera *The Mother*

Of Us All, featuring Susan B. Anthony and other American voices from the last century. But for most her career she had characterized her identity as hybrid, saying things like, "I am an American and I have lived half my life in Paris, not the half that made me but the half in which I made what I made" ("American" 62). She repeatedly made the case that she lived in France for the freedom she felt: "Your parent's home is never a place to work" (*How Writing* 51); indeed, living in France "has left me more intensely alone with my eyes and my english" (*Autobiography* 70). We see this search for freedom most clearly when we picture her in the countryside: she went to Paris to be "alone . . . with [her] english," and when Paris was teeming with Americans in the 1920s, she escaped to Belley.

One final suggestion: read *The Autobiography of Alice B. Toklas* but do not rely solely on it for the story of Stein's life and work. Approach the book with some caution, as the Stein-Toklas perspective is not always historically accurate; the anecdotes are told as they were remembered, not necessarily as they happened. Stein biographies, the collections of her letters, and critical books such as Richard Bridgman's *Gertrude Stein in Pieces*, Bruce Kellner's *A Gertrude Stein Companion*, and Ulla Dydo's *Gertrude Stein: The Language That Rises* offer useful and necessary contexts for her story. The *Autobiography* aside, Stein usually wrote in the present about the present, and these books inform us where she was and who she saw when she wrote. Even at its most opaque her work was rooted in her life, and the two—like America and France—were mutually constitutive.

Alice Toklas

In 1950, four years after Stein's death, Alice Toklas was visited by John Malcolm Brinnin, who intended to write the first Stein biography.[24] After his visit, she wrote to Carl Van Vechten:

> I got him to exclude me from his book because the atmosphere of [Gertrude's] home was a private matter—that if my existence had ever made the slightest difference to her work it was nothing to equal the effect—for example—of landscape. . . . It was agreed my name could not be ignored in connection with the Plain Edition but not elsewhere. (Burns, *Staying* 205)

On the issue of her "existence" making a "difference" to Stein's work, then, Toklas was skeptical, and perhaps with good reason. Even though she and Stein were inseparable from 1907 to 1946, and *The Autobiography of Alice B. Toklas* suggests an intimate dialogue of perspectives, it remains an open question how much a knowledge of their relationship might help us understand Stein's writing.[25] Toklas was unquestionably essential to Stein's life and career, managing her days so that Stein was free to write, typing her manuscripts, and offering devotion to her craft and purpose. Just one form this devotion took was the one she acknowledged to Brinnin: the Plain Edition press in the early 1930s. At Toklas's initiative they published five Stein books.

That letter to Van Vechten had two parts, Toklas's self-effacement and the report that Stein's unpublished novel *Mrs. Reynolds* might appear in *Elements*, a new literary magazine. Toklas may not have directly affected Stein's compositional practice as much as, for instance, Stein's studies in psychology or the landscape around Bilignin, but during Stein's life and after it was Toklas who helped move the work from manuscript to print. After 1946, working with Van Vechten and Donald Gallup, who was the librarian at Yale University Library in charge of Stein's archive, Toklas was instrumental in publishing many texts never before available to readers: after *Four in America* (1947) and *Things As They Are* (1950),[26] eight volumes appeared from Yale University Press (1951–58). She also encouraged Donald Sutherland, whose *Gertrude Stein: A Biography of Her Work* (1951) was the first critical study of Stein's work, and stoked the Toklas legend with *The Alice B. Toklas Cook Book* (1954), a mixture of recipes and sharply observed reminiscence, and with *What Is Remembered* (1963), which reprises the earlier *Autobiography*. Edward Burns's *Staying On Alone: Letters of Alice B. Toklas* (1973) reveals not only Toklas's care with Stein's legacy but also her wit and evocative commentary. The letters (1946–66) are evidence that Toklas's voice determined the style of Stein's monumental *Autobiography*.

Alice Babette Toklas was born three years after Stein, on 30 April 1877, in San Francisco. The Stein family settled across the bay in Oakland three years later. Although they did not meet until 1907, when Toklas arrived in Paris with her friend Harriet Levy, a childhood friend of Stein's sister-in-law Sarah, this shared California background endeared each to the other.[27] Toklas was an only child when she toured Europe with her parents in 1885, her brother, Clarence, being born 1887 (he died in 1937, a suicide). From 1890 to 1895 the Toklas family was in Seattle, and in 1897, now back in San Francisco, her mother Emma died. For the next decade Toklas ran the household, raising her brother and tending to her father, Ferdinand (who died in 1924), and when the door to Paris opened in 1907, she flew through it. Toklas and Levy were roommates until July 1910, when Levy returned to America, but by the summer of 1908, in Italy, Toklas and Stein had pledged themselves to each other. It can be said that they became engaged then. Toklas became Stein's typist and primary reader: in the evenings "Gertrude talked over her work of the day [on *The Making of Americans*], which I typed the following morning. Frequently these were the characters or incidents of the previous day. It was like living history. I hoped it would go on forever" (*What* 54).

In 1910 Stein wrote "Ada," telling the story of Toklas back in San Francisco in a household of men. After finally leaving home, Ada began "telling stories that were charming" to "one who was loving" and "listening," and "certainly Ada all her living then was happier in living than any one else," except perhaps the one loving, listening, and writing (103).[28] This was Stein's first love poem for Toklas. She probably wrote "Ada" shortly after Toklas moved into 27 rue de Fleurus with her and Leo, late in 1910. By that point brother and sister had grown apart—Leo did not like the direction Stein's work was taking with *The Making of Americans* and the portraits—and Toklas's faith ("I hoped it would go on forever") both helped Stein and drove the wedge between the siblings more deeply. The Saturday evening salon was soon hosted by the two women exclusively. Stein and Toklas took summer holidays on their own—to Spain, not Italy, as had been the Stein family tradition—and when Leo left Paris permanently, moving to Italy in 1913–14, the long engagement was over and Stein and Toklas were, as it were, married.

In 1932, when Stein wrote the *Autobiography* from Toklas's perspective, she told what sounds like an old joke between them: "Before I decided to write this book my twenty-five years with Gertrude Stein, I had often said that I would write, The wives of geniuses I have sat with. I have sat with so many" (14). Apparently Stein could be the only woman among men when the male "geniuses" visited with their wives, and it was Toklas's responsibility to entertain the latter. Yet if Stein played the husband and Toklas the wife, and if Stein could appear more masculine than feminine, Stein was also utterly dependent on Toklas. Generally speaking, Toklas rose early and managed the routine of the day. Back in San Francisco, Toklas did this sort of domestic work for her brother and father, but now it was not just in service to a person but a career: Stein's success would be theirs together. And many more texts like "Ada" were to come after 1910, expressing their love and desire for each other, especially in 1915–16, when they lived on Mallorca: "Alice was everywhere" in what Stein wrote that year, including "Lifting Belly" (Simon 99).[29] The collaborative spirit is perhaps best conveyed in the story behind the famous Stein motto:

> Speaking of the device of rose is a rose is a rose is a rose, it was I [Toklas] who found it in one of Gertrude Stein's manuscripts ["Sacred Emily" (1913)] and insisted upon putting it as a device on the letter paper, on the table linen and anywhere that she would permit that I would put it. I am very pleased with myself for having done so. (*Autobiography* 138)

The most famous Steinism was put forward by Toklas.

After reading and typing the manuscripts,[30] managing the household and mottos, playing lover and muse, and influencing where they lived,[31] Toklas asserted her authority through her oversight of Stein's personal relationships. If she did not care for someone or felt jealous, summary dismissal could be the result.[32] Recently, critical attention has focused on the moment when, in 1932, Toklas discovered that an old friend of Stein's, May Knoblauch, née Bookstaver, had been more than just a friend; after learning that Stein had once been in love with May and had based *Q. E. D.* on their affair, Toklas demanded that Stein remove the word "may" from her then-in-composition *Stanzas in Meditation*.[33] Stein's revising her writing over a lovers' quarrel reminds us that Toklas's power should not be underestimated. And neither should their mutual devotion. Stein's death made Toklas a lonely widow, and in 1957 she converted to Catholicism in part because—odd though the logic may be, since both women were secular Jews—she took comfort in the idea that she and Stein could be reunited in heaven (Simon 238).[34] Toklas was almost ninety when she died, on 7 March 1967, after four decades of life with Stein and two decades of faithfully curating Stein's reputation after her death.

Yale Archive

"The story of Miss Stein's presentation of this material to the Yale Library goes back to 1937 when, after depositing some of his own manuscripts at the University Library, Thornton Wilder went to France and persuaded Miss Stein to do likewise" (News bulletin). So said the Yale University News Bureau in 1947, promoting the exhibit of Gertrude Stein materials then on display. The exhibit celebrated the fundamental completion of a decade-long process: the making of the Stein archive. Composed of manuscript notebooks, typescripts, correspondence, clippings, photographs, and much else, the archive is both immense and comprehensive. Stein saved practically everything, and almost all of it is at Yale's Beinecke Rare Book and Manuscript Library. Gallup, the archive's curator from 1947 to 1980, speculated in 1947 that "far from being dead, Gertrude Stein has perhaps only just begun to live" ("Always" 258). No dust has settled on these materials.

This archive has played four roles. First, in its early years, it advertised just how much Stein writing was still awaiting publication. Second, it documents her creative process and the vision she had of her career's work, how systematically she made her way through a series of aesthetic styles. Third, its materials—the correspondence especially—have reinforced the perception that she was a central figure in the modernist world. And fourth, Yale's promotion of this archive played a significant role in the turn to underrepresented groups—Jews, women, blacks. The emergence of modernist gender and race studies later in the century owes a debt to the collecting work that Stein's archive inspired.[35]

The Stein archive began in 1937, when Wilder visited Stein in Bilignin and brokered an arrangement with Yale. For the next eight years, the understanding was that the materials would be held for safekeeping, along with a few gifts outright (Gallup, "Gertrude Stein Collection" 22). In 1945 she "formally relinquished title" to the materials and affirmed her intention that Yale would receive everything she still had (25); her 23 July 1946 will reiterated this arrangement. Shortly before her death, she sent the materials that had accumulated since 1940 (the war years had halted her construction of the archive), and thereafter Toklas would forward the rest.

When Wilder returned to the United States, he brought with him two "large valises full of her MSS which she is donating to the Yale University Library. There are several 'layers' of parts of The Making of Americans; there is A Long Gay Book; Tender Buttons, etc." (Burns and Dydo, *Letters* 184n).[36] By 1938 the manuscripts were cataloged and were "in number about half the total now [1947] owned by the library" (Gallup, "Gertrude Stein Collection" 22). In 1941 Yale held its first exhibition of her materials, and to accompany it Gallup co-wrote, with Robert Bartlett Haas, *A Catalogue of the Published and Unpublished Writings of Gertrude Stein* (Haas and Gallup). Its final section listed all 533 titles. The texts that had been published were highlighted in small capitals; most had not been published. The catalog and exhibition were an open invitation to readers and publishers. In *Everybody's Autobiography*, Stein had said, "I wanted printed all the things that have not been printed" and "if it is not printed [now] some one will discover it later" (94, 110). The archive was to be the place for such discovery.

Stein embraced this archive project. She had long been collecting and preserving her manuscripts and letters alongside collecting and curating visual art in her home, and so her sense of how Yale could promote her work as a writer as a gallerist promotes the work of a painter was three decades in the making. She had hung notebook sketches by Picasso alongside his paintings, a curator's decision equivalent to what visitors to the 1941 and 1947 exhibitions beheld: the juxtaposition of published texts with related manuscripts and letters.[37] With the help of friends, she placed at Yale a collection of materials that allows us to contextualize her writing in two ways: with a chronology of composition established, we can compare texts from across her career, as variations or departures, and we can delve into her fashioning of a public personality. In the archive, private and public intimately intersect. Shortly after the 1941 exhibition closed, Norman Holmes Pearson argued that a

> full comprehension of the meaning of Miss Stein's work requires, far more than for that of most writers, an acquaintance with all that she has written. The knowledge of where she was makes easier the understanding of where she is. Many of these steppingstones of Miss Stein's literary progress have been mentioned by her in her autobiographies and discussions of her own work. They have never before, however, been available to the student and critic of literature. (46)

As Dydo would later reformulate the Pearson argument, Stein's "life's work is not only a series of discrete pieces but also a single continuous work" (*Gertrude Stein* 78); with the archive we can "follow her progress" and "represent her development" (420–21). With its relative completeness and the comparative possibilities it offers, within itself and with other collections at Yale, the archive has been an ideal and necessary context in which to read Stein.

Publication History

Gertrude Stein wrote nine books of fiction and three of poetry, three autobiographies, two produced librettos, three books for children, three books that articulate her creative principles, and, in her lifetime, five collections with various pieces (plays, operas, portraits, and other prose poetry)—a number of like collections came out posthumously. She wrote a lot of letters. She wrote books about Picasso and her adopted French home, and books that defy categorization (e.g., *How to Write*, *Four in America*, and *The Geographical History of America*). In "the time of the composition" no one of these was for her more important than the others; each was "a thing made by being made" ("Composition" 497, 495).[38]

1909–25

Writing from this period has been particularly appealing to teachers and scholars. *The Making of Americans* (written in 1903–11, published by Contact Editions in 1925) is a 925-page novel, but despite its daunting length it has been popular in the classroom, both in full and in excerpted form (the Heath and Norton anthologies of American literature include sections, as does Dydo's *A Stein Reader*). Much of what Stein wrote in this period was relatively brief or, as in the case of *Tender Buttons* (written in 1912, published by Claire Marie in 1914), can be excerpted for students. Some of her first publications were portraits, including "Picasso" and "Matisse" (written in 1909–10, published in *Camera Work* in 1912). Along with *Tender Buttons* and the portraits, Stein's first published book, *Three Lives* (written in 1905–06, published by Grafton Press in 1909), is frequently taught; many instructors report, in the survey distributed for this volume, teaching one of its three stories, "Melanctha," on its own. Other pieces from this period frequently mentioned by survey respondents are "Ada," "Sacred Emily," "Susie Asado," *Ladies' Voices*, "Miss Furr and Miss Skeene," and "Pink Melon Joy," all of which were collected in *Geography and Plays* (written in 1908–20, published by Four Seas in 1922) and are relatively brief.

1926–32

Stein continued publishing with small presses, including Leonard Woolf and Virginia Woolf's Hogarth Press, which issued *Composition as Explanation* after Stein gave it as a lecture at Cambridge and Oxford in June 1926, and Laura Riding and Robert Graves's Seizin Press, which brought out *An Acquaintance with Description* (written in 1926, published in 1929). She was also published by the little magazines associated with modernism, including *Transition*, *Broom*,

The Little Review, and *The Transatlantic Review*, as well as more mainstream magazines like *Vanity Fair*. As *Geography and Plays* had done, *Useful Knowledge* (written in 1915–27, published by Payson and Clarke in 1928) collected various pieces. Stein's collaborations with artists resulted in editions featuring lithographs by Juan Gris (*A Book Concluding with As a Wife Has a Cow A Love Story* [written in 1923, published by Galerie Simon in 1926]) and by Elie Lascaux (*A Village Are You Ready Yet Not Yet A Play In Four Acts* [written in 1923, published by Galerie Simon in 1928]). She worked with translators (Georges Hugnet and Virgil Thomson) on an abridged French edition of *The Making of Americans* (Éditions de la Montagne, 1929) and *Dix Portraits* (written in 1913–29, published by Éditions de la Montagne in 1930). Stein and Toklas then started their own imprint, Plain Edition. Beginning with the novel *Lucy Church Amiably* (written in 1927, published in 1930), they then published *How to Write* (written in 1927–31, published in 1931); *Before the Flowers of Friendship Faded Friendship Faded* (written in 1930, published in 1931), a book of poems; *Operas and Plays* (written in 1913–30, published in 1932); and *Matisse Picasso and Gertrude Stein with Two Shorter Stories* (written in 1909–12, published in 1933). The books did not sell particularly well, but they did get reviewers' attention.[39] According to our survey respondents, writing from this phase of Stein's career is less commonly taught, although some instructors pair "Composition" and selections from *How to Write* with other Stein texts.

1933–37

At age 59, after years of small print runs and parodies, Stein finally received public credibility and the backing of major commercial publishers with *The Autobiography of Alice B. Toklas* (written in 1932, published in 1933). According to our survey, the *Autobiography* is one of her most widely taught texts. First serialized in *The Atlantic Monthly* and *Harper's Bazaar* (London), the book was published by Harcourt, Brace, and was the September 1933 selection of the Literary Guild, a competitor to the Book-of-the-Month Club. The acclaim spurred Stein's return to America for the first time in forty years; her sold-out lectures were collected in *Lectures in America* (written in 1934, published by Random House in 1935). As important as the money and fame for Stein was a resulting standing contract with Random House, and most of what she published from 1934 to 1946 was with them—including *Four Saints in Three Acts* (written in 1927, published in 1934), *Portraits and Prayers* (written in 1909–33, published in 1934), *The Geographical History of America or the Relation of Human Nature to the Human Mind* (written in 1935, published in 1936), and her follow-up to the *Autobiography*, *Everybody's Autobiography* (written in 1936–37, published in 1937). Her return to the United States led her to reflect on the experience in shorter pieces, some of which appeared in the *New York Herald Tribune* in 1935 and some in *The Saturday Evening Post* in 1936.[40]

Stein's writing about writing has been especially helpful to instructors, and many report assigning, along with "Composition as Explanation" and *Lectures In America*, two other lectures, "How Writing Is Written" (written in 1935, published in *Choate Literary Magazine* in 1935) and "What Are Master-pieces and Why Are There So Few of Them" (written in 1935, published in *What Are Masterpieces* in 1940) as well as *Narration* (written in 1935, published by U of Chicago P in 1935), a volume containing four lectures. During this period Stein also gave several interviews; her conversations with William Lundell, broadcast on radio in 1934, and John Hyde Preston, published in *The Atlantic Monthly* in 1935, are especially useful for instructors looking for information about Stein's view of creativity and her relation to readers. These lectures and interviews from 1934–35 were a serious attempt at explaining her poetics.

1938–46

This period, when the threat of war turned to war itself, was neglected in the scholarship on Stein until fairly recently. It begins with her slim monograph *Picasso* (written in 1937, published by B. T. Batsford in 1938), on his work and life; *Paris France* (written in 1939, published by B. T. Batsford in 1940), a reflection on her adopted home; and *Ida A Novel* (written in 1937–40, published by Random House in 1941), about a woman celebrity and woman as celebrity. At the invitation of Margaret Wise Brown, Stein wrote her first book for children, *The World Is Round* (written in 1938, published by William R. Scott in 1939, illustrated by Clement Hurd). She thought of her *The First Reader & Three Plays* (written in 1941–43, published by Maurice Friberg in 1946) as another book for children, but its humor is almost absurdist, Beckett-like. *What Are Masterpieces* (Conference Press, 1940) included the lecture of that title and reprinted "Composition As Explanation." *Wars I Have Seen* (written in 1943–44, published by Random House in 1945), a memoir and journal on the year and a half before liberation, again garnered a wide readership. She then wrote *Brewsie and Willie* (written in 1945, published by Random House in 1946), a fictional series of conversations among American GIs and nurses.

Posthumous Publications to 1958

Shortly after Stein died, the first major anthology of her career's work, *Selected Writings of Gertrude Stein* (Random House, 1946), edited by Van Vechten, appeared. It has remained in print and, as an affordable paperback containing many of her most recognizable texts, is a popular choice for instructors. From 1947 to 1958, much of the backlog of her unpublished texts made it into print. Toklas, Van Vechten, and Gallup were or became, through the Yale archive, familiar with this backlog and worked to honor Stein's vision that it all be published. After *Four in America* (written in 1933–34, published by Yale UP in 1947)—the "four" being

Ulysses Grant, Wilbur Wright, Henry James, and George Washington—and *The Mother Of Us All* (written in 1945–46, published by Music Press in 1947)—the "mother" being Susan B. Anthony—were two short novels: *Blood on the Dining-Room Floor* (written in 1933, published by Banyan Press in 1948), a detective story; and *Things As They Are* (written in 1903, published by Banyan Press in 1950), an autobiographical roman à clef about a lesbian love triangle (also known as *Q. E. D.*). Rosalind Miller's *Gertrude Stein: Form and Intelligibility* (Exposition Press, 1949) printed Stein's undergraduate writing, and *Last Operas and Plays* (written in 1930–46, published by Rinehart in 1949), edited by Van Vechten, contained many of her major dramatic works, including *Photograph* (1920), *Doctor Faustus Lights the Lights* (1938), and *Yes Is For A Very Young Man* (1946).

Yale University Press then began issuing what would be eight volumes of previously unpublished materials: *Two: Gertrude Stein and Her Brother and Other Early Portraits* (written in 1908–12, published in 1951), *Mrs. Reynolds and Five Earlier Novelettes* (written in 1931–42, published in 1952), *Bee Time Vine and Other Pieces* (written in 1913–27, published in 1953), *As Fine as Melanctha* (written in 1914–30, published in 1954), *Painted Lace and Other Pieces* (written in 1914–37, published in 1955), *Stanzas in Meditation and Other Poems* (written in 1929–33, published in 1956), *Alphabets and Birthdays* (written in 1916–40, published in 1957), and *A Novel of Thank You* (written in 1921–26, published in 1958). Each volume was prefaced by one of Stein's friends, including Janet Flanner, Virgil Thomson, and Natalie Barney. This series marks the first appearance of a number of book-length texts: *A Novel of Thank You* (1925–26), *Stanzas in Meditation* (1932), *To Do: Alphabets and Birthdays* (1940), which is a book for children, and *Mrs. Reynolds* (1940–42), a loosely autobiographical novel that has been called "a hate-letter to Hitler" (Axelrod 262). *Bee Time Vine* included poems that have become well known, such as "Yet Dish" (1913), "Lifting Belly" (1915–17), and "Patriarchal Poetry" (1926–27). These volumes quickly went out of print, but in 1980 Richard Kostelanetz selected texts from them for *The Yale Gertrude Stein* anthology.

After 1958

Those eight volumes did close the circle, making available the work Stein wanted published, but the Yale archive held much more—manuscripts, letters, photographs. Gallup and Leon Katz edited a book representing Stein's so-called apprentice work, *Fernhurst,* Q. E. D., *and Other Early Writings* (written in 1903–05, published in 1971). In addition to a corrected edition of *Q. E. D.*, this volume included draft material that Stein incorporated into *The Making of Americans*. Robert Haas edited three volumes: *A Primer for the Gradual Understanding of Gertrude Stein* (1971), *Reflection on the Atomic Bomb* (1973), and *How Writing Is Written* (1974). *Primer* is notable for the wide-ranging 1946 interview Haas did with Stein, and *How Writing Is Written* reprints many of Stein's essays from 1933 to 1945. There are numerous collections of her correspondence with others, including Sherwood Anderson (1972), Samuel Steward (1977), Van Vechten (1986), Wilder (1996), Mabel Dodge Luhan (1996), Picasso (2008), and Thomson (2010). An edition of love notes between Stein and Toklas, *Baby Precious Always Shines* (1999), is available. Some of the many photographs in the Stein archive have appeared in Renate Stendhal's *Gertrude Stein: In Words and Pictures* (1994) and Wanda Corn and Tirza True Latimer's *Seeing Gertrude Stein: Five Stories* (2011). *Four Americans in Paris* (1970) and *The Steins Collect: Matisse, Picasso, and the Parisian Avant-Garde* (2011) reconstruct the art collections of Leo, Gertrude, Michael, and Sarah Stein in the early 1900s.

Other anthologies of Stein's work include Patricia Meyerowitz's *Look at Me Now and Here I Am: Writings and Lectures, 1909–45* (1967); Judy Grahn's *Really Reading Gertrude Stein* 1989); Dydo's *A Stein Reader* (1993), which provides helpful introductions to each piece; the Library of America's two-volume *Gertrude Stein: Writings, 1903–46* (1998), edited by Catharine Stimpson and Harriet Chessman; Kostelanetz's *The Gertrude Stein Reader* (2002); and Retallack's *Gertrude Stein: Selections* (2008), which contains a long introductory essay. In recent years, several of Stein's texts have been reissued, sometimes as corrected and archivally grounded editions and often with an eye toward the classroom—*Three Lives* and *Q. E. D.* (2006); *Ida A Novel* (2012); *Stanzas in Meditation* (2012); and *Tender Buttons* (2014). *Narration* (2010) and *Paris France* (2013) were also reissued, with new introductions. There are illustrated editions of *To Do: A Book of Alphabets and Birthdays* (2011, illustrated by Giselle Potter) and *Tender Buttons: Objects* (2013, illustrated by Lisa Congdon).

Critical Reception

For more than a century now, tension has existed between Stein the writer and Stein the personality. Her 27 rue de Fleurus address in Paris was well known before World War I for its modern art collection and Saturday salon, and after the war it became legendary; the younger generation of writers, if they did not know her personally, knew of her; everybody, it seemed, had an opinion on her appearance, her talk, and her writing (even if they had hardly read it). Her name had currency.[41] The avant-garde magazines welcomed her work, but only with her autobiographical writings were commercial publishers able to market her gainfully. Stein worked tirelessly to maintain her identity as a writer first, insisting in 1934, for instance, when Random House was about to become her publisher, that it offer her "real kind of books" alongside her "open" or "illustrative" ones (Holbrook and Dilworth 238). She maintained that "if it were not for my work they would not be interested in me so why should they not be more interested in my work than in me" (*Everybody's Autobiography* 50). Every successful writer experiences consumer demand for life stories or public appearances, but this pressure was a distinct tension for Stein because, even if it made no sense to her, it could seem as if people were interested in her life alone.

As Stein told an interviewer in 1946, "I became fairly early in the game a writer's writer" ("Transatlantic Interview" 31). Because many of her first critics were fellow writers, the critical reception of her work overlapped with her influence (a topic we address in the next section). Of course not all writers agreed in their estimations, not even with themselves. Katherine Anne Porter, for instance, penned a glowing review of *The Making of Americans* for the *New York Herald Tribune Books* in 1927 but wrote a parody of her own review the following year (251–55). In *Axel's Castle* (1931) Edmund Wilson complained about "[Stein's] soporific rigamaroles, her echolaliac incantations," but concluded, "we are always still aware of her presence in the background of contemporary literature" (252). In 1935, on the heels of the success of *The Autobiography of Alice B. Toklas*, Stein found herself and that work denounced in *Transition*, a magazine that had previously published her writing, in a special pamphlet entitled *Testimony against Gertrude Stein*. That she could command such attention suggests her significance. Her distinctive writing style was also widely parodied; Stein-inspired doggerel appeared in newspapers from New York City to Detroit to South Carolina. As Van Vechten pointed out in 1946, her work was both "widely quoted and ridiculed by friends and enemies in the American press" (Stein, *Selected Writings* 460)—easy to mock but impossible to ignore. Natalia Cecire has summed up this polarized response, saying that Stein's style "has been taken as evidence of her genius and of fraud in equal measure. Indeed, it has been praised as innovative and condemned as nonsense on exactly the same formal grounds" (284). Celebrated, dismissed, vilified, and embraced, Stein and her work have occupied nearly as many positions as are available in modern literature. "[T]he creator of a new composition in the arts is an outlaw until he is a classic," Stein observed ("Composition" 496).

Since Sutherland's *Gertrude Stein: A Biography of Her Work* (1951), more than forty critical books solely on Stein's work have appeared, as well as two groundbreaking dissertations, six collections of essays, and two Stein issues in journals.[42] After Sutherland's, the next major study was Bridgman's *Gertrude Stein in Pieces* (1970). Like Dydo's *Gertrude Stein: The Language That Rises* (2003) more recently, Bridgman's helps readers understand the relation of one text to the whole. Wendy Steiner's *Exact Resemblance to Exact Resemblance* (1978) was the first book on Stein's portraits, and Betsy Alayne Ryan's *Gertrude Stein's Theatre of the Absolute* (1984) was the first on her plays.[43] Jayne Walker's *The Making of a Modernist: Gertrude Stein from* Three Lives *to* Tender Buttons (1984) relates well with Lisa Ruddick's *Reading Gertrude Stein: Body, Text, Gnosis* (1990) and Steven Meyer's *Irresistible Dictation: Gertrude Stein and the Correlations of Writing and Science* (2001). All three books study the early writing; the latter two in particular address the influence that Stein's education—and her relationship with William James—had on her approach to writing.

Although in *Axel's Castle* Wilson devoted an entire chapter to only one woman writer, Stein, she was easily elided from many literary histories. In the late 1970s, however, the academic sea change involving feminist and sexuality studies firmly established her significance. Stimpson's essays, Marianne DeKoven's *A Different Language: Gertrude Stein's Experimental Writing* (1983), Chessman's *The Public Is Invited to Dance: Representation, the Body, and Dialogue in Gertrude Stein* (1989), and Elizabeth Fifer's *Rescued Readings: A Reconstruction of Gertrude Stein's Difficult Texts* (1992) all read Stein as a major modernist writer. She was also embraced as a protopostmodernist, someone whose work inspired literary experiments of the later twentieth century—see, for instance, Marjorie Perloff's *The Poetics of Indeterminacy* (1981), Ellen Berry's *Curved Thought and Textual Wandering: Gertrude Stein's Postmodernism* (1992), and Peter Quartermain's *Disjunctive Poetics: From Gertrude Stein and Louis Zukofsky to Susan Howe* (1992). Feminist, queer, and avant-garde poetics approaches to Stein's work continue to flourish.[44] According to the *MLA International Bibliography*, there was less scholarship on Stein in the first three decades after World War II than on peers such as T. S. Eliot, Ezra Pound, or James Joyce, but by the 1980s and 1990s she began keeping pace with, if not outpacing, them.[45]

Since Stein's death in 1946, attention has gone to the writer and legend about equally. Although book-length studies of the writing vastly outnumber the biographies, our sense generally is that scholars have been drawn to both approaches. Four recent books represent this bifurcation. On the personality side are Karen Leick's *Gertrude Stein and the Making of an American Celebrity* (2009) and Barbara Will's *Unlikely Collaboration: Gertrude Stein, Bernard Faÿ, and the Vichy Dilemma* (2011); on the writer side are Dydo's *Gertrude Stein: The Language That Rises* (2003) and Janet Boyd and Sharon Kirsch's *Primary Stein: Returning to the Writing of Gertrude Stein* (2014). That said, and as much as Stein has remained relatively easy to caricature, in the years since her death the range of her writing has become far better known than it was in her lifetime. In the field of modernist or even twentieth-century American literature, she stands as a major figure both in the history of women writers and in the poetics of indeterminacy. This background helps explain her continued popularity in the twenty-first century. What strikes us today is not so much Stein as exception (the only woman in the room, so to speak, or the most extreme among the avant-garde) as the networked Stein, the one whose writing can fit into so many different humanities courses.

Influence

While Stein's status as a major modernist writer is secure, the critical reception of her work can be called a long history of polarized responses. By contrast, her influence has always been strongly felt. Even the critics of her time who decried her work as nonsense illustrated the power of her influence: many chose the parodic mode, imitating the style of the Stein text under review. What they worried about especially was that she would be taken seriously and affect the younger generation of writers.[46]

It may have been in France where she was first widely accepted as a serious writer. In 1920 Richard Aldington noted her influence there, particularly with *Tender Buttons*, listing poets such as Guillaume Apollinaire, Blaise Cendrars, Pierre Reverdy, Jean Cocteau, and André Breton as "French disciples of Miss Stein" (37).[47] In the United States her influence seemed to be on fiction writers (e.g., Anderson, Hemingway) primarily.[48] While *Tender Buttons* received attention, her contemporaries tended to cite *The Making of Americans* and *Three Lives* as the most exciting (and readable) models for them.[49] After 1950, however, poets, playwrights, and artists were more likely to mention her as a significant influence. Including Stein when teaching the New York School (Barbara Guest, John Ashbery, Frank O'Hara) or Language poets (Lyn Hejinian, Ron Silliman, Charles Bernstein) or a post-Oulipo poet like Harryette Mullen seems useful if not mandatory, and as these writers have become more canonical, so has Stein.[50] As inspiration and vexation, her writing has served as both "an extraordinary source of creative energy" and as a source of "critical consciousness" for many writers (Mullen, "If Lilies" 26–27).

In his introduction to *The Yale Gertrude Stein* (1980), Kostelanetz asserts that Stein's writing has been influential to Ashbery, John Cage, Allen Ginsberg, and bpNichol (xxx). (Kostelanetz also hypothesizes that her "preference for denotative language" indirectly influenced "American newspaper writing and . . . crime fiction" [xxxi].) As this list suggests, there has clearly been an avant-garde tradition, in literature and music, in which Stein figures as a key influence, a tradition overtly articulated by experimental poets' engagement with her work. In the December 1978 issue of Bruce Andrews and Charles Bernstein's *L=A=N=G=U=A=G=E* magazine, a number of poets, including Larry Eigner, Jackson Mac Low, Steve McCaffery, Bob Perelman, Rae Armantrout, and Robert Grenier, responded to selections from *Tender Buttons*. In *My Emily Dickinson* (1985), Susan Howe identifies Stein as "among the most innovative" writers in Anglo-American literature (11), and Retallack's work has consistently acknowledged Stein's radicality as a touchstone.

In an essay in the feminist experimentalist journal *How(ever)* in 1986, DeKoven argued that scholars had begun recognizing Stein as an important figure "for female modernism, for the female aesthetic, for the avant-garde, for American experimentalism, for lesbian writing, for theoretical study of gender and culture, [and] for the literary matrilineal descent" ("Second Reappreciation" 13). Note that Kostelanetz's 1980 list included men only; by 1986, history was being rewritten. As Hejinian explained in her introduction to "Two Stein Talks" (1986), knowing that her father recognized Stein as a "genius" meant that "gender would not be a bar" to achievement (84). Mullen wrote *Trimmings* (1991) and *S*PeRM**K*T*

(1992) to extend and complicate Stein's own critique of assigned identities for women (Interview). In other cases Stein's influence is more implicit, as with the writers published by LeeAnn Brown's Tender Buttons Press (established in 1989): Bernadette Mayer, Hannah Weiner, Rosmarie Waldrop, and Jennifer Moxley.[51] Though Stein did not acknowledge her lesbianism publicly, a lesbian eroticism can be found in her writing, and she has figured in a lesbian tradition in literature as a source of permission and inspiration for writers such as Judy Grahn, Nicole Brossard, Daphne Marlatt, and Betsy Warland.

Sarah Bay-Cheng has pointed out that although Stein's plays are not especially well known, "the history of experimental theater and drama in America is virtually inconceivable without her influence" (1–2). In a similar vein, Arnold Aronson has argued, considering the dramatic work of John Cage, "Along with Zen, Stein would have the most profound influence upon a man who in turn exerted the greatest influence on the development of the American avant-garde" (31). Notable playwrights who have drawn on Stein's sense of time and repetition are Richard Foreman, Robert Wilson, and Suzan-Lori Parks. Bay-Cheng sees Stein's drama as influential to performance artists like Laurie Anderson and Karen Finley in their "Steinian exploration of the spoken word and the breakdown of human communication" (117). Stein's plays have been performed by some of the most important avant-garde theater groups, including The Living Theatre, which staged two of them in its first year (1951), including *Ladies' Voices* (1916); the Judson Poets' Theater, led by Lawrence Kornfield and Al Carmines (in 1964 they received three Obie Awards for their production of Stein's *What Happened* [1913]); and The Wooster Group, which adapted Stein's *Doctor Faustus Lights the Lights* (1938) as *House/Lights* in 1998. Dancers and choreographers—the Mark Morris Dance Group, for instance—and visual artists too, such as Ellsworth Kelly, Agnes Martin, and Ellen Gallagher, have found her work to be generative for their own.

Finally, Stein herself has often been used as a character, whether in Monique Truong's novel *The Book of Salt* (2003), which imagines the life of Stein and Toklas's Vietnamese cook; *Loving Repeating* (2006), Stephen Flaherty and Frank Galati's chamber musical based on Stein and Toklas's lives; or Woody Allen's *Midnight in Paris* (2011), in which Stein appears as a gnomic adviser to young male writers. Perry Miller Adato's documentary *Gertrude Stein: When This You See Remember Me* (1970), which includes interviews with a number of Stein's friends, is another, earlier instance of Stein's representative authority in film narratives that have shaped our sense of the legendary 1920s. In a 2013 video, Adato recalls that her first impulse was "to do a film about Paris." She was told, however, that "Paris" was "too broad" and was asked, "Can't you find one person whose life and whose work encompass that period?" Her answer: "Well it had to be Gertrude Stein. Who else? Who else was it going to be?" And in making her film, she realized "that Gertrude Stein was not just some esoteric person that lived in the first part of the twentieth century"; "she was very current."

NOTES

[1] Of the Stein biographies, we recommend Mellow; Hobhouse; Wagner-Martin; and Wineapple.

[2] Simon died in 1913, Bertha in 1924, Michael in 1938, and Leo in 1947. Not until *The Autobiography of Alice B. Toklas* became a best seller in 1933 did Stein make any significant income from her writing, and before and after 1933 she was at times forced to sell some of the art she had collected. In 1929 she wrote to her agent William Bradley, "I did inherit a very small income on which I have lived with great care but one grows older and life is harder and it diminishes and the need of earning is definitely there" (Dydo, *Gertrude Stein* 544). In 1935 Michael wrote to her, "You have not made a [tax] declaration for years because you did not have enough income above your personal exemption to make you liable. . . . You were living on capital and selling paintings, which you owned" (Wagner-Martin 215).

[3] Out of these experiments came two articles by Stein: "Normal Motor Automatism" (1896), cowritten with Leon Solomons, and "Cultivated Motor Automatism" (1898).

[4] From 1893 to 1899 she visited California most summers. Her attraction to Italy, Spain, and (from 1924 to 1944) southeastern France was in part due to this California background. Thinking back to the 1880s, she remembered the residents as racially diverse: "[S]chool in California meant knowing lots of nationalities" (*Wars* 8).

[5] The dates here are of composition. *The Making of Americans* "contains within its schemes and diagrams of personality some four hundred people whom Stein had known, and almost everything that had happened to her. All of these were built in one way or another into the book's elaborate and peculiar mosiac" (Katz, "First Making" v). The *Autobiography*, though different in style and on a reduced scale, likewise offers a mosaic of "people whom Stein had known."

[6] "Even though Leo and Gertrude combined their funds for their purchases, they simply could not afford major works by established artists" (Rabinow 26).

[7] Two major museum exhibitions have documented these collections: *Four Americans in Paris* (1970–71) and *The Steins Collect* (2011–12).

[8] The abridged version we get of their meeting in the *Autobiography*—"There I went to see Mrs. Stein who had in the meantime returned to Paris, and there at her house I met Gertrude Stein. I was impressed by the coral brooch she wore and by her voice" (5)—is amplified in Toklas's 1963 memoir, *What Is Remembered* (see 22–25).

[9] For another early attempt at championing Stein, see Van Vechten, "How." A devoted friend, he later supplied introductions to her books: a 1933 reprint of *Three Lives*; *Four Saints in Three Acts* in 1934; *Selected Writings* in 1946; *Last Operas and Plays* in 1949; and *A Novel of Thank You* in 1958.

[10] *Three Lives* received 19 reviews in 1909–10; in 1914–15 Stein was referred to in 44 articles; in 1923, after *Geography and Plays*, 34 did so; and 275 articles addressed her writing in 1933–34 (R. White, *Reference*).

[11] In 1922 she wrote of her portraits that "always she was translating the rhythm of the spoken personality as directly as possible, using every form that she could invent to translate the repeated story of everybody doing what, what they are being" (Stein, Literary notes).

[12] One of them, William Rogers, later reconnected with her after she mentioned him in the *Autobiography*. He would go on to write a memoir about their friendship, *When This You See Remember Me: Gertrude Stein in Person* (1948).

[13] In 1924 Hemingway helped arrange for the serialization of *The Making of Americans* in *The Transatlantic Review* across nine issues, and in 1927 Thomson began collaborating with Stein on the *Four Saints in Three Acts* opera, a creative relationship revived in 1945–46 for *The Mother Of Us All.*

[14] She helped Hugnet and Thomson with *Morceaux choisis de la fabrication des Américains* (1929), a selection (16 passages) from *The Making of Americans*, and with *Dix Portraits* (1930), ten of her portraits. She provided her collaborators with almost word-for-word translations (Dydo, *Gertrude Stein* 291). For Hugnet she wrote a film scenario, *Film deux sœurs qui ne sont pas sœurs* (1929), and translated—she called them reflections—a thirty-poem sequence of Hugnet's "Enfances," which in 1931 she published as *Before the Flowers of Friendship Faded Friendship Faded.* Faÿ, with Renée de Seillière, translated about a third of *The Making of Americans* for *Américains d'Amérique* (1933), and Faÿ translated *The Autobiography of Alice B. Toklas* in 1934. Stein did not like writing in French. Having written *Picasso* in 1937, she said to a friend, "I have just written a french book in french about Picasso and it was a frightful struggle it is not natural not at all natural to write french, English is what I write" (qtd. in Wagner-Martin 234).

[15] Over her career she wrote more than 130 portraits (Steiner 209–15) and more than 75 plays (Ryan 157–60).

[16] In 1929 Stein wrote, "I am very busy finding out what people mean by what they say. I used to be interested in what they were I am now interested in what they say" (*Primer* 105). Although this remark comes long after she started writing plays, it applies to her shift from fiction and portraits to plays.

[17] Stein had given her first public lectures in June 1926, reading "Composition as Explanation" at Cambridge and Oxford. In 1936 she returned to those universities to read "What Are Master-pieces."

[18] Thornton Wilder's three introductions to works by Stein—*Narration* (1935), *The Geographical History of America* (1936), and *Four in America* (1947)—were informed by his conversations with her about publicity's threat to creativity.

[19] On Stein and race, see Blackmer; Hovey; E. Miller; Smedman; Sollors. Readers today will wrestle with her use of racist stereotypes, but Nella Larsen and Richard Wright both applauded "Melanctha," Larsen calling it a "truly great story" that "accurately" represented "the spirit of this race of mine" (qtd. in Blackmer 408) and Wright commenting that it was "the first realistic treatment of Negro life I'd seen when I was trying to learn how to write, and from my first reading of the story, I wished I had written it and I still do. . . . [T]his story made me see and accept for the first time in my life the speech of Negroes, speech that fell around me unheard." On Stein's response to the New Deal, see Mix, "Gertrude Stein's Currency." Her comments made in 1936 conflate Roosevelt with Hitler and Franco: "There is too much fathering going on just now and there is no doubt about fathers are depressing. Everybody nowadays is a father, there is father Mussolini and father Hitler and father Roosevelt and father Stalin and father Lewis and father Blum and father Franco is just commencing now and there are ever so many more ready to be one" (*Everybody's Autobiography* 137).

[20] Susan Zuccotti believes that as "Americans and thus enemy nationals, Stein and Toklas, if caught, would have been interned [in France] but probably not deported" to a concentration camp outside France (303). On Stein's war years, see Bridgman 317–18; Wagner-Martin 246–47; Burns and Dydo, "Gertrude Stein"; Van Dusen; Gallagher; Davis, "Even Cake"; Malcolm; Zox-Weaver; Will; Whittier-Ferguson; Axelrod; Galvin; Bernstein, *Gertrude Stein's War Years.*

[21] In 1943 Stein wrote, "[S]omebody wrote to me and said that in America everybody said that there was no difference between the occupied and unoccupied zone but we who lived in the unoccupied we knew there was a difference all right" (*Wars* 87). While Jews throughout France were subject to loss of employment and assets and to internment or deportation, Stein's comment suggests that she felt significantly safer in the "free" zone.

[22] Stein claimed that "it was the mayor, the subprefect, and the townspeople who chose to look the other way when official anti-Jewish legislation trickled down to the villages of Bilignin and Culoz" (Will 127). On the other hand, as she notes in *Wars I Have Seen*, the people of Belley could expose too: for instance, a drugstore owner was "sent a coffin" for being "what they call a collabo" (132).

[23] Stein drafted an introduction (addressed to American readers) in January 1942, started translating in spring or summer 1942, and, after completing a rough translation of about three-fifths of the book, abandoned the project by January 1943 (Burns and Dydo 405–10). None of this was published in her lifetime. In 1996 the introduction was published twice ("Introduction to Pétain's *Paroles*" and "Introduction to the Speeches"). Besides heeding Faÿ, two other likely prompts for this translation project were the Belley region being a "bastion of Pétainism" (Will 129) and wanting the United States to continue its diplomatic relations with Vichy.

[24] Brinnin's *The Third Rose*, not published until 1959, was preceded by Elizabeth Sprigge's *Gertrude Stein* (1957).

[25] For more on their relationship, see Simon; Souhami; and K. Turner.

[26] *Things As They Are* is Stein's novella *Q. E. D.* (1903).

[27] They first heard of each other in 1906, when Michael and Sarah Stein returned to San Francisco after the 18 April earthquake, bringing with them a copy of Alfred Jarry's *Ubu Roi* that Gertrude had signed and giving it to Toklas (Burns, *Staying* 115–16). Michael and Sarah returned to Paris with Annette Rosenshine, and for the next year Rosenshine shared Toklas's letters with Stein and wrote to Toklas about the Steins (Simon 49, 43). They were thus acquainted before they actually met in September 1907.

[28] "Because 'Ada' is as much a celebration of their union as it is a portrait of Alice, it suggests that her character is fulfilled only in this relationship" (Burke 554). The text of "Ada" may have been a "collaborative effort": the extant manuscript contains the handwriting of both women (Bridgman 210). For more on what it might mean to consider Toklas a writing partner, see Hobhouse 93; Stendahl 64; and Laird 185.

[29] See "A Sonatina Followed By Another" (1921) as well.

[30] An example of what Stein might receive from Toklas as a reader is a note Toklas wrote to her after having typed her work: "Sweet pinky, you made lots of literature last night didn't you. . . . You are doing most handsomely" (Dydo, *Gertrude Stein* 31).

[31] The move to spending half the year in the countryside was made in part to satisfy Toklas's wishes: "For fourteen successive years [1929–1942] the gardens at Bilignin were my joy, working in them during the summers and planning and dreaming of them during the winters. The summers frequently commenced early in April with the planting, and ended late in October with the last gathering of the winter vegetables" (*Alice B. Toklas Cook Book* 265).

[32] A list of those dismissed at Toklas's prompting would include Etta Cone, Leo Stein, Mabel Dodge Luhan, and Ernest Hemingway. Toklas also kept many of Stein's pre-1904 friends from seeing Stein during the 1934–35 American lecture tour.

[33] See Dydo, *Gertrude Stein* 488–502; Stein, *Stanzas*; and the essay in this volume by Hollister and Setina.

[34] When Leon Katz interviewed Toklas in 1952–53 about Stein's notebooks for *The Making of Americans*, he noticed that Stein had referred to Toklas as Saint Therese and asked, "'In what sense were you St. Therese to Gertrude?' . . . Alice with enormous reluctance and some anger responded, pained and hesitant, 'Because I felt toward Gertrude as St. Therese felt toward the Christ. For me, it was the same experience and the same relation" ("Year" 17).

[35] Many other collections went to Yale in the wake of Stein's: those of Mabel Dodge Luhan, Alfred Stieglitz, Marsden Hartley, and *The Dial* (Gallup, "Du Côté de Chez Stein" 169). Van Vechten, after helping organize Stein's archive, started a James Weldon Johnson archive at Yale, which in turn attracted the papers of W. E. B. Du Bois, Langston Hughes, Richard Wright, Jean Toomer, Countee Cullen, Zora Neale Hurston, and Claude McKay. See Braddock.

[36] Katz unpacked those "several layers" of *The Making of Americans* in his 1963 dissertation ("First Making").

[37] See *The Steins Collect* for photographs of the Stein salon with Picasso sketches on the wall (Bishop 268–69, 370). The 2012 Yale University Press edition of *Ida*, edited by Logan Esdale, offers archival materials to contextualize the novel. For more on Stein's making of her Yale archive, see Esdale, "Gertrude Stein's Twin."

[38] Much of Stein's work is currently in print. The Library of America's two-volume *Gertrude Stein: Writings, 1903–1946* alone contains twelve of her books (as well as excerpts and shorter pieces). Bibliographies of her works are available in R. Wilson; Kellner.

[39] Robert Coates, writing about *Lucy Church Amiably* in *The New Yorker* in 1932, observed that Stein "has attained the curious position of being more talked about by more people who have never read a line of hers than any other author" (qtd. in Leick 136). For more on Plain Edition, see Dean.

[40] Haas included these shorter pieces in *How Writing Is Written*.

[41] In January 1923, Stein was included in a *Life* magazine illustration of "112 writers, politicians, and celebrities," including Calvin Coolidge, Sherwood Anderson, Babe Ruth, and Charlie Chaplin (Leick 69). *Vanity Fair* nominated her for its "Hall of Fame" the previous year, suggesting that she was recognizable to its readership. In 1934, when she arrived in New York, her name appeared in lights in Times Square: "Gertrude Stein has arrived in New York, Gertrude Stein has arrived in New York" (Mellow 382). Her name and writing were pressed into service for advertising copy and store window displays (Tischler 14–15; S. Watson 5).

[42] The two dissertations are Katz's "The First Making of *The Making of Americans*: A Study Based on Gertrude Stein's Notebooks and Early Versions of Her Novel (1902–1908)" (1963) and Rosalind Moad's "1914–16: Years of Innovation in Gertrude Stein's Writing" (1993). Shirley Neuman and Ira Nadel's *Gertrude Stein and the Making of Literature* (1988), Janet Boyd and Sharon Kirsch's *Primary Stein: Returning to the Writing of Gertrude Stein* (2014), and Sarah Posman and Laura Luise Schultz's *Gertrude Stein in Europe: Reconfigurations across Media, Disciplines and Traditions* (2015) all contain new essays, but Harold Bloom's *Gertrude Stein* (1986), Michael Hoffman's *Critical Essays on Gertrude Stein* (1986), Richard Kostelanetz's *Gertrude Stein Advanced: An Anthology of Criticism* (1990), and Kirk Curnutt's *The Critical Response to Gertrude Stein* (2000) offer reception histories from the early twentieth century on. The Stein issues in *Twentieth Century Literature* (vol. 24, no. 1, Spring 1978) and in *Modern Fiction Studies* (vol. 42, no. 3, Fall 1996) remain excellent resources.

[43] Ryan's work on Stein's theater was followed by Jane Palatini Bowers's *"They Watch Me as They Watch This": Gertrude Stein's Metadrama* (1991), Sarah Bay-Cheng's *Mama Dada: Gertrude Stein's Avant-Garde Theater* (2004), and Leslie Atkins Durham's *Staging Gertrude Stein: Absence, Culture, and the Landscape of American Alternative Theatre* (2005).

[44] Nicola Pitchford cautions that identifying a feminist or postmodern Stein has sometimes dehistoricized her, as if she existed outside or transcended the circumstances in which she produced her writing (643). Pitchford offers useful examples of Stein's inclusion in and exclusion from mid-century studies of modernism.

[45] The most recent monographs are Lorange; Kirsch, *Gertrude Stein*; Peters; and Voris, *Composition*.

[46] T. S. Eliot in 1927 worried that "Miss Stein is going to make trouble for us. . . . [H]er work is not improving, it is not amusing, it is not interesting, it is not good for one's mind. But its rhythms have a peculiar hypnotic power not met with before. It has a kinship with the saxophone. If this is the future, then the future is, as it very likely is, of the barbarians. But this is a future in which we ought not to be interested" ("Charleston").

[47] Aldington claimed that Edgar Allan Poe's "The Raven," Walt Whitman's *Leaves of Grass*, and Stein's *Tender Buttons* are "[t]hree impingements of American genius upon the mind of Europe" (36).

[48] Wendell Wilcox wrote in 1940 that Stein's "prosody is most usually just the ordinary diction of her prose, and since by her style, her manner, and her approach to subject matter she has influenced in no way the poets but only the prose writers, it is far more natural to think of her as belonging to prose" (255). Although overstated ("in no way . . . but only"), his claim spoke for many writers of that time.

[49] In addition to recognizing her influence on Hemingway and Anderson, we should consider the ways her writing intersects with that by Mina Loy, William Carlos Williams, Marianne Moore, Nella Larsen, F. Scott Fitzgerald, Thornton Wilder, William Faulkner, Laura Riding, Richard Wright, and Paul Bowles.

[50] For readings of Stein's influence on later twentieth-century poets, see Spahr, *Everybody's Autonomy*; E. Frost; Mix, *Vocabulary*; and Robbins.

[51] See also the work of Alice Notley, Leslie Scalapino, Sonia Sanchez, and Theresa Hak Kyung Cha.

Part Two

APPROACHES

Introduction

Logan Esdale and Deborah M. Mix

Stein is best known for the stories in *Three Lives*, the prose poems of *Tender Buttons*, her memoir *The Autobiography of Alice B. Toklas*, and lectures such as "Composition as Explanation." That she wrote across so many genres explains both her continuing popularity and the difficulty in teaching her. Students encounter multiple Steins: storyteller, poet, librettist, aesthetic leader, art collector, pop-culture figure, and queer icon. They study her in composition, literature, creative writing, linguistics, women's and gender studies, theater, history, and American studies courses; they see her cited as an influence by a diverse range of contemporary writers and artists.

Although professors are obviously writing about Stein and teaching her work, there have been few places to find discussions of how to teach her. The *MLA International Bibliography* lists just a handful of articles on the subject.[1] Indeed, what Kirk Curnutt pointed out back in 1996—how surprising it is that Stein critics have largely ignored the pedagogy issue "given the formidable challenges of teaching her work"—remains true ("Parody" 2). What sets Stein apart from other so-called difficult writers is that she remains well known and so many of her books are still in print. The popularity of her work must be at least partly the result of excellent teaching, yet teachers have not had, in one book, the resources they need to dispel the myths about Stein and demonstrate the extraordinary depth and variety of her writing experiments.

The essays in this volume define Stein's role in modernism and her legacy; highlight familiar titles, placing them in the field of her long career; and suggest strategies for teaching some of her less familiar pieces. The purpose is to expand the number of Stein texts that teachers enjoy, understand, and feel ready to assign. This collection builds on critical and popular enthusiasm for Stein in the last forty years, but as a volume on teaching it also looks ahead to the discoveries of teachers and students alike.

Our surveys and our own experiences suggest that Stein can be a challenge to teach for several closely related reasons: she undermines the notion of a static or singular identity; she privileges the pleasure of reading over the knowledge it provides; and she dismantles in radical ways the linguistic conventions that result from "automatic copying" and "indolent" living, and so it can feel as if, with her writing, we are reading a foreign language (Stein, *Making* 192). (These actions are not necessarily unusual in the twentieth century, but she often appears to be pushing them to an extreme.) Such challenges are not easily overcome. People who have read Stein's writing for years face them as much as (if not more than) the student encountering *Tender Buttons* for the first time. If conventional ways of knowing can impede enjoyment and if teachers are knowers, then teachers may ironically have more trouble with Stein than their students do. She observed that people who were young, either literally or figuratively, were her ideal readers.[2] One goal of this volume, then, is to help teachers enjoy being the equal of their students.

Another challenge facing teachers, the decontextuated, message-in-a-bottle, or dehistoricized aspect of Stein's language, is more easily addressed. The contributors to this volume offer multiple contexts for her writing and career. For instance, Corinne Blackmer includes the psychology of William James and discourse on race around 1900 as background for "Melanctha," Roger Gilbert discusses *Tender Buttons* as a response to the language of *Mrs. Beeton's Book of Household Management*, Linda Voris locates Stein's portrait-poems in relation to contemporaneous changes in the visual arts, and Susannah Hollister and Emily Setina reveal the role that Alice Toklas played in revisions to *Stanzas in Meditation*.

Identity

Stein avoided identifying labels as much for herself as for her work. As Rajiv Krishnan put it in response to our survey, "Stein requires one to suspend one's ideas about what constitutes art and poetry." When she explicitly called something a poem or play or novel, as she often did, it was usually a sign that she had in fact troubled the normal identity of the genre. Her *A Novel of Thank You*, for instance, takes on the structure of the Victorian triple-decker novel even as it dismantles a host of other conventions, most notably linear plot and the hierarchical relationship between author and reader. Or her book *The Autobiography of Alice B. Toklas*—whose story is it? Both Stein's and Toklas's? Stein's resistance to static or singular notions of voice and identity, both human and generic, came from an exceptional sensitivity to their oppressive power, and she was always thinking of ways around the modes, such as expectation and memory, that delimit one's perception of immediate reality. She wanted people to read a text and discover what it was rather than read it according to their preexisting ideas of the genre. A text like "Patriarchal Poetry" offers the flowers we might expect from a love poem, but in a playful upending of genre, it also includes "Day-light and wishes and apples and fishes, dedicated to you all the way through," nourishing readers in order to encourage them to relinquish notions of identity as fixed and independent and instead, as she puts it, "be we to be to be we to be to be to be we" (575). As James Peck and Kelly Howe state in their article on teaching Stein in a theater classroom, "the process of identification—insisting upon borders between who you are and who you're not—inscribes far too many limits on the process of creation" (395). Stein's creative practice, her texts as relatively unmediated instances of creative thinking, opens borders in exhilarating ways.[3]

Pleasure

Stein said that if readers find pleasure in her writing, then they understand it.[4] Her comment has an unmistakable echo in literary theory. As many critics have argued, literary writing often provides us with an uncanny and seemingly perverse pleasure: as we find the unfamiliar in the familiar and the familiar in the unfamiliar, the experience of that dissolution of identity provides a pleasure that is not always comfortable. To the extent that we understand identity as a limiting force that operates both on and in us, we enjoy having our assumptions unsettled because they are not really our assumptions at all: they were constructed for us, and we adopted them out of habit, not choice. As we read Stein's play with grammar and see her movement within and between genres, we know the pleasure of deconstruction. Yet, as many of our survey respondents pointed out, it can be difficult for students to enjoy writing that alienates. In her response to our survey, Rachel Blau DuPlessis admitted that it can be a challenge to get students to see the value in "non-semantic (or better, semi-semantic) and non-extractive reading strategies."

Stein goes beyond defamiliarizing literary fundamentals (character and plot) to deconstruct language itself, its basic units (sentence and word). As Sherwood Anderson's brother said of Stein's uncanny writing style, "it gives words an oddly new intimate flavor and at the same time makes familiar words seem almost like strangers" (Anderson 5). In Stein's own optimistic formulation, "there is no such thing as putting [words] together without sense" ("Transatlantic Interview" 18). The history of a word typically determines its meaning, its identity, but Stein wanted use the act of writing to create meaning: "The only way to say what is the meaning of anything is to say that thing" ("Long Gay Book" 226–27). She would "say that thing" repeatedly and in various ways. This openness to new meanings is partly why nonnative or nonnormative English speakers are drawn to Stein: her language is democratic, making room for everybody (see, in this volume, the essays by Kaufman and by Malcolm; see Spahr, *Everybody's Autonomy* 45–47).

We can look to creative writing and theater for strategies that generate an understanding of literature that differs from the familiar hermeneutic (see, in this volume, the essays by Frank, by Peck, and by Mullen). These disciplines use Stein to make new work (poetry, fiction, plays, creative nonfiction), and bringing these strategies to bear in the classroom can help move students from bafflement to enjoyment. For example, we taught *Tender Buttons* to literature students by asking them to write formalist poems that used only her words.[5] Their poems and accompanying essays, which describe discoveries about her technique, are invariably remembered by students as a highlight of the semester and offer clear evidence that with Stein the challenge is not so much in her writing as in our approach to it. In a theater classroom what is practically mandatory—having various voices read the text aloud and experimenting with tone and pacing—is generally essential for Stein: many of the essays in this volume show that what can seem flat or merely repetitive on the page can become filled with nuance when performed. Reading aloud becomes a strategy for understanding.

Reading

During her wildly successful 1934–35 lecture tour of the United States, Stein was asked by a reporter why she did not write the way she presented her work to audiences. Stein said, "Oh, but I do. . . . After all, it's all learning how to read it" (Mellow 380). Reading the way Stein writes presents a challenge for students (and often for their teachers) in part because she wrote in so many different ways. She astonishes her fans by her continuous growth from decade to decade. The continuity of her work over her career is not obvious: an early work of fiction like *Three Lives* bears little resemblance to a later novel like *Lucy Church Amiably*; her representation of World War I in "Lifting Belly" is quite different from the way she presents World War II in *Mrs. Reynolds* or *Brewsie and Willie*; the radical repetitions of "Patriarchal Poetry" threaten to unhinge words from their familiar meanings, as "before" and "be for" intermingle (567); and the sonic play of "Yet Dish" seems to redistribute meaning through what Maria Damon has described as Stein's playful use of the "*idea* of Yiddish" (499).

Stein's inventive texts invite us to be similarly inventive as readers. Her experimentalism, however, can be off-putting to students, resulting in their resistance and frustration. Student responses to reading Stein can tend toward two extremes: students either see her work as utterly meaningless, all play, or see it as filled with meaning, all code, from which they are excluded. Steven Axelrod wrote in his survey response that "[t]he challenge is to get [students] over their preference for clarity and succinctness. It's to get them to see the fun in language play and the seriousness in language play." Instead of eschewing or encoding meaning, Stein turned to formally innovative writing as a way to open up the possibilities for how meaning works. She truly did (as she said) "hope that they will like it" (*How to Write* 158), and we have learned that students who are encouraged to experiment with their ways of reading Stein ultimately find significance and pleasure too in that reading. In *The Making of Americans*, Stein asks her reader to "arm yourself in every kind of a way to be patient, and to be eager" (34).

Context

Although stylistic, political, and cultural themes connect Stein to her contemporaries when one is describing the person, her biography, and her role in the modernist avant-garde, the connection weakens when one turns to her actual writing. Her texts rarely appear to have literary antecedents and often do not supply straightforward illustrations, for example, of her feminist sensibility or politics. Rather, she made her demand for change through career moves and by upsetting the expectations of readers trained by a patriarchal or Enlightenment-based system. Stein's texts were not created in a vacuum, as if her work and her life (or culture or bookshelf) were strictly separate, nor are they closed systems, referring solely to themselves; however, they can suspend what is normally the referential nature of language and literature. Readers might encounter a person's name and expect it to refer to a character, someone with a discernible role in a story; instead, Stein may be describing (not narrating) things that exist, so that a person's name, while it means something different from "umbrella" or "lemon," is one object among others. Toklas said of *Tender Buttons* that the aim was "to describe something without mentioning it" (qtd. in Thomson, *Virgil Thomson* 173). Stein can indefinitely defer as well, using the pronouns "she" or "it" without giving the antecedent.

Her seemingly unreferential writing has therefore often been called abstract. Ulla Dydo comments on this quality:

> With a minimal, monotonous vocabulary and great economy of means, she arranges the world in words that are not representations but analogues. For she writes not of the order of things but of the order of composition. I call her work on description abstract because out of the objects of the world of nature, she creates arrangements that do not exist in nature and are unlike any we have ever seen. (*Gertrude Stein* 131)

On the one hand, then, readers may learn not to search for a typical explanatory context; reaching beyond the text to explain may be a frustrated effort. On the other hand, as Dydo's *Gertrude Stein: The Language That Rises* makes abundantly clear, we can trace out "many apparently obscure references to immediate daily life—people, places, events, observations, letters" (7). Scholarship on Stein has long operated in this contradictory atmosphere, telling us that while contextual details may not explain the text or make us like it, they can shed light on the conditions of its creation. We have learned a great deal about the women behind *Three Lives*, for example; about the relationships that prompted Stein's portrait-poems; and about the influence of the Ain department (in eastern France)—where she spent half the year for the last two decades of her career—on her writing generally. The context matters but has limits; the text is foremost.

Structure

The essays in this collection are grouped into four sections: narrative prose, poetry and portraits, plays and operas, and creative principles. The organization is by genre, mainly, rather than by theme or chronology, to make the diversity of Stein's work clear to teachers working in a variety of classroom contexts. Creative writing teachers, for instance, will be pleased to see the myriad ways Stein can fit into courses or units on fiction, poetry, playwriting, and creative nonfiction. Teachers are encouraged to link Stein texts. A poem or lecture could be taught with one of her autobiographies; *Tender Buttons* could be taught with a portrait-poem or an excerpt from her fiction. This volume is designed to speak to all Stein's work, not just the texts most commonly taught. It travels the whole length of her career, from her student essays in 1894 and her first book-length text in 1903, *Q. E. D.*, to *The Mother of Us All* in 1946.

Respondents to our survey felt that this wide range is "crucially important," one wrote, because "it reveals her desire to remake and challenge definitions." "For me the range is everything," another said. A third asserted that the range is "precisely what I love about Stein." A fourth wrote, "One of the key ways in which Stein is an innovator lies precisely in this production of writing which engages and expands previous categories." A fifth argued, "Stein wants us to see that we don't read all texts the same way, that there's a multiplicity of ways of reading, oftentimes determined by the genre/form of the text." These responses accord with our claim that a fundamental aspect of Stein's career was her drive to renovate the genres, and invent new ones along the way. Stein was never just one writer, never just a novelist, poet, playwright, or theorist of the avant-garde.

Stein's critics have long recognized the importance of reading any Stein text in relation to the texts that come before and after it. As Dydo has argued on the basis of years of studying Stein in print and manuscript, "Always one Stein piece engenders the next, so that each becomes a context for the next" (*Gertrude Stein* 78). Linda Voris put it this way in her survey response:

> I tell [students] that [reading Stein in context] is much like standing in a really rich art gallery that has so many Cubist paintings that one can see the method change abruptly—that's it—the year or the month that Picasso shifted the compositional question. Stein's work is similar in that we can trace a compositional question as it spills over a range of texts and we can follow it because there are tag lines that recur across neighboring texts. This is extremely important in my teaching because I want to convey the excitement of open-ended innovation.

In using genre to structure this volume, we show how typical and generative it was for her to write across the genres, that everything she wrote has a synchronic aspect, and that she hoped that her readers would see any one piece in the context of the whole.

This volume focuses on Stein's writings but does not neglect her personality. Part 1, "Materials," includes a full biographical picture, and we encourage teachers to use anything in addition that can fill in the context for a Stein book and enliven class discussion, be it photographs, anecdotes, reviews, or parodies.[6] We take seriously the critical efforts to understand Stein's celebrity, her art collecting, her relationships with other modernist and popular writers and artists, and topics such as her life during World War II. The essays in this volume show teachers how to approach Stein so that the life and the writing are inseparable. The old life-work binary led to the conclusion that her life was accessible and interesting but her work was neither; in this volume, instead, we bring out the complexity of her life and the accessibility of her work.

Approaches

There are strategies for teaching this notoriously difficult writer, and they can be summarized in this way:

> Close listening: read the text aloud word by word, hear the rhythms, and listen to Stein recordings. The plays are especially useful for bringing a class together to decide how to voice a text.
>
> Close reading: note how repetition, disjunction, anaphora, punning, and the lack of punctuation defamiliarize words. Follow the changes in Stein's writing practice across texts, focusing on her use of sentence structure or conversational language and on her unsettling of the laws of genre.
>
> Contextualization: compare one Stein text with another. Study the literary, intellectual, and cultural history of her time. Compare a parody of Stein with a Stein original. Find a context for a Stein innovation. Become acquainted with the wildly divergent reception of her work.
>
> Creative exercises: write imitations or transformations; stage the plays.

Readers may look first for the particular text they are teaching—"Melanctha," *Tender Buttons*, or "Pictures," for instance. Or they may look for ideas on how to teach Stein in a particular course—creative writing, theater, or composition. Or they may have a topic in mind, such as gender, sexuality, race, the visual arts, war, celebrity, the archive, or Stein's influence on other writers. In what follows, we suggest some connections. We hope that readers who come to the volume with one text or approach in mind will leave with others.

Most of the contributors to this volume are in English departments, but some teach women's studies (Lamm), creative writing (Mullen), theater (Peck), and history (Schechter) courses. The essays by Patricia A. Schechter, by Stacy Hubbard, and by Rebecca Walsh draw on interdisciplinary approaches associated with American studies. We have contributors who work primarily with lower-level students: two in the first-year writing classroom (Foster, Kaufman), one (Rumbarger) teaching an introduction to fiction, and one (Goodspeed-Chadwick) teaching Stein in a survey course. Half the essays should work well at either the lower level or the upper level (Blackmer, Bollinger, Albrinck, Hedrick-Moser, Lamm, Gilbert, Diepeveen, Hollister and Setina, Brazier, Malcolm, Stec, Kirsch), but a number are aimed at upper-level undergraduate courses or graduate seminars (Goldberg–Moon–Guo, McCallum, Walsh, Voris, Cardinal, Frank, Peck, Schechter, Hubbard, Mullen).

Most of the essays situate Stein in her sociohistorical time, but some reach back to writing or figures before her (Albrinck, Gilbert, Schechter, Hubbard) or make connections to late-twentieth-century, Stein-influenced poetry and drama (McCallum, Peck, Mullen, Kirsch). Readers might compare Laurel Bollinger's description of Stein's influence on Hemingway with Michelle J. Brazier's description of Stein's collaboration with Virgil Thomson. There are essays that address Stein's life with Alice Toklas (Lamm, Cardinal, Hollister and Setina), and one on Stein as a student (Rumbarger). Issues of gender and sexuality are a focus (Goldberg–Moon–Guo, Blackmer, Bollinger, Rumbarger, Goodspeed-Chadwick, Lamm, Gilbert, Cardinal, Hollister and Setina, Schechter), as are issues of race and ethnicity (Blackmer, Hedrick-Moser, Schechter, Walsh). Some essays deal with modernist representation, including Stein's relation to the visual arts (Foster, Albrinck, Voris, Stec). The J. Ashley Foster and Meg Albrinck essays offer two different approaches to one text, *The Autobiography of Alice B. Toklas*; the Roger Gilbert, Julie Goodspeed-Chadwick, and Len Diepeveen essays offer three different approaches to *Tender Buttons*. The Kimberly Lamm, Voris, and Loretta Stec essays read *Tender Buttons* in the context of Stein's portrait-poems. Sharon J. Kirsch's essay also takes up Stein's portraits. Jane Malcolm's essay describes teaching Stein in a multilingual classroom (in Montreal, Canada). Several essays offer suggestions for creative exercises (Hedrick-Moser, Gilbert, Hollister and Setina, Frank, Peck, Mullen, and Kirsch). Three explore the trope of wandering (Blackmer, Walsh, Mullen). Susannah Hollister and Emily Setina explain in their essay how Stein's archival materials can affect our understanding of her writing and creative process. Hubbard addresses the effect of celebrity on Stein's notion of authorship. Elisabeth Hedrick-Moser explores Stein's late autobiography and her struggle to witness—indeed, a career-long question of Stein's was, What does seeing know? Readers can compare genres from the same period: for example, the essays by Hollister and Setina (poem), Foster (autobiography), Lee Rumbarger (novel), Hubbard (lecture), and Walsh (multigenre) all deal with Stein's writing in 1932–35.

The contributors close the gap between the description of a Stein text and the reading experience of that text by including excerpts as much as possible. So that we understand how Stein's writing usually performs rather than represents an idea, the teaching and reading strategies offered in the essays feature practical demonstrations and specific assignments. At the same time, as much as this volume offers pictures of actual classrooms—not every student is going to love Stein, nor is the analytical essay always the most effective assignment—readers are asked to consider the claim that Stein in the classroom may be greater than the Stein one reads on one's own. The contention sparked by these difficult texts can be pedagogically productive, as students (and teachers too) express their enthusiasm for or rejection of Stein. The task of learning how to read Stein can motivate a class to work together. Reading Stein teaches us that meaning is not just inherent in or derived from what others have done with words and forms. Meaning also depends on what we do today.

In 1926 Stein lectured at Cambridge and Oxford, and in 1934–35 she lectured at colleges across the United States and accepted an invitation to teach a two-week course at the University of Chicago. Despite some trepidation about public speaking, she ultimately embraced the teaching experience because she felt that students understood her work better than literary critics and fellow artists did. She "look[ed] to students as her most promising audience" (Dydo, *Gertrude Stein* 602). Teachers can draw at least some reassurance from that idea.

NOTES

[1] According to the *MLA International Bibliography*, from 2000 to 2017 more than 475 books and articles addressed Stein's work, as well as more than 120 dissertations. On teaching Stein, see Curnutt, "Parody"; English; Esdale, "Unoriginal Genius"; Kane; Keith; Peck and Howe; and Young.

[2] In 1928 Lindley Hubbell wrote a letter to *Transition* thanking the magazine for publishing Stein: "I do not think that you realize how widely accepted Miss Stein is in America—not by the articulate middle aged, but by the young ones" (Holbrook and Dilworth 111n). Shortly thereafter Stein wrote in a letter to Virgil Thomson: Hubbell "wrote transition a nice letter in which he said that one should not be discouraged by the remarks of the articulate middle aged which I thought a nice phrase" (110).

[3] Stein said in a 1935 interview, "The great thing is not ever to think about form but let it come. Does that sound strange from me? They have accused me of thinking of nothing else. Do you see the real joke? It is the critics who have really thought about form always and I have thought about—writing!" ("Conversation" 194).

[4] In a 1934 radio interview Stein said, "Look here, being intelligible is not what it seems, after all all these things are a matter of habit. . . . You mean by understanding that you can talk about it in the way that you have a habit of talking . . . putting it in other words . . . but I mean by understanding enjoyment. . . . If you enjoy it you understand it, and lots of people have enjoyed it so lots of people have understood it" ("Gertrude Stein" 89).

[5] Esdale's "Unoriginal Genius" describes this assignment in more detail.

[6] For parodies, see Diepeveen.

NARRATIVE PROSE

Teaching *Q. E. D.*

Jonathan Goldberg and Michael Moon, with Wenwen Guo

In the spring 2015 semester, we (Jonathan Goldberg and Michael Moon) taught *Q. E. D.* in a graduate seminar on Henry James, Willa Cather, and Gertrude Stein. Wenwen Guo, a student in the course, submitted a final paper that discussed *Q. E. D.* in ways that illuminate the goals of the course. We will be quoting from it later in this essay. The aim of the course was to consider how the three writers offer competing versions of queer modernisms. We were interested in pursuing a number of questions, as the course description indicated: "questions of relations between sexuality and writing, influence and imitation, visual and verbal modes of representation." To explore these issues we focused not only on the fiction but also on critical writings by the three writers, especially pieces in which they reflect on their own aims as writers. To narrow the focus further, we initially concentrated on James's *The Wings of the Dove* (1902), the late and experimental novel of his that Stein quotes directly in her novella *Q. E. D.* (1903). Stein was composing *Q. E. D.* only a year after James's novel was published, a notable instance of an immediate literary response.

Different in many ways as the fictional texts that we read in the course are from each other, several lines of convergence between and among these novels and novella emerged in the course of our discussions over the semester. These included a concern manifested by several of the texts, including *Q. E. D.*, with the dynamics and effects of triangulation on characters and plots. We also noticed a recurrent tendency in a number of these texts to produce and privilege moments of excess—emotional, epistemological, and affective—in which intense perceptions, the acquisition of exciting or frightening kinds of knowledge, and acute emotional responses are depicted and, to varying extents, analyzed by the character or characters involved. A related tendency to acquire knowledge by means of certain kinds of visual and nonverbal perception (as in unexpected social encounters in public or semipublic spaces, as a tourist or flâneur, or in unusually intense experiences of visual art) led us to repeated discussions of the pervasiveness of queer forms of looking and gazing. This last ongoing concern of the course was taken by Guo as the research topic of her final paper.

We began the course by looking at the first preface (1907) to the collected New York edition of James's fiction, introducing *Roderick Hudson* (1875), the novel that James retrospectively made his first, thereby dropping *Watch and Ward* (1871) from his oeuvre (Preface). This gesture of James's, in fact, shaped the readings we did subsequently. We considered Cather's *Alexander's Bridge* (1912)—reading it the week before *Q. E. D.*—and *O Pioneers!* (1913) along with the preface Cather wrote when *Alexander's Bridge* was republished in 1922, and finally an essay from 1931 titled "My First Novels (There Were Two)," at once including and yet trying to efface her first effort. In Stein's case, there are two first fictional works not published in her lifetime, *Q. E. D.* and "Fernhurst" (although Stein did publish material from "Fernhurst" in *The Making of Americans* and *Q. E. D.* lies behind "Melanctha"). Our decision to read *Q. E. D.* was in part a result of its inclusion with *Three Lives* in a convenient Norton Critical Edition. So, from the first, we were interested in how these writers came to decide where and how their careers began; a backward glance at (or suppression of) beginnings was a gesture that all three shared. It was possible, also, we thought, that Stein and Cather, in very different ways, to be sure, were following the example of James.

By the time we turned to *Q. E. D.*, the seminar had developed its skills in closely attending to difficult texts. Each week, we invited members of the class to open discussion by raising questions, tracing patterns, making connections; class discussion unfolded from these promptings. The class on *Q. E. D.* began by considering the passage from Shakespeare's *As You Like It* (in act 5, scene 2) that serves as its extended epigraph. Among the connections we saw was the transportation of a group of courtiers to a pastoral milieu not their own, intimating questions of politics and of exile that play out in Stein's novella as its three American women cross the Atlantic. This pattern also reminded us of similar trajectories in *The Wings of the Dove* and *Alexander's Bridge* (the latter novel charts the movements of bridge-builder Bartley Alexander between the United States, England, and Canada). The passage that Stein quotes from *As You Like It* also is one about the crossing of desire. Each character announces desire for another, who in turn announces desire for yet another. These crossings of desire are further crossed by the fact that one character, Rosalind, is cross-dressed as Ganymede. The audience knows that, and therefore knows that the desires all the characters might believe to be heterosexual are complicated by Rosalind's gender. Indeed, to say that Rosalind has one is to misstate: to the very end of the play, s/he maintains herself as both he and she. Her drag name, Ganymede, is period slang for a male prostitute, named after the Trojan boy that Zeus ravished and made his cupbearer. The female character's assumption of a male name may have reminded members of Shakespeare's initial audience, or the historically informed reader now, that the actor playing Rosalind is a boy actor.

Complications about the nature of desire, about the nature of the object of desire, and about its expression—everyone in the lines Stein cites saying the same thing, the same words, about desires that are differentiated by the nature of the one desired, and yet are articulated as if that difference made no difference—were some of the points that seemed key to Stein's choice of Shakespeare to evoke some of the tensions and stylistic features of the text that lies ahead. Our discussion proceeded to consider how Stein's novella reconfigures the ostensible heterosexual triangle of Milly Theale, Kate Croy, and Merton Densher in *Wings*. The prompt at the beginning of *Q. E. D.* describing Helen as the "American version of the English handsome girl" (179), for instance, associates her immediately with Kate Croy, whom James repeatedly describes as "handsome," rather than beautiful, positioning her somewhat equivocally in terms of gender norms (110, 112, 119). When Adele places Helen in Kate's position, she does it in a brutal recall of James: " 'What a condemned little prostitute it is,' Adele said to herself between a laugh and a groan. 'I know there is no use in asking for an explanation. Like Kate Croy she would tell me "I shall sacrifice nothing and nobody" and that's just her situation, she wants and will try for everything' " (219). We were rather taken aback by the note that Marianne DeKoven, the Norton editor, supplied at this point, identifying Kate as a "[s]elfish, hypocritical character" (219n8). When we concluded our discussion of *Wings*, we read Eve Kosofsky Sedgwick's "Is the Rectum Straight? Identification and Identity in *The Wings of the Dove*," in which what Sedgwick describes as Kate's "double-sidedness, presented and averted, recto and verso" (84) locates her not in the position of moral opprobrium that DeKoven offers as a gloss on Adele's version of Helen, but rather as a figure made by and to complicate hetero-homo difference. Sedgwick's positive reading of Kate is compatible with Adele's further thoughts about Helen: "I am so fond of her and do somehow so much believe in her that I am willing to help as far as within me lies. Besides I certainly get very much interested in the mere working of the machinery" (219).

Sedgwick argues that Kate's position as the daughter of the much-shamed Lionel Croy shapes her sexuality in the shadow of his unnamable difference; in this position, she radiates both same-sex desire for Milly and a cross-sex desire for Densher, a crossing and/or doubling of desire only further complicated by the degree to which Lionel Croy's situation (as a character who has suffered an indelible disgrace that Sedgwick interprets in relation to the trope of "unnamability," "the love that dare not speak its name," stigmatization and shaming) facilitates the author's erotic attachment to him.

We had noted similar crossings when we discussed *Alexander's Bridge*. In Cather's novel, Bartley Alexander's affair with Hilda Burgoyne transports him back to the "boy" he was when he first knew her. His affair with the English actress is also an affair with the western boy he left behind when he became a successful and married man. Cather's novel performs a kind of retrospect that also facilitates her inclusion of a same-sex desire that could as easily be read as her own fascination with Hilda as it is Bartley's fascination with a boy. These complications of sexual identity through cross-identification, we noticed, were treated in a rather blunt manner by DeKoven, who labels moments in *Q. E. D.* where the women in the text are identified as male as a code for their being lesbian. Although such cross-gender configurations are one way in which same-sex desire is registered in modernist writing (Sedgwick's *Epistemology of the Closet* further unfolds these complications), DeKoven's translation of Adele's "I always did thank God I wasn't born a woman" (181) into a "[r]eference to lesbian gender indeterminacy" (181n2) seemed to us rather too quickly to determine (and delimit) the range of meanings that indeterminacy might encompass.

Moreover, as DeKoven's note goes on to say, Adele here also is citing a Jewish prayer in which men express happiness that they were not born women. The complication of ethnic identity with sexual identity led us to discuss the ways in which the Americanness of the three young college-educated women in *Q. E. D.* is complicated by class and ethnicity (forecasting thereby the ways in which Stein would recast *Q. E. D.* in "Melanctha" across race and gender). It also led us to wonder to what degree it is fair to describe *Q. E. D.* as an overtly lesbian novella or to suppose that is the reason Stein did not publish it. DeKoven also appears certain, judging from her editorial apparatus (and following earlier scholarship on the text, such as Leon Katz's [Introduction]), that Adele is Stein herself, Helen Thomas is May Bookstaver, and Mabel Neathe is Mabel Haynes; such certainties about identity led us to discussions about epistemology, about how and what we as readers know and how and what characters know in this novella, questions of course that relate it to James, where such questions are always central. The circulation of knowledge about which character desires whom (or what), the kinds of strategies that arise for attempting to keep this knowledge secret or restricted to an intimate circle, and the sometimes fateful consequences of its becoming available to characters beyond this circle, is a primary focus of James's late fiction that Stein rigorously explores.

In *Q. E. D.*, the fact that Adele, Helen, and Mabel seem related to each other anagrammatically—the "el" they share is perhaps the L word—and the fact that they fetch their existence from other texts as well as from biographical sources further complicate the question of knowing and also open additional possibilities for pedagogy, such as (for example) drawing on the students' knowledge of novel tradition to discuss how characters such as those in *Wings* or in *Q. E. D.* differ in their relation to questions of knowing from those depicted in various realist, regionalist, or naturalist fictions. For a second example, the explicit intertextuality of *Q. E. D.* with *Wings* may raise questions in the classroom about other texts with which *Q. E. D.* may be intertextual, such as other fiction of the time about groups of young women students or travelers, the "new woman" novel, or the emergent lesbian novel of the time.

Discussions in class of such matters as the relation of coming to knowledge to narrative sequencing and temporality, sexuality, desire, and identity—either in one of the works of fiction that we read for the course or between one of these works and some other work of fiction that promised to make for productive comparison with it—provided ample leads for students to form research questions for their own writing projects. Students were required to submit brief, focused research statements in writing the week after midterm break in the course in order to choose a restricted topic and to begin writing on it for the research paper that was due at the end of the semester. Wenwen Guo's final essay took up and explored some of these questions, trying to puzzle out the "queer form of directness" in James (168) and the oblique "wonderful system" that joins Kate and Densher (358). Guo writes of the beginnings of her interest in writing about these questions: "Reading Cather's *Alexander's Bridge* impressed on me the importance of looking and failing to look (between Hilda and Bartley, between Winifred and Bartley). I then investigated similar instances of looking between characters in *The Wings of the Dove* and *Q. E. D.* and was struck by its peculiar appearance in several key relationships."

Against the complications in Stein's novella as Adele tries to puzzle out Helen's relation to Mabel (and to herself), Guo analyzed the brief moment in *Q. E. D.* when Adele seems relieved of these stresses as she enjoys a pastoral moment with a Spanish girl she happens to meet at one point in her travels. Here is an excerpt from her paper:

> The encounter between Adele and a Spanish girl sheds light upon the constituents of a communicative rapture, "a feeling of complete companionship." One day, while "looking down at Granada desolate in the noonday sun," Adele comes upon a young Spanish girl: "As she came nearer they smiled at each other and exchanged greetings. The child sat down beside her." Adele is inexplicably but unquestionably overwhelmed by what one might call the perfection of this interaction, despite or because of "their ignorance of each other's language." The suddenness and the intensity of such an emotional surge is not incomparable to an ecstatic religious experience: "For some time they sat there, finally they arose and walked on together. They parted as quiet friends part, and as long as they remained in sight of each other they turned again and again and signed a gentle farewell." What has transpired between Adele and the Spanish girl besides smiles, greetings and other gestures, is a sustained flow of visual exchanges. There is both bodily side-by-sideness and a repetitive turning. Adele and the Spanish girl, prompted by an unwillingness to part from one another, arguably forever, will themselves to turn, time and again, to cast as many glances as they can, before their inevitable farewell. This desire to engage in prolonged visual exchanges is a key to what Adele characterizes as a "simple" but "perfect" experience that infuses one with "real joy" (187).

The incident overall raises the question of whether it is possible for such a character as Adele to enjoy what she has experienced as the absolute pleasure of her brief but intense encounter with the Spanish girl on a more prolonged basis. A point of comparison here for Guo's paper is not only the relatively turbulent relationship that Adele appears to have with Helen in the novella, but also the relatively enduring romantic relationship that James's narrator describes as arising between Kate Croy and Merton Densher as a product of their exchanging a series of glances in the course of a short journey on the London underground (50–51).

The theoretical framework of Guo's paper was an eclectic assemblage of concepts drawn from such sources as Jean-Paul Sartre's phenomenological account of the look or *le regard*, Jacques Lacan's formulation of the mirror stage and the importance of looking in the process of ego formation, Jacques Rancière's discussions of the effects of disconnections in looking in his *The Intervals of Cinema*, and Sedgwick's discussions of the dynamics of the "beside" in her *Touching Feeling*. Discussions in class regarding the rendering of visual phenomena and of the relation of sexuality to looking and the kinds of knowledge that come of gazing, including mutual or reciprocal gazing, helped her select the kinds of analytical terms and tools that she wanted to bring to bear on her analysis of looking in Stein and James.

We end with some retrospects:

I (Michael Moon) taught *Q. E. D.* in 1990, in the English department at Duke University, in one of the first undergraduate courses I offered on gay and lesbian literature. We read Stein's novella alongside Radclyffe Hall's *The Well of Loneliness* (1928), discussing the very different versions of lesbian desire that the two texts present. We also speculated about Stein's possible reasons for not publishing the book during her lifetime: a question partially, but perhaps not entirely, answered by noting the storm of controversy with which Hall's overtly lesbian novel had been received a quarter of a century after Stein wrote her book (we also discussed some of the defenses of Hall's novel, by such writers as Virginia Woolf and E. M. Forster, whom we were also reading in the course). I am at present preparing a senior seminar on Stein scheduled for academic year 2015–16, in which we shall be studying writings from throughout her career, and I am struck as I was in coteaching our recent graduate course, by the inadequacy of judgments that assign *Q. E. D.* to an allegedly earlier and simpler time in Stein's career before she began producing the "difficult" writing for which she is famous: the complexities of *Q. E. D.* present their own kinds of challenges to readers, even ones who have also encountered *Tender Buttons* and *Stanzas in Meditation*.

More than twenty years ago, when I (Jonathan Goldberg) last taught *Q. E. D.* in a graduate seminar at Johns Hopkins University on the history of sexuality, I had come to Stein by way of James, and to both of them by way of Michel Foucault and Sedgwick, and more immediately, when we turned to Stein, through contextualization in essays by George Chauncey, on the emergence of homosexuality from an inversion model (the one DeKoven assumes); by Carroll Smith-Rosenberg, on female friendship and the emergence of lesbian difference around the figure of the New Woman of the early twentieth century; and by Esther Newton ("The Mythic Mannish Woman"). The point of such historical contextualization, in that class, was not to arrive at a vision of history as one in which identities emerge with a name and a distinctness from past ways of comprehending the nature of desire. Teaching *Q. E. D.* now, it seemed possible to imagine that point was well established and could be presumed, as seemed to be the case as our discussions developed. Still, students who are unfamiliar with queer work or the history of sexuality are ill served by the apparatus of the Norton *Wings*, which does not include Sedgwick's essay on James, while the apparatus for *Q. E. D.* and *Three Lives* is almost entirely about questions of race and ethnicity. All of this prompts questions about how best to historicize Stein's practice: intense reading of her work as it exemplifies modernist practices of the attempt to make it new, rather than slotting it into prefabricated notions of identity.

To put this a different way, and to return to something we (Michael Moon and Jonathan Goldberg) noted in class, let's take the 1950 title for *Q. E. D.*, "Things As They Are," as an answer to the last words of *Wings*, the declaration that Kate and Densher "shall never be again as we were" (407). This temporal prompt, we would conclude, is a project that speaks to queer theory, to Sedgwick's embrace of sidedness (and besideness), but also to Michel Foucault's claim that it was the work that still lay ahead for friendship to become—to invent—a way of life. *Q. E. D.*, in its title, offers the promise of a geometric proof, but it is perhaps closer to say that the "quod" to be shown remains a *Q* whose answer is in the making.

Teaching Race, Gender, and Narrative Form in "Melanctha"

Corinne E. Blackmer

As "Melanctha" opens, the eponymous heroine acts as a nurse, doing "everything that any woman could" to help her erstwhile friend Rose Johnson give birth to her baby, who dies shortly thereafter. As the narrator, who initially seems gleefully naive and bumptious, relates, "[Melanctha Herbert] tended Rose, and was patient, submissive, soothing, and untiring, while the sullen, childish, cowardly, black Rose grumbled and fussed and howled and made herself to be an abomination and like a simple beast" (*Three Lives* 53). Perhaps to elicit a kind of shocked attentiveness to the text, Gertrude Stein launches her story by doubling down on egregiously unapologetic and deliberately provoking racial stereotypes. When students first approach this text, however, they do not know that it neither pretends to authoritative knowledge nor intends to make racial, gendered, or sexualized sense. The text's final evaluation of Rose reverses this opening description; the result is ironic dissonance, with ostensible racist discourse in the process.

Students will need to traverse almost the entire novella—moving through Melanctha's miserable childhood, her youthful "wanderings" (61), her tutelary lesbian relationship with Jane Harden, her troubled heterosexual bond with Jefferson Campbell, her romance with the "reckless" gambler Jem Richards (135), and her masochistic, daughterly bond to Rose—to see the description repeated (138). Then, after Rose ejects Melanctha from her house for flirting with her husband, the narrator describes Rose, from Melanctha's point of view, as always "so simple, solid, decent" (145). Miming the winding confusions and uncertainties experienced by characters who question received racial and sexual knowledge, the narrator alternately describes Rose Johnson as "black" (137), "real black" (53), and "black but raised by real nice kind of white folks" (129). Other African American characters are either praised or blamed for being "pale yellow" (56), "very black" (132), "pale brown" (70), "light brown" (70), "half white" (125), "colored" (56), "mulatto" (57), or "a negress [but] so white that hardly anyone could guess it" (65). Because these characters exhibit contentment, cruelty, alcoholism, recklessness, caring, childishness, desire, sorrow, or selfishness, racial stereotypes fail to make sense. Does Stein stoop to blatant racist language, or does she employ racial and gendered stereotypes of separate spheres with sardonic insistence to draw the reader's attention to their status as incoherent social fictions?

The dystopian opening can repel our desire to engage with this cultural object. Thus contextualization is needed for teaching "Melanctha," from *Three Lives*,[1] particularly since many students come to Stein doubting their ability to understand this modernist author. As the text jettisons narrative conventions of depth, cause and effect, and linearity, students can, like Melanctha, become more open to the world and the self's potential. They can imbibe the idea that identities are not cultural or biological givens but rather are created, sought after, and modified through time, experience, and formative epistemological encounters.

When teaching "Melanctha," I make use of the ancient Jewish pedagogical practice of *havruta* ("fellowship"), which, originally designed for study of the Talmud, works particularly well with challenging texts. Dividing students into groups of two, I give each pair close reading and research assignments and ask them to participate in and lead class discussion. Not isolated, the students struggle together to understand the meanings of passages, apply their learning to larger issues in the text (and in their lives), and correct the biases or limitations in each other's vision. The class, through *havruta*, assumes responsibility for understanding three seminal factors that informed how Stein crafted her narrative design and represented her African American characters: scientific racism, discourses of homosexuality, and Jamesian psychology. All three implicate her in creating a masklike self-portraiture in "Melanctha" to identify with and distance herself from a bourgeois moral background.

Scientific racism. From the 1880s to 1920s, the heyday of scientific racism, this theory was used to exclude and control nonwhite races and prove the superiority of the Caucasian race. Caucasians were intelligent, strong, beautiful, and, according to social Darwinist ideology, destined to survive as the fittest. Other ethnic groups, including Jews, were subject to negative classifications, but African Americans represented the inverse of the superior Anglo Saxon race.[2]

Stein, born in 1874, lived in a culture saturated with this racism. However, she also interacted with African Americans in Oakland and as a medical student in Baltimore. Moreover, as a Jewish lesbian she was a target herself of odious classifications. With the exception of a few fixed types (James Herbert as the "brute," for instance [70]), "Melanctha" undoes the pseudo-logic of scientific racism, revealing it to be an ironic farce. Students, working in *havruta*, can be asked to track one or more characters in "Melanctha" and analyze how they diverge from a racial type and also how other factors—gender, sexuality, social class, education, respectability, and social marginality—complicate, challenge, and enrich the representation of character in the text. In addition to the major characters, Melanctha Herbert and Jefferson Campbell, students can construct concise portraits of, for instance, Jane ("hardened") Harden. Jane, Melanctha's first lover, is an alcoholic lesbian schoolteacher who "wanders widely" (65), who "had power and liked to use it," and who had "much white blood that made her see clear" (66). But the *havruta* will observe, as they read, how notwithstanding the supposedly ameliorative effects of her "white blood" and despite her "good mind" (71), Jane was fired from her job because of her drinking and lives a marginal existence. Eventually, having learned from Jane how to "use power" and feeling "ready now herself to do teaching" (68), Melanctha turns the tables and deserts the lovelorn Jane in "her trouble" (67). Asking the *havruta* to examine the relation between gender and race can reveal to them how and why race as a construct of scientific racism is connected to modes of power and powerlessness. The *havruta* may also note that fictions of identity based on scientific racism distract attention from the more substantive problems—lovelessness, maternal alienation, class limitation, and moral dogma—that the text explores.

Discourses of homosexuality. By the time Stein wrote "Melanctha," she was eager to put her middle-class background behind her through a daring narrative about African Americans that challenged scientific racism and sexual taboos. But she was still working through societal perceptions of her sexual orientation. She had explored these conflicted feelings in what might be called the earlier lesbian version of "Melanctha," *Q. E. D.* I teach *Q. E. D.* alongside "Melanctha" in LGBT-themed upper-division and graduate courses and have the *havruta* lead class discussions about the transformations Stein made in adapting the Adele-Helen relationship to the Jeff-Melanctha one.[3] The *havruta* conduct research on the period to report on how the public saw lesbianism as a criminal vice and how medical sexology perceived *inversion* as a biologically inherited anomaly, a form of insanity, or a neurological disorder (see Terry and Urla; Rosario). Stein's conflict over her lesbianism was manifested in her love affair with May Bookstaver. Stein was aware of the establishment view of homosexuality and also the belief, expressed by such writers as Charlotte Perkins Gilman (*Women and Economics* [1898]), that sexual passion, which led to marriage and dependency, prevented women from achieving social equality. When Stein finally accepted and expressed her feelings, Bookstaver had lost romantic interest, just as Melanctha eventually wandered away from Jeff. Bookstaver was exhausted by Stein's moral dithering and, as Melanctha says of Jeff, "wanting to have it all clear out in words always, what everybody is always feeling" (107). Stein addresses discourses of homosexuality in Melanctha's relationship with Jane Harden. Students can also study the relationship with Rose Johnson ("real black"), which is infused, for Melanctha ("pale yellow"), with considerable homoerotic and racial desire. In these two texts, what might have been a pathological vision of lesbianism is instead compelling and complex human tragedy.

Jamesian psychology. The character dynamics of race, gender, and sexuality also emerge from her debt to her teacher William James, whom she met when she was an undergraduate at Radcliffe. Influenced by him and his textbook *Principles of Psychology* (1890), she did experiments testing modes of attention that led to two articles, including "Cultivated Motor Automatism" (1898). The *havruta* can read selected passages from that article and explore, in research papers, how her science background informed "Melanctha," particularly around gender and gendered relations. According to James, habits of attention allow human beings to focus on certain things at the expense of the welter of sensations that bombard them. These random sensations transfix children, who are much more open to perceptions that are interesting and exciting and much less utilitarian and self-centered than adults, who have more rigidified habits. Adults judge sensations according to existing schema that, for instance, reinforce racial and gender stereotypes. Habits of attention therefore have ethical consequences—for instance, adults, who have lost the antiutilitarian perceptual habits of children, can reflexively prejudge minorities.

In a Jamesian view of "Melanctha," Melanctha and Jeff are opposed psychological types locked in a hopeless standoff (see Ruddick 134–58). Melanctha is putatively childlike in her desire for "wisdom" (60), "excitements," and taking care of others with no care for herself, whereas Jefferson lives according to the adult preconceptions that make him want to have "his" colored people "live regular" and stop "this running around business" (73). At first, Jeff represses sexual passion by blinkering his perception to include only secure parental love, his status as a doctor, and a bourgeois ethos of self-control. He learns, however, the wisdom of greater openness to sexual and intellectual experience from Melanctha and, with his mind improved, incorporates what he has learned into an epistemology: "Jeff always had strong in him the meaning of all the new kinds of beauty Melanctha Herbert once had shown him, and always more and more it helped him with his working for himself and the colored people" (129). Above all, he learns about the conflicted nature of the complex self—a lesson that the *havruta* can develop through an assignment on how Jamesian psychological theories of perception inform the representation of the relationship between Jeff and Melanctha.

Jamesian psychology can also help the *havruta* analyze the female-female dynamic in the relationship between Melanctha and Rose. The narrator blithely inquires why the "subtle, intelligent, attractive, half-white girl Melanctha loves and demeans herself in service to the coarse, decent, sullen, ordinary, black, childish Rose," who, unlike Melanctha, is "regularly married" (54). According to a Jamesian reading, Rose, as an adult, has learned middle-class codes of conduct and has the perceptual habits of an unreflective and selfish adult. The childlike Melanctha does not feel safe in the world, so she clings to Rose for protection. When Rose expels Melanctha from her house, Melanctha feels lost, and "all the world went whirling in a mad weary dance around her" (145).

Students should be cautioned—and they should also learn it through their analysis of the story in conjunction with the reading of cultural-context articles—that Stein rejected James's belief in separate spheres. A lesbian, she identifies herself not only with Jeff but also with the bisexual Melanctha. Melanctha's masochistic dependence on the "childish" Rose also seems related to Melanctha's orphan status and abusive childhood. As Rose reports to her husband, Sam, Melanctha's mother had told her father that "it was awful sad to her, Melanctha had not been the one the Lord had took from them stead of the little brother who was dead in the house there from fever" (133). Jeff asks Melanctha to be his teacher, and she does all the teaching and giving and most of the risk-taking. Hence only Jeff benefits, while the "complex, desiring" Melanctha eventually wanders away in boredom, hurt, and frustration, her sexual feelings for him eviscerated by his inquisitions. She is the same person she was before meeting him yet discernibly more "blue" and despairing at "the thought of how all her world was made" (54). The *havruta*'s class dramatization represents the perspectives of both Jeff and Melanctha, putting select passages from the text in their own words. In this exercise the *havruta* not only reflect on how Stein's narrative style differs from the realist norms but also investigate the topics of teaching and learning, racism and pseudo-racist discourse, spontaneity and middle-class mores, and gender and separate spheres.

In my experience, students are frustrated by the interpretive challenges arising from the representations of race, gender, sexuality, and modern psychology and by the lack of narrative cause and effect. They often express fatigue at the length, repetition, and miscommunication in the romantic saga between Melanctha and Jeff, which is the philosophical center of the novella and extends dialectically for over fifty pages. Stein's claim that "Melanctha" marks "the first definite step away from the nineteenth century and into the twentieth century in literature" (*Autobiography* 54) explains both difficulties. As a modernist, Stein jettisons traditional literary cause and effect, so the only conclusion we can draw from the conjunction of the facts that Melanctha begins to "live regular" (146) and then dies of consumption is that poor women often died from this disease. Without a narrative causal nexus, the episodes in the text careen from one to another.

I explain to students that they can understand the text through the episodic relationships Melanctha has with others and through the motifs: wisdom, blues, real experience, excitement, living regular, and power. The *havruta*, tracing the characters' shifting attributes, examine how phrases like "real experience" and "world wisdom" change according to the epistemological, philosophical, and linguistic concerns Stein is addressing. For instance, both caregiving and caretaking are forms of failed "real experience" and major motifs. A systolic-diastolic movement of reconciliation and alienation informs all Melanctha's relationships: she "was always being left when she was not leaving others" (56). Like the Hebrew Bible, Stein's text repeats a word and thus multiplies its connotations. Meaning becomes determined by the specific context. The rhythmically repetitive language disconnects words from what they describe (see North 73). Stein's innovative prose raises doubt about the relation between noun and referent, sign and signifier, and cognitive process and artistic representation. Her repetition questions, undoes, and remakes meanings.

The best pedagogical approach to the exhausting conversation between Jeff and Melanctha is to have the *havrutas* lead class discussions on the contrast between the complex and unified self, reason and spontaneity, the function of putatively "remember[ing] right" (114), and the fearful pull of passion. Such discussions can lead to jointly produced close-reading papers in which, for example, the *havrutas* respond to a prompt about the representation of the conflicted Freudian self and the morally unified pre-Freudian self. At a central moment of the text, Melanctha wanders away from her first love, Jane, during the final illness of Melanctha's mother, Mis Herbert, and becomes acquainted with Dr. Jefferson Campbell, who has never had "real trouble" (70). As Jeff admires Jane, a bemused Melanctha points out to him the contradiction between his avowed wish that the "colored people" stop "running around" and "all the time being in excitements" (73) and his preference for the company of a woman like the "roughened" Jane (66):

> But Melanctha Herbert had listened to him say all this. She knew he meant it, but it did not mean much to her, and she was sure some day he would find out, that it was not all, of real wisdom. Melanctha knew very well what it was to have real wisdom. "But how about Jane Harden?" said Melanctha to Jeff Campbell, "seems to me Dr. Campbell you find her to have something in her, and you go there very often, and you talk with her much more than you do the nice girls that stay at home with their people, the kind you say you are really wanting. It don't seem to me Dr. Campbell, that what you say and what you do seem to have much to do with each other." (113)

She goes on to say that she "knows" such "real wisdom"—one of many other resonant verbal clusters that can refer to sexual knowledge, insight into power, worldly experience, or self-understanding. Stein shows how abstract, multivocalic thought coalesces in vernacular language with a limited vocabulary.

Attempting to move too fast through a text that has such rich meanings will only confirm that "Melanctha" is difficult, but the practice of *havruta* can help eliminate this stumbling block. The extra time spent will enable the students to bond with one another and become much more sophisticated about language, reading, and writing.

NOTES

[1] The other two stories, "The Good Anna" and "The Gentle Lena," are stellar examples of American naturalist fiction about the immigrant experience for lower-class women. "The Good Anna" is an example of lesbian experience as well. I like teaching "Melanctha" together with *Q. E .D.* (1903) and feminist African American texts such as Nella Larsen's *Passing* (1929). I have long remained fascinated by Stein's treatment of appearance versus reality, sexual liberation, and middle-class world wisdom.

[2] For an excellent discussion of issues of race and sexuality, see S. Gilman.

[3] When teaching a non-LGBT-focused class in modernism, I take excerpts of *Q. E. D.* dealing with the conflicts between feeling and reason in the relationship between Adele (Stein) and Helen (Bookstaver) (183, 200, 227) and have students compare them with analogous passages on the relationship between Melanctha and Jeff (86, 93, 123), where Stein provides herself with a middle-class male persona interested in helping "his people" to "avoid trouble" (70, 77).

Americans Aloud

E. L. McCallum

Why teach *The Making of Americans*? Why not choose something shorter, like *Ida* or *Tender Buttons*, or more accessible, like *Everybody's Autobiography* or *Three Lives*? Admittedly, *The Making of Americans* is long and unwieldy to work into a semester, much less a quarter. But its length is precisely why we should teach it, and teach the entirety. The book exploits the novel form, pushing the limits of time and attention, needing room to recount three generations of two American families and all the people they knew and know. In the process, it fundamentally changes our understanding of the novel form and of reading. The evolving styles for which the book is known mark shifts in focus from grandparents to parents to children. Stein develops an expanded, nonlinear consideration of time and being that transforms the novel from a linear narrative into a spatial, durational, layered, and relational one. She picks up the tools of the nineteenth-century novel, initially interleaving first-person-plural narration and third-person-tagged discourse, gradually complicating free indirect discourse, only to invent her own mode of storytelling, refracting the perspectives of narrator and character across a spectrum marked by the third-person impersonal ("one" or "some"). To fully experience this transformation requires reading the whole book.

To read Gertrude Stein is to be inescapably aware of *The Making of Americans*. The book hinges between her early experimental efforts in *Three Lives* and the full flourishing of her genius in *Tender Buttons* and other later works. This novel is pivotal not only in her oeuvre but also in literary history: as Jayne Walker observes, "the trajectory of Stein's writings from *Three Lives* to *Tender Buttons* should come to be regarded as a crucial episode in the history of representation" (xix). *The Making of Americans*, written between 1903 and 1911, occupies the middle of that trajectory—Stein rightly compares her novel with James Joyce's and Marcel Proust's twentieth-century masterpieces, observing that "in the three novels written in this generation that are the important things written in this generation, there is, in none of them a story. There is none in Proust in *The Making of Americans* nor in *Ulysses*" ("Portraits" 184).[1]

The novel's seeming lack of story and our expectation that it should have one provoke us to reflect on how we read. English majors may be adept at consuming a long novel over two or three weeks, but Stein's demands a slower reading pace. I use a few strategies to help students embrace that pace. First, I teach the book over seven weeks in a course on women writers for undergraduate English majors, pairing one section of the novel each week with other texts, from Emily Dickinson's poems to works by contemporary experimental writers—such as Harryette Mullen's *Sleeping with the Dictionary* (2002) or *Recyclopedia* (2006), Lyn Hejinian's *The Language of Inquiry* (2000), Anne Carson's *Autobiography of Red* (1998), Carole Maso's *Ava* (2002)—who have been influenced by Stein.[2] This approach lets students see how writers today, in their work with language, form, and genre, have learned from Stein. The juxtaposition with Dickinson places Stein's work in a larger historical trajectory, provocatively questioning who is a twentieth-century writer, since much of Dickinson's work came to be available only in the twentieth century, and her originality has famously complicated the publication of her poems. While I make no claim that Stein read Dickinson—indeed, a key reason for this collocation is to wrest the Stein text from the tenacious grip of the biographical—the pairing shows students how Stein's experimenting with ordinary language and representing experience is part of a longer tradition.

The second strategy I use is to have students read Stein's novel aloud in class.[3] Fortunately I have a three-hour seminar block, so I use the first fifty minutes for reading aloud, the second fifty minutes for a discussion of Stein (with a brief written reflection to launch that discussion), and the third fifty minutes for a discussion of the paired text. We read aloud the beginning of the section assigned for the upcoming week; students will finish reading on their own by the next class. The class sits in a circle and takes turns, each student reading a page while all the others have their books closed to focus on listening. I read in my turn with the students, modeling for them how to make sense of the underlying rhythms of the text, or how inflection can convey emotion or implicit meanings, which some students find difficult to discern in Stein until they hear the text. Yet student readings often reveal an intuitive, sure-footed understanding of the language, if not of the novel, far beyond what the students will articulate in discussion; their readings bring out inflections or rhythms I did not notice before.

Depending on the difficulty of the style, we can generally cover twelve to fifteen pages in fifty minutes, stopping at the end of the page when the clock is up. I ask students to write down briefly their observations of what they heard and also what they noticed as they took their turn reading aloud. What rhythms or sounds or other patterns did you hear? How did the language feel in your mouth? Were the sentence rhythms natural or challenging? How is the act of reading aloud itself a mode of interpretation, as one decides how to color the text in performance? Where did you feel you stumbled or had to reach in order to finesse smoothness in reading?

The feeling of reading a page aloud changes markedly as we progress through the novel, as conventional sentences give way to more repetitive and less clearly punctuated ones. Students particularly notice the absence of commas. In the late middle sections, they feel precariously on the edge as they read, having to slow down in order to say everything accurately and in the right order. I may bring specific passages to their attention—for instance, when a reader has tripped over a word, misread, or changed pace, I ask what the text is signaling by making this moment difficult to read. Whatever such passages elicit, I invite discussants to consider how the difficulty of the form leads to questions of content: What is the novel doing in this passage?

Students frequently offer fruitful insights. They remark, for instance, on how much easier the David Hersland chapter (723–904) is to read aloud than the Alfred Hersland and Julia Dehning chapter (479–719), although when reading silently they often find the opposite to be true. I agree with them: the second section of the Alfred Hersland and Julia Dehning chapter (598–719) is particularly challenging to get through; therefore I provide no paired text that week. Whereas this chapter is very detailed and discusses many people whom the characters know (not to mention the cresting of the narrator's emotional obsessing about her ability to write), the David Hersland chapter shifts to simple language and has less detail and far fewer names. Since the David Hersland chapter aims both to play with variations in language—as in Stein's parsing of an idea ("completely liking that thing . . . almost completely liking that thing . . . quite liking that thing . . . not liking that thing" [822])—and to foil conventional novelistic referentiality, reading aloud helps students appreciate and even revel in it and the last chapter. The fun of saying, "He was one being living in being one being living," can outweigh a reader's anxiety about what that means (827). Close attention to Stein's precision in parsing "completely" versus "almost completely" versus "quite" helps students see that Stein is being equally precise in describing a particular mode of existence as "one being living in being one being living." The practice of reading aloud directs attention to these details of the text, and reflecting on their experience helps students cultivate a sense of aesthetic relation to the text, so that these details matter. From week to week, reading aloud gives students a kind of geological sampling of the text: comparing the strata shows them how and why its styles and purposes evolve. That sense of evolution can be gained only by reading the whole book.

After reading aloud, we consider critically the reading that students completed in preparation for class. This retrospective look at what leads up to what we just read aloud follows the method of the novel itself: an open-ended tension between beginning again and evolving into something new. By considering the difference between the text read aloud and what the students read at home, we observe how Stein gradually shades from one style to another. Although each chapter has its distinct mode, the differentiation of modes does not align with section or chapter breaks, as they do in a realist novel, where a new chapter often signals a shift in plot, narrator, focus, and so on. Keeping students mindful of the earlier sections is vital, so that they can experience the queer temporality[4] that Stein later described in her 1934 lecture: "I was faced by the trouble that I had acquired all this knowledge gradually but when I had it I had it complete at one time. . . . And a great deal of *The Making of Americans* was a struggle to do this thing, to make a whole present of something that it had taken a great deal of time to find out" ("Gradual Making" 147).

This peculiar interplay between the duration of a novel—how long it takes to read—and the sense that one has of "a whole present" is the essence of the aesthetic experience of *The Making of Americans*, in which text is transformed into performance. Notably, a number of stage performances have been developed from Stein's novel, including an opera and a musical.[5] The gradual reading of *The Making of Americans* enables students to reach this "whole present" and make it their own.

We read aloud because listening is an overlooked mode of critical understanding that needs concerted practice. Reading aloud as a collective activity takes us back to a time before networked media; it also takes us back personally, to when we were very young and our parents read to us. Reading aloud defamiliarizes students from their habits of silent reading and cultivates a different mode of attention. They must tackle firsthand Stein's syntax, rhythms, diction, and punctuation. So much of the work of Stein's novel is bodily: it uses language to call attention to the rhythms of the body, especially to how breathing and phrasing collaborate in the spaces between words to create meaning.[6] Reading aloud helps students learn the cadences of the sentences in *The Making of Americans*. It also calls attention to Stein's formal, insistent use of "As I was saying" (393) or the subtle shift in prepositions or pronouns from one phrase to the next, as from "a whole one to me" to "a whole one in me" (291). These are details that silent readers may overlook, focusing instead on characters, events, and themes. Reading aloud emphasizes the performative aspect of interpretation: the novel performs what it narrates. An example is how the narrator obtrudes more and more into the story; by the middle chapters, the narrator's histrionics about writing punctuate the text, often mirroring the readers' own feelings, whether of frustration or delight.

Outside class, students complete a reading register, which has a two-part structure and a length of at least seven hundred words. Each entry starts with a close reading of the text, usually a sentence, although given Stein's inflection of sentences within a paragraph, it is often useful to close-read a paragraph's patterns. Then students are asked to write about what registers with them in the week's reading assignment, whether it intrigues, puzzles, confuses, is creatively inspiring, or offers some insight.[7]

The narrator's own formation and deformation especially engage students and thus serve as an important pedagogical hook. In the early sections, which tell how Julia Dehning came to marry Alfred Hersland and how their grandparents immigrated, we deliberate whether the novel is recounted in first person or third person. We consider the distinction between story and discourse, tagged and untagged speech, and how focalization works. As we move further into the novel, the story of the families opens out into a description of the people around them—the Hersland neighbors, servants, governesses—and gradually yields to the narrator's effort to tell, which becomes the new story, alongside the narrator's increasing concern with the philosophical project of categorizing people in their "bottom nature" as either "resisting being" or "attacking being." Some students are frustrated that the family history they found so appealing turns into philosophy; others like the philosophy and are drawn in by the narrator's personality. As the novel progresses, this taxonomy in turn breaks down, and the narrator's struggle to tell the story comes to a crisis. Finally the first-person narrator disappears, and so do the boundaries of individuality in characterization. The actors engaged in events become "some" or "one," and it becomes difficult to discern whether the "one" is focalized or not. Some students miss the narrator; others embrace this multisubjective representation, feeling that it brings them closer to David Hersland.

Focusing on the narrator helps students manage the novel's innovations by giving them familiar tools to guide their reading and detach them from the presumed protagonists and the appeal of the family story. It keeps them from being frustrated by, for instance, the announcement "This is now a history of Martha Hersland" (290), a story that is really given only in the second Martha Hersland section (382–476) and even then not completely. But focusing on the narrator raises an interesting problem: What do we do with the gender of the narrator? If we ascribe the feminine pronoun, we risk conflating Stein and the narrator, which we should not do, because this book is a novel.[8] "It" is too impersonal. I ask students what marks the gender of the narrator. Some argue that the way the narrator emotes and chooses certain words indicates that she is feminine. In an early and vivid address to the reader, the narrator describes the writing material as "this scribbled and dirty and lined paper that is really to be to me always my receiver . . . my scraps of paper" (33), which they feel is a feminine mode of description. "A man would never diminish his writing paper with words like as 'scribbled' and 'scraps,'" one student observed. Others opine that the narrator's affinity for describing women (205) indicates her own womanhood. We consider how a persona is created by the narrator and what other attributes we perceive—is the narrator positioning herself as part of the family whose tale she recounts? Is she a resisting being or an attacking being—two core terms of the novel's typology? This last question is best asked before the narrator confesses (573). That the narrator claims to be a resisting being, when "[g]enerally speaking those having resisting being in them have a slow way of responding" (347), may help us appreciate the novel's own slow accretion of meaning and understanding, the emphasis on description rather than action, or how its style evolves as an evasion of or way around an obstacle to the narrative.

Teaching *The Making of Americans*, although it affords pleasure and serendipitous experiences, is unquestionably a matter of managing frustrations. The sheer length of the novel makes even graduate students chafe at reading more slowly and more reiteratively. I remind students how John Ashbery remarked that in reading the novel the first time, he essentially "read it about three or four times, since I had to read every sentence, I think, at least that many times" ("Being" 84); I encourage them to take inspiration from his experience. Constantly beginning again is a trope of the narrator, yet when students have reflected on how "loving repeating" or "always I am beginning again and again and again" (337) is her methodology, they start to appreciate the way that the accretion of sentences and paragraphs gradually affects our perception of the people whom the narrator describes.[9] In their evaluations of the course, students overwhelmingly say that it improved their critical thinking, reading, and language skills. While a few remain detractors of Stein, most are excited by her work and the possibilities she opens up, and they feel a great sense of accomplishment in completing the book.[10] In particular, aspiring writers have come away from reading this novel with their creative practice transformed. The methodology of the novel teaches students to be aware of being in the moment as it unfolds, to be present with our perceptions and patient with our observations, attentive in and to all our senses. In an age of distraction, this is a most valuable lesson indeed.

NOTES

[1] Early in the course, I assign Stein's lectures "Portraits and Repetition" and "The Gradual Making of *The Making of Americans*" to orient students.

[2] I pair texts that resonate with what is going on in Stein's novel: *Autobiography of Red* fits with the second Martha Hersland chapter, for instance, since both are about betrayal of a lover, and *Ava* with David Hersland, since both are about dying.

[3] Scott Pound argues that reading the novel aloud renders it accessible. There is a long-standing tradition of reading it aloud—at the Paula Cooper Gallery in New York City (from 1974 to 2000), for instance. *Triple Canopy* magazine in Brooklyn offered live streaming and live tweeting of a three-day reading (from 2012 to 2014). A solo reading by Gregory Laynor is available online at ubu.com. Stein herself can be heard reading an excerpt in a recording available online at the PennSound archive.

[4] For a discussion of Stein's queer time, see McCallum, *Unmaking* 1–26, 223–74 and "Stein."

[5] Among these performances are Leon Katz's *The Making of Americans: An Opera and a Play* (published by Something Else Press in 1973); the Music Theater Group–Lenox Arts Center's production in 1985, directed by Anne Bogart (libretto by Leon Katz, music by Al Carmines); Heiner Goebbels's *Hashirigaki*, first performed at Théâtre Vidy–Lausanne in 2000; and Jay Scheib and Anthony Gatto's 2008 staging of the novel as an opera at the Walker Art Center.

[6] This bodily relation to language is central to Lisa Ruddick's incisive reading of the novel (55–136).

[7] One student, a former Marine, compared the world of Stein to the Camp Lejune training grounds, and observed astutely that "[i]t wasn't that the characters didn't seem real; they do, and are very valid figures even today. The problem felt like the universe they lived in was not really real or alive [like the training town]," because they are so set off from diegetic space. But as the relations among them become more in focus, the characters became more real to this reader.

[8] Critics have often read the novel through a biographical lens. See George Moore on Leo Stein as the model for David Hersland (145); Janice Doane's qualified view of the narrator as Stein (103).

[9] Doane's admirably meticulous reading makes "beginning again" its central concern (82–144).

[10] Some typical comments: "I read the hardest book I have ever encountered. I'm glad I did because I would otherwise never had read anything by Stein. All the class discussions contributed to the advancement of my critical reading skills"; "Everything was challenging. This made me smarter overall. . . . I pretty much loved Stein"; "What I enjoyed was that this class, more than others, focused on grammatical elements of language and how it affects the meaning of the text"; reading Stein "intensely encouraged critical thinking"; and "*The Making of Americans* was an epic challenge. I hated it at the time, but now I love that I've read it."

Teaching Comparative Stylistics: Gendered Language in Stein and Hemingway

Laurel Bollinger

> As Pablo [Picasso] once remarked, when you make a thing, it is so complicated making it that it is bound to be ugly, but those that do it after you they don't have to worry about making it and they can make it pretty and so everybody can like it when the others make it.
>
> —Gertrude Stein,
> *The Autobiography of Alice B. Toklas*

Students often read for plot and character, considering stylistics at best a subordinate concern. Because Gertrude Stein's work centers on style, they often have trouble appreciating it. Ernest Hemingway's work they appreciate but focus so fully on its surface events that they overlook his stylistics, some of which Hemingway clearly absorbed from Stein. Both writers share a commitment to style not as decoration but as the fundamental mechanism for creating meaning. In this essay I argue that their style also performs and interrogates gender and sexuality. Teaching them together productively illuminates both: Stein the innovator, Hemingway the writer who "can make it pretty and so everybody can like it" (Stein, *Autobiography* 23).

I teach a semester-long course for upper-division and graduate students on Stein and Hemingway but at lower levels have taught segments of a few weeks on the subject. I first establish the writers' interconnections through Stein's *The Autobiography of Alice B. Toklas* (1933) and Hemingway's *A Moveable Feast* (1964).[1] The pair's complex relationship becomes visible in their mutual attacks and counterattacks, as each takes credit for the other's accomplishments. Stein refers to Hemingway as a "pupil who does it without understanding it," insists that Alice Toklas introduced him to bullfighting (the year after he published his book on it, *Death in the Afternoon* [1932]), and recounts her criticism of his first novel: "Begin over again and concentrate" (213). She also suggests that Hemingway withholds a story, "the real Hem" (216), to protect his career—a suggestion that may connect to her reported conviction that Hemingway was secretly gay.[2] For his part, Hemingway describes Stein as a "lazy writer" unwilling to do the editing necessary "to make her writing intelligible" and claims that he "forced" *The Transatlantic Review* to publish *The Making of Americans*, which he read in proofs because Stein herself refused (*Moveable Feast* 18–19). While he sidesteps his claim from *Green Hills of Africa* (1935) that he taught Stein to write dialogue (66–67), the memoir clearly seeks to quash assertions that he was her pupil. Such insistence parallels his work to separate himself from other mentors, particularly Sherwood Anderson (whom he brutally parodied in *The Torrents of Spring* [1926]).[3]

To turn student attention to style-related issues, I discuss the two texts as artifacts of each writer's attempt to manage public image. For Stein, I assign an essay from Helga Lénárt-Cheng, who explains the *Autobiography* as enacting techniques later offered as textbook recommendations for advertisements. Stein uses product placement, often repeating her name many times on a page and establishing the circumstances of her composition (complete with excerpts as teasers), and she includes testimonials from her many famous friends and acquaintances. In my experience, students who initially found Stein's style off-putting express much greater interest in the book once they recognize these advertisement features. I then ask them to look for similar features in Hemingway's *Feast*.

Such comparisons open attention to influence, the most obvious example of which is Hemingway's adaptation of Stein's use of repetition.[4] I introduce this feature of Stein's style with "Melanctha," where slight variations in phrasing across otherwise repeated sentences trace the characters' emotional growth. For example, Jeff Campbell initially rejects Melanctha's complaint that he is unfeeling: "I certainly do think I feel some, Miss Melanctha, even though I always do it without ever knowing how to stop with my thinking" (83). But as their relationship progresses, he sits "with only a little thinking and sometimes a beginning feeling" (84), until eventually "[s]ometimes Jeff would lose all himself in a strong feeling. Very often now . . . he did not know how or what it was he had been thinking" (96). Such repeated verbs and gerunds illuminate his developing appreciation of emotion.

This repetition reflects the influence on Stein's stylistic practice of her scientific work as a medical student in the 1890s, which she took quite seriously despite her dismissive remarks in the *Autobiography* (81–83). Both Steven Meyer and Maria Farland explain that a primary research project for Stein involved drawing precise representations of fetal brain cross-sections. After assigning excerpts from Farland, I ask students to consider Stein's repetition as a similar project in a different medium.[5] Just as each brain cross-section differs only slightly from the section before, with major structural differences emerging gradually across the different slices, Stein's depiction of character development through repetition captures each phase of the transformation instead of focusing on the outcome. Stein's writing may be described in many productive ways, but seeing Stein as a scientist working in language helps students (particularly at my STEM institution) take her explorations more seriously and sympathetically. She herself rejected the language of experimentation, insisting to Thornton Wilder, "Artists do not experiment. Experiment is what scientists do. . . . An artist puts down what he knows and at every moment it is what he knows at that moment" (Wilder vii). Much as she analyzed brain tissue, she analyzed mental processes by segmenting experience into individual moments.[6] Hemingway's use of incremental repetition, modeled after Stein's, is more limited. When Nick falls asleep at the end of "Big

Two-Hearted River: Part I," "[h]e turned on his side and shut his eyes. He was sleepy. He felt sleep coming. He curled up under the blanket and went to sleep" (*Complete Short Stories* 169). Like "Melanctha," Hemingway's "Soldier's Home" and "Up in Michigan" use repetition to represent shifting emotions.[7]

For both authors, style is a mechanism to replicate but also challenge existing gender stereotypes. Stein's treatment of gender vexes students, forcing them to confront the distinction between articulating a feminist position (which Stein resists) and engaging in gender slippage (which her writing does). Stein rejects the antipatriarchal, political features of feminism, described as "the cause of women" in the *Autobiography*, because "it does not happen to be her business" (83), implying a rejection of political involvement and even of biological sex. The terms "genius" and "wife" (5, 14) allow her, the genius, to evade her own gendered identity by emphasizing Alice's. I ask students to notice the way she relegates the domestic to the feminine throughout the *Autobiography*, making Alice the figure concerned with entertaining wives and managing the household, too encumbered to become a writer: "I am a pretty good housekeeper and a pretty good gardener and a pretty good needlewoman and a pretty good secretary and a pretty good editor and a pretty good vet for dogs and I have to do them all at once and I found it difficult to add being a pretty good author" (251–52).

The narrator's voice, however, complicates this evasion of the feminine. As Ulla Dydo explains, "[i]n joining the substance of Stein to the voice of Toklas, [Stein] is both distinguishing the two and making them one" (*Gertrude Stein* 540). The voice, clearly replicating Toklas's vocal patterns, represents a commitment to placing a specific woman on the page.[8] Stein, in selecting and ordering the anecdotes to be included, retains control over the structure of the narrative as a whole. Voice and structure fuse, however, in the phrase "but to return" (echoed over two dozen times in the *Autobiography*), each time signaling a moment when, having interrupted one story to tell a different one, Alice returns to the main narrative thread. The narrative thus refuses linearity or even the sense that it must tell a single story. In such a commitment to repetition and play, Stein enacts what the French feminist philosopher Hélène Cixous would later describe as a feminine text: "[I]t's the beginning, or beginnings, the manner of beginning, not promptly with the phallus in order to close with the phallus, but starting on all sides at once, that makes a feminine writing. A feminine text starts on all sides at once, starts twenty times, thirty times, over." The narrator's "but to return" phrase signals a moment when a story starts again, circling back to a new beginning instead of concluding an anecdote. If we accept Cixous's assessment that such structure should be celebrated as a "feminine textual body" that embraces a "female libidinal economy" (53), then Stein, by joining her own narrative substance with Toklas's voice, simultaneously evades and reinscribes the feminine throughout her text.

Hemingway too constructs gender as subject to negotiation, although he focuses on masculinity. He codes something like Stein's use of language, which depends more heavily on repetition than his does, as feminine, while his tightly edited language functions as normatively masculine. Verbal reticence is masculine for him. "Nick said nothing" appears throughout the Nick Adams stories, for instance, and in "Soldier's Home" Krebs silently endures his mother's verbose fretting over his wartime morality. In "Cat in the Rain," the American wife offers a veritable litany of desires, each prefaced by "I want," until her husband tells her to "shut up and get something to read" (*Complete Short Stories* 131). In "Mr. and Mrs. Elliot," Mr. Elliot writes "very long poems very rapidly" (123)—in contrast to Hemingway's short stories written slowly—and the unmasculine Elliot soon finds himself replaced in his marital bed by his wife's lesbian lover.

I suggest to students that Hemingway was well aware of gender identity as performative and of his and his characters' often uneasy position relative to such performance.[9] Far from being an essential or biological characteristic, masculinity must be mediated and policed, and language is a primary field of that effort. Much like Stein's, Hemingway's work shows moments of gender instability, in some cases through challenging the very language dichotomy he constructs. In "Hills like White Elephants," Jig's request for the man to "please please please please please please please stop talking" reproduces the excess language Hemingway generally constructs as feminine (214). However, the textual moment also signals a power shift in the couple's relationship: after Jig's words, the man moves the couple's luggage to the fertile side of the station, implicitly endorsing Jig's wish to have the baby.[10] Here and elsewhere, Hemingway destabilizes masculine codes by creating female characters who "subtly [inhabit]" otherwise masculine roles (Strychacz 65).

He also severs verbal patterns from biological sex by establishing that trauma evokes uncontrolled language. In "A Way You'll Never Be," a shell-shocked Nick Adams cannot stop himself from talking, leading the adjutant and major to recognize his ongoing struggle with brain injury. Even when presented as an iconically masculine figure in "Big Two-Hearted River," Nick finds that his control over language requires constant vigilance, as he "chokes" the desire to think, speak, or write (*Complete Short Stories* 164–69). Surplus language, signaling gender instability, always threatens to emerge, be it in the "silly, talky time" when he is put under anesthesia after his injury in "A Very Short Story" (107)—modeled after Hemingway's wartime hospitalization—or simply in being a writer at a time when writing itself could be coded as an unmanly pursuit.[11] Hemingway's public performance of masculinity in extraliterary activities (big-game hunting, boxing, and so forth) may protect the Hemingway brand, but an attention to his style prompts questions that destabilize strict gender dichotomies.

In a related focus, both writers use stylistic devices simultaneously to engage and to obfuscate the erotic. To provide students with relatively shorter Stein texts to clarify specific stylistic features, I start with the textual rhythms in her "A Book Concluding With As A Wife Has A Cow A Love Story." (*Tender Buttons* and "Lifting Belly" can also be used.) Slow, almost incantatory repetitions of words and phrases at the outset build to breathlessness by the final paragraph, where commas replace earlier end marks. The rhythm of the final staccato sentence suggests resolution and echoes orgasm. The shift from "a wife" to, in the final paragraph, "my wife" is telling, given Stein and Toklas's public reserve about their sexual relationship and the legal barriers to actualizing the term *wife* (503). Although the word *cow* functions in the private vocabulary Stein constructs to invoke her sensory life, repetition creates a smokescreen, shielding the text's central revelation by burying it beneath so much language that a reader may miss it.[12] When students recognize this use of repetition and substitution, they can unpack it elsewhere in Stein's oeuvre, where wordplay across French and English often encodes the erotic.[13]

Once attuned to Stein's treatment of the erotic, students are better prepared to see through Hemingway's similar obfuscations—the same students who before would have felt that an instructor's identification of such moments was overreading. As Nancy Comley and Robert Scholes explain, "the complexity of human sexuality—especially the potential bisexuality of all humans—were issues that . . . were in the air that Hemingway and other artists of his time were breathing," and Hemingway's exploration of sexuality is markedly "more sensitive and complex" than he is generally credited with (144).[14] To address this feature of Hemingway's style, I turn to specific stories, particularly "Mr. and Mrs. Elliot," where lesbian eroticism is encoded in the phrase "a good cry"—an encoding that students often miss but identify readily if they are experienced readers of Stein. "The Sea Change" (*Complete Short Stories* 302–05) addresses bisexuality directly: Phil grudgingly comes to terms with his partner's desire for a lesbian relationship, even as she reminds him of their own gender-crossing sexual experimentation—all of which happens below the surface of a conversation where nothing is spelled out for the reader.[15] Hemingway's evasive language in the story (particularly his use of an unglossed, exophoric *it* to refer to heterosexual and lesbian desire alike) serves the same function as Stein's repetitions: to camouflage the erotic so that only those who already anticipate its presence will recognize the topic under discussion. Indeed, without careful attention to style, readers may miss the studied neutrality of moments where Hemingway evokes homoerotic attraction. What Gerry Brenner characterizes as the "radical ambiguity" of "A Simple Enquiry" has led critics to disagree as to whether we should understand the main character as a lecherous gay man or "exemplary professional figure" (202–03). Readers have no difficulty understanding Hemingway's negative construction of the consequences of female sexuality in stories such as "Up in Michigan" and "Hills like White Elephants" (rape and unplanned pregnancy, respectively), but careful attention to his stylistics reveals a more complex treatment of the erotic than students suspect.

By looking at these two writers closely and together, students encounter both the stylistic innovations of Stein and the more conservative and occasionally mildly derivative—and more accessible—stylistics of Hemingway. They can also explore style as a mechanism for performing gender without oversimplifying how that performance should be understood. As a result, they become more adept readers of style in all their literary encounters. When students can both decode and problematize complex literary texts, we have served them well.

NOTES

[1] To cover only interactions between the two writers, use Stein's final chapter of her *Autobiography* or just the relevant pages (212–20) alongside these three chapters in Hemingway's *Moveable Feast*: "Miss Stein Instructs," "Une Génération Perdu," and "A Strange Enough Ending" (11–21, 25–31, 117–19). Lyle Larsen's *Stein and Hemingway* offers useful biographical and critical detail. Teachers may want to include the two portraits Stein did of Hemingway, both of which Ulla Dydo includes in *A Stein Reader*: "He and They, Hemingway," written in 1923 (449–50), and "Evidence," written in 1929 (541–46). Dydo's notes in the *Reader* and, on "Evidence," in her *Gertrude Stein: The Language That Rises* (see 379–86), are illuminating.

[2] Samuel M. Steward reports a conversation in which Stein claimed, "[W]hen I ran down the male [homosexuals] to Hemingway it was because I thought he was a secret one" (56).

[3] See Daniel Pollack-Pelzner on Hemingway's Stein parodies, which include his "Mr. and Mrs. Elliot" (1924) as a response to her "Miss Furr and Miss Skeene" (1911).

[4] Robert Paul Lamb cautions that Stein's influence on Hemingway "has been exaggerated and misunderstood" and that Hemingway had "to adapt rather than adopt" Stein's techniques (*Art* 113–14). For a discussion of Hemingway's craft, see Lamb's *The Hemingway Short Story*.

[5] Farland uses her research into Stein's scientific career to examine *The Making of Americans*. To apply her insights to other early Stein texts, pages 120–27 are particularly helpful.

[6] In other texts, *Tender Buttons* particularly, I identify for students the way Stein segments time, space, and attention, as she segments mental processes in "Melanctha."

[7] While outside the scope of this essay, in Hemingway's novel *Garden of Eden* David Bourne describes his writing process as requiring a segmenting of experience, with each moment reflecting only what happened "untinctured by how he had felt later" (174). The novel thus describes a Steinian compositional technique.

[8] For a discussion of the difficulty Stein initially had in constructing that Toklas voice and the revision work—unusual for Stein—she undertook to maintain it, see Dydo, *Gertrude Stein* 535–43.

[9] For a detailed discussion of Hemingway and performative masculinity, see Strychacz.

[10] For arguments complicating prior critical assumptions of Jig's powerlessness or the indeterminate quality of the story's ending, see Renner; Justice.

[11] Hemingway's typical compositional technique involved writing long passages that would be cut in revision, fusing the style he otherwise constructs as masculine (concise) and feminine (wordy).

[12] On the different usages of *cow*, see Bridgman 151–54.

[13] For such bilingual wordplay, see "Patriarchal Poetry," where Stein uses "chose" (571) as both a past-tense English word and what Lisa Ruddick identifies as French slang for vagina, which she argues Stein puns on throughout *Tender Buttons* (226). For instances of cross-language jokes in Hemingway's *The Sun Also Rises*, see Hinkle.

[14] *The Garden of Eden*, even in its published, bowdlerized form, offers his fullest exploration of bisexuality. Interestingly, Hemingway started the novel the year Stein died and so could be a response to her admonition in the *Autobiography* that he be bolder in telling "the real story" about himself (216).

[15] In a 1952 letter to Edmund Wilson, Hemingway wrote that Stein "talked to me once for three hours telling me why she was a lesbian. . . . It was this knowledge, gained from G. S., that enabled me to write A Sea Change" (qtd. in Bennett 227).

Cultivating a Critical Edge: Teaching *The Autobiography of Alice B. Toklas* in the College Writing Classroom

J. Ashley Foster

> [T]he single text is valid for all the texts of literature, not in that it represents them (abstracts and equalizes them), but in that literature itself is never anything but a single text: the one text is not an (inductive) access to a Model, but entrance into a network with a thousand entrances.
>
> —Roland Barthes, *S/Z*

Recounting Gertrude Stein and Alice Toklas's life together from prewar Europe to the early 1930s, *The Autobiography of Alice B. Toklas* tells how "two americans happened to be in the heart of an art movement of which the outside world at that time knew nothing" (28). Written by Stein in Toklas's voice, it is a text that, with its narrative circumlocutions and frequent references to the people and events of the time, college freshman can find difficult to follow. Yet it is this very difficulty that makes it so rewarding as a central text in writing courses. Stein's experimental mode makes *The Autobiography* an unusual but apt choice for introducing students to the nuances of language and narrative. And as the story of an era, it provides a gripping initiation into the networks of literature. Informed by writing across the curriculum (WAC) and feminist pedagogy, I argue that teaching the *Autobiography* in writing courses helps develop the necessary researching, close-reading, and analytic skills that are foundational to a flourishing college career. The *Autobiography* introduces students to still-pertinent social and ethical issues and challenges them to find their own academic voices.

Using Stein's book as a map for a syllabus, I give readings and assignments that are prompted by the artists, writers, and themes that the book introduces, and I indicate historical and conceptual points of intersection. Tracing references teaches students to read intertextually, in the context of the interdisciplinary artistic networks of the era, and models how to pursue scholarly questions across the humanities. When selected readings that relate to the people, art movements, and historical events discussed in the text are paired in the syllabus alongside the *Autobiography*, students cultivate a critical edge. This essay offers strategies for using the *Autobiography* as an entrance into discussions of war, gender, and colonialism—topics that prepare students for conducting ethical lines of study across many fields.

Conceptual Pairings

Jane Marcus, whose model of feminist pedagogy has influenced my own, avers that "[l]iterary criticism is inescapably political" (*Art* xvii). Part of teaching students to become engaged in academic writing is helping them account for the politics they seek both to uncover and put forth in their essays. Inspired by Marcus's methodology and Jessica Berman's work on feminism and ethics, I use Stein's text as a point of departure to open conversations that explore intersections between the ethical and political. This approach is underwritten by the work of Emmanuel Levinas and attends to the ways in which we are responsible to one another. Berman outlines a Levinasian ethics in *Modernist Commitments*, saying that "'the first and final question' is not 'how being justified itself' but how it responds to a preexisting ethical responsibility to another" (14). This relationship between the self and other, I contend, is both embedded and unveiled in art and literature. My teaching begins from the premise that students, through reading and writing about literature and art, can explore their relationality and responsibility to and within the world as global citizens. The feminist teacher, or any instructor concerned with a developing a praxis of ethics, can help them read Stein "against the grain"[1] by highlighting those places in the text that raise ethical and political questions. This highlighting is accomplished through conceptual pairings, by studying Stein contextually and in conversation with the other people of her day.

Teaching Stein's story of "the african statues," for example, and how "it was Matisse who drew Picasso's attention" to them introduces young thinkers to the troubled relations between modernism and colonialism and between modernism and race (63). Pairing chapter 3 of the *Autobiography*, "Gertrude Stein in Paris, 1903–1907," with the Metropolitan Museum of Art's *African Influences in Modern Art* Web site allows students to interrogate how Pablo Picasso and Henri Matisse incorporated elements of sculpture from West and Central Africa into their work. Using the annotation application *BaiBoard*, which can be downloaded for free on tablets or smartphones, a class can compare artworks side by side, such as the Dan mask photographed by Charles Sheeler (c. 1918; www.metmuseum.org/art/collection/search/283270) with Picasso's painting *Bust of a Man* (1908; www.metmuseum.org/toah/works-of-art/1996.403.5/). *BaiBoard* allows students to coannotate as a group and identify the relationships between the pieces. If one student annotates the images, the entire class can see the annotations. The physical interaction and visualization of the art makes real to students the way in which European modernists pulled upon a variety of traditions and facilitate conversations concerning cultural appropriation. This activity, conducted in conversation with Susan Jones's "Savage and Superb" chapter, explores the modernist fetishization of the problematic concept of primitivism. Jones's chapter gives students insight into the complicated and ambivalent way in which European modernists, searching for a vocabulary for liberation from a restrictive and repressive occidental tradition, adopted aesthetics from a variety of African cultures.

The appropriation of sculptural forms from various regions in Africa is a gateway to a larger conversation concerning racialized modernist tropes and the European appropriation of resources, peoples, and cultures. One student, writing her final paper on the statues and masks that Picasso and Matisse incorporated into their art, found a personal connection to the Met's *African Influences* site. Having moved to the United States from the Ivory Coast, she was descended from the Baule people. When she gave her in-class presentation, she brought to class art that her mother had collected from the region, drawing a parallel between her household art and the *Bell Mallet* piece on the Met's site (www.metmuseum.org/art/collection/search/506764), and pointed out symbolism and meanings that the European artists may not have understood. Considerations of modernism and colonialism, and connections that students have made between modernist art and literature and their own histories, encourage ethical reflection on and excavation of social narratives central to the field of literary analysis.

Stein's representation of the Great War invites a number of ethical inquiries, through conceptual pairings, about trauma and the liminal place of the relief worker in war. Reading the *Autobiography* as a war narrative in the context of related modernist texts allows students to fill in some of the gaps in Stein's story. For instance, in chapter 6, "The War," vignettes about driving through the French countryside delivering supplies for the American Fund for French Wounded are offered with a strangely cheerful air: "We had a few adventures, we were caught in the snow and I was sure that we were on the wrong road and wanted to turn back. Wrong or right, said Gertrude Stein, we are going on" (173). The Battle of the Marne is described, in part, as the failure to find a taxi (150). Ostensibly callous, these moments suggest that war offers excitement, that, disrupting the status quo, it encourages travel and new connections.

By reading Stein alongside Sigmund Freud's *Beyond the Pleasure Principle* (1920), students can consider the effects of war on people and society that Stein does not describe, including shell shock, the relation between pleasure and pain, repetition compulsion, repression, and traumatic symptoms such as flashbacks, nightmares, and temporal displacement. In class, we look at the images that compose Otto Dix's *Der Krieg* (1929–32), which depicts the violence that Stein withheld, and we read an English soldier's account in Robert Graves's *Good-Bye to All That* (1929). A Freudian approach can help students situate the work of Dix, Graves, and Stein in the language of trauma. Reading the *Autobiography* with Freud and art and literature from veterans, including Siegfried Sassoon's *"Counter-attack" and Other Poems* (1918), students start to suspect that, as Janet Malcolm has argued, in Stein's "grotesque gaiety" there is "the low hum of melancholy," and her writing can be an "exercise in whistling in the dark" (208–09). Many detect a distressed pathos behind Stein's happy facade, and images of refugees and the dead seep through cracks in her jolly tale. Students might also compare her relief work with Olaf Stapledon's in the Friends' Ambulance Unit, described in his contribution to *We Did Not Fight: 1914–18 Experiences of War Resisters* (1935), a collection edited by Julian Bell. Although Stein and Stapledon both describe relief work as a way of being involved in the war without fighting, he emphasizes his service as a form of pacifist commitment. Reading the *Autobiography* alongside the work of Stein's peers allows students to explore ethical questions related to enlistment, humanitarian effort, and the violence of war, as well as to compare a female civilian's voice with male soldiers' voices in the narration of war experience.

Scaffolding Assignments

When using the *Autobiography* in writing courses, I employ WAC pedagogy to guide students from discussions in the classroom to a research paper, helping them develop writing-with-sources and analysis skills. WAC pedagogy approaches writing as a process that requires time and repetition. Susan McLeod describes WAC as a "movement" defined by its use of writing as a mode of learning, a way of working through material.[2] WAC posits that through subject-oriented, short, frequent assignments that build to a larger research paper, a student can both learn the content of a subject and hone writing skills. WAC emphasizes writing to learn in addition to writing to communicate (153). In class, I teach imagining, speaking, brainstorming, reading, and note-taking as essential stages in the drafting process and draw on these techniques to help students engage, understand, analyze, and deconstruct the *Autobiography* through contextualizing the text historically.

Many students have never been to Paris and are unfamiliar with the cultural landscape of the modernist era. Taking them outside the classroom and to the museum can create an imaginative bridge between the twenty-first-century United States and early-twentieth-century Europe. I was lucky enough to be teaching the *Autobiography* in New York when *The Steins Collect: Matisse, Picasso, and the Parisian Avant-Garde* was exhibited at the Metropolitan Museum of Art in 2012. Attending this exhibition with my City College students allowed them to visualize the text's references in a concrete and palpable way. Many museums contain collections of early-twentieth-century art, and visiting them with a class can establish the aesthetics of the era and provide students with points of reference, even if the pieces that the Stein family owned are not displayed. (If a museum visit is not possible, a *Steins Collect* exhibition catalog is available [Bishop et al.], and students can view "selected highlights" at the Met's Web site.) Clips from Woody Allen's *Midnight in Paris* (2011) can also be an effective tool for creating a bridge to Stein's time and place.

The *Autobiography* encourages students to think deeply about gender and sexual identity, to question what we mean when we label something masculine or feminine. How and why does Stein transcend her assigned gender, forming a category for herself? How does she represent gender roles in a lesbian relationship? In a passage that often generates lively in-class discussion of gender representation, Stein writes in Alice's voice:

> I have sat with wives who were not wives, of geniuses who were real geniuses. I have sat with real wives of geniuses who were not real geniuses.

> I have sat with wives of geniuses, of near geniuses, of would be geniuses, in short I have sat very often and very long with many wives and wives of many geniuses. (14; see 87 for another instance)

Together we interrogate the gender dichotomy that Stein creates and then transcends in aligning herself with the (male) geniuses and not the (female) wives. Students, when asked to find further textual examples, usually enjoy the sense that they are conducting detective work. This mode of active reading leads to the first stage of their writing process. I ask them to write a two-page essay on a passage (of their choosing) using the close-reading methodology modeled in class.

Another assignment asks students to practice writing descriptively and with evidence while thinking through the ways in which artists and writers produce in an intellectual network of influences. They analyze Picasso's portrait *Gertrude Stein* (1905–06) in the light of Stein's account of the painting's creation (12, 45–57). We begin with the portrait, looking at it together in class. What does it make us think or feel? Then the students discuss the relevant passages from the *Autobiography*. They look for traces of Picasso's difficulty representing Stein and of the growth of the friendship between the artist and the author, seeing in the expression of her face how she "meditated and made sentences" (49). Finally students write a two-page essay on the painting, using quotations from the text. This assignment teaches them how to generate an argument from evidence in a text or image and how to use citations to make a point and convince the reader.

These assignments move students toward an in-class presentation and their research paper. As current writing pedagogy recognizes speaking as a stage in the drafting and brainstorming process (see Hacker and Sommers 13), the presentation offers students a bridge between the short essays and the research paper. In the presentations, they discuss the research material that they compiled in tracing Stein's references, based on their choice of topic. (I offer a list of topics that have been discussed in class, but students are invited to develop their own.) They may use sources from academic book chapters, peer-reviewed journal articles, primary source material, and sources that are nonliterary art forms, such as a performance, a musical score, or a painting. I discourage the use of online sources that are not academic or artistic—for example, a piece from the Metropolitan Museum of Art's Web site would count as an artistic source, as would a video clip of the reconstruction of Vaslav Nijinsky's *Rite of Spring* (mentioned in the *Autobiography* on pages 135–37)—and ask that they instead familiarize themselves with library resources and include a variety of types of references in their paper. After a seven-to-ten minute presentation on sources, the students participate in a question-and-answer session with their fellow students. Any class member may ask a question. If a group is reticent, I assign two respondents. Such questions allow the students to engage with one another in a way that is relatively independent of the instructor.

This research builds into a final eight-to-ten-page paper. Students are required to use at least five sources, three of which they have found on their own. They offer a critical reading of a theme in the *Autobiography*. I have seen community college students seriously engage with scholarly articles such as Helga Lénárt-Cheng's "Autobiography as Advertisement: Why Do Gertrude Stein's Sentences Get under our Skin?" and E. Okechukwu Odita's "African Art: The Concept in European Literature."[3] Some students become intrigued by Stein's experimental mode and explore her modernist techniques, and some become intrigued by Alice and Gertrude's relationship and explore that connection and its context. Through these assignments, students start to develop their own critical edge and writerly voice.

Creating Community

Ultimately, teaching *The Autobiography of Alice B. Toklas* opens the classroom up to creating the communities described in the text. In response to the world of artistic exchanges students see in it, they collaborate with and support one another, sharing not only their labor but their creativity too. In the mise-en-scène of modernist art and literature established in the *Autobiography*, Stein's network of friends and the way Stein illuminates her creative exchanges with figures like Picasso demonstrate the collaborative nature of imaginative production and the benefit of working intellectually with others. For the composition classroom, with its writing and workshopping processes, a sense of community is essential. Stein offers a model of what has been called "communal modernisms"; this image of artistic interaction "resonates with the classroom as a community and enables reflection on this shared space" (Hinnov et al., "Introduction" 14).

Stein's modeling of community also enables the instructor to apply feminist pedagogical methods, creating classrooms where, as Marcus describes it, "the students do not relate individually to the teacher. They form a common bond with the teacher and the other students to read and critique race, class, and gender issues from Virginia Woolf to WikiLeaks" ("Afterword" 190). As students study the *Autobiography*'s account of an intellectual network, they can create aspects of it in the classroom. Discussions, peer-review workshops where the students read and comment on one another's papers, and the question-and-answer sessions after presentations all contribute to a collaborative environment that brings everyone's work forward. The personal, ethical nature of the conversations and of the critical engagement with scholarly sources develops a certain gravitas in the work that we do as a group and includes students in the rigors and labors of the field.

Student projects often echo this emphasis on communal influences in artistic production, reading contextually, developing analytic skills, and opening lines of inquiry that address ethical questions. The semester usually culminates in especially creative and inclusive presentations. One student took a map of Paris and traced Hope Mirrlees's peripatetic wanderings throughout the city as described in her experimental work *Paris: A Poem* (1920). Another, using *The Alice B. Toklas Cook Book* (1954) in conversation with the *Autobiography*, presented on the significance of food in French culture and, from an Alice recipe, baked a dessert and shared it with the class. The *Autobiography*, though at times challenging to teach and fatiguing for students, captures the spirit of community that, when brought into a college writing course, can shape the classroom into a creative and collaborative universe of its own.

NOTES

This essay is based on my experience teaching the *Autobiography* in a number of college writing classrooms and one women's studies course. My thanks goes to students at Haverford College, Highline Community College, Borough of Manhattan Community College, and City College, Center for Worker Education.

[1] This phrase references Walter Benjamin's "task" for the historical materialist, which is to "brush history against the grain" (257).

[2] WAC pedagogy is often integrated with writing in the disciplines (WID) and operates from the premise that those ensconced in a particular academic discourse are the best ones to teach the conventions of that discourse, but here I apply WAC pedagogy to interdisciplinary models of literary studies, following the current trend in modernist studies to create conversations among artistic media. This approach helps a class of non-English majors find points of personal connection to the material and diversifies the discourses of the classroom. It also helps those who will become literature majors practice reading contextually.

[3] A complementary resource for the Odita article is the Web site *Africa Is a Country* (africasacountry.com), which "challenge[s] the received wisdom about Africa from a left perspective."

"The Picture Seemed to Her Perfectly Natural": Portraiture as Teaching Strategy in *The Autobiography of Alice B. Toklas*

Meg Albrinck

As one of Stein's most accessible works, *The Autobiography of Alice B. Toklas* provides an entry point for discussions of literary modernism and for exploring Stein's life and her relationships to the modern art world, Paris, other writers and artists, war, and of course Alice Toklas. In a course on Stein, the text can serve as a marker in her emergence as a celebrity and support explorations of her ever-changing aesthetics.

I teach the *Autobiography* in an capstone course on American autobiography. The course offers an introduction to genre theory by pairing theoretical explorations of a genre with literary examples of it. My syllabus is organized in a roughly chronological manner, beginning with a monolithic vision of identity and genre and then complicating that vision with questions of race, gender, sexuality, and media. The time line reflects not only the production of the autobiographies we read but also the theoretical discussions of autobiography. We begin with *The Autobiography of Benjamin Franklin*, paired with readings from Georges Gusdorf and from William Howarth. We then complicate the notion of autobiography as the story of the representative man by reading *The Narrative of the Life of Frederick Douglass*, incorporating articles by Robert Sayre and by Roger Rosenblatt. Stein's *Autobiography* appears midway through the term and is paired with Philippe Lejeune's discussion of the autobiographical pact and with readings by feminist critics such as Susan Stanford Friedman and Estelle Jelinek. At the end of the term, we discuss visual autobiography, using Elizabeth Bruss's "Eye for I" to frame a graphic narrative from Alison Bechdel and a film from Ross McElwee. For teachers interested in exploring the genre of autobiography as a course topic, *Reading Autobiography* (2001), by Sidonie Smith and Julia Watson, is invaluable, providing historical overviews of the genre and its critics, comprehensive bibliographies, distinctions between types of life writing, and sample assignments.

In the arc of the course, Stein's *Autobiography* serves as a pivotal text—in part because it destabilizes the notions of genre, identity, authorship, and representation that shape the first half of the course, in part because its preoccupation with visual portraiture anticipates questions that arise in the second half. Specifically, it raises the question of whether autobiography or portraiture can represent a person and a life, when that person, that life, is both constantly changing and staying the same.

I provide more apparatus for students to encounter the *Autobiography* than I do for other texts, primarily because I know that Stein's disruption of grammatical and narrative conventions—even in this accessible work—can be frustrating to first-time readers. Students often enjoy her anecdotal stories about famous contemporaries, but they are surprised by her unpunctuated and repetitious prose, nonlinear narrative, and adoption of Toklas's point of view. It is not unusual for students to question the use of the term "autobiography" in the book's title, given the blending of the authorial voice in the Stein-Toklas narrative. To provide a platform for informed consideration of her work, I situate the *Autobiography* in the contexts of Stein's literary career and of her patronage of avant-garde art.

For the literary career, I provide two glimpses into Stein's broader work: a brief section from "Composition as Explanation" and the poem "Susie Asado" (*Selected Writings* 549). My purpose is to buy some trust (if you can read these works, the *Autobiography* will be a piece of cake) and to introduce two of Stein's broader experimental techniques—using repetition to define a continuous present, her "lively words" portraiture (DeKoven, *Different Language* 68)—that shape her method in the *Autobiography*. Like her predecessors, Stein commits to the autobiographical convention of representing a great person or genius; but she challenges the autobiographical convention of linear time through her explorations of the continuous present in the prose portraits that make up the first half. Discussing these techniques helps students see that she is approaching the genre in a way that is different from that of her predecessors: in the spirit of aesthetic innovation instead of having social or political goals in mind.

We could spend the entire unit exploring questions of subjectivity and authorship, but I cannot imagine asking students to read the *Autobiography* without considering the visual arts. In the first sixty pages, the text covers Toklas's initial reaction to the Steins' atelier, the response to the public exhibition of Henri Matisse's *La femme au chapeau*, and Pablo Picasso's struggle to paint Stein's portrait. Examining these spaces and canvases drives the narrative and also supports comparisons between Stein's literary style and these painters' work.

After establishing Stein's interest in and treatment of portraiture through our discussion of "Susie Asado," we examine portraiture in the *Autobiography*. In the first chapters, students notice that Stein documents contradictory assessments of the paintings and painters she knew intimately. Toklas exemplifies the shift between derision and appreciation, recognizing that her initial dislike of the pieces collected by Gertrude and Leo Stein gives way to comfort: "It is very difficult now that everybody is accustomed to everything to give some idea of the kind of uneasiness one felt when one first looked at all those pictures on these walls" (10). Although students may feel uneasy with Stein's prose style, many of them are "accustomed" to the kind of painting that Toklas describes. Some have seen the originals in museums or have had access to reproductions, and posters of impressionist and postimpressionist masterworks are sold regularly on college campuses. Many students therefore see this art as classic rather than avant-garde. To help them appreciate the "uneasiness" of Toklas, I invite them to enter the visual space of the Steins' atelier and of fin de siècle Paris.

We begin with the Steins' atelier at 27 rue de Fleurus. Toklas describes how the paintings filled the room, saying, "[T]hey completely covered the white-washed walls right up to the top of the very high ceiling" (10). Her reaction to this space is telling: "Now I was confused and I looked and I looked and I was confused. Gertrude Stein and her brother were so accustomed to this state of mind in a guest that they paid no attention to it" (11). Toklas reveals that she looked "at some snap shots" to remind herself of her first impressions of the room (9), and I invite students to follow her journey by showing them photographs of the atelier, available online and through the wonderful catalog for the comprehensive 2011–12 exhibition *The Steins Collect* (Bishop et al.). The photographs reveal what Toklas describes, that paintings were arranged tightly, extending horizontally and vertically from the walls' midline, with very little space between them. The confusion of images and frames is in contrast with the symmetry and spacing of current exhibition practices. Students who have experience viewing art in museums will understand that this was no typical gallery. These images provide an opportunity for students to engage with the complex array of visual stimuli that surrounded Stein on a daily basis, to visit her social and authorial spaces, and to see Stein and Toklas positioned in them. Such tours also help students understand 27 rue de Fleurus as a key narrative environment in the *Autobiography* and provide a starting point for discussing Stein's later claim, "I write with my eyes" ("Transatlantic Interview" 31).

Once the exhibition style of the Steins is established, I ask students to consider the specific works they collected. The confusion of Toklas is as much about the kind of art she sees as its volume. For most of my students, the art is neither new nor "strange" (9). I try to make it new for them by showing them nineteenth-century portraits by George Frederic Watts, John Singer Sargent, and James McNeill Whistler, all of which are readily available online. The fine brush-strokes, somber colors, and realist approaches introduce students to the generic conventions of the time before Stein's. But it is important to note that even some of these works caused controversy on their release and that impressionists such as Paul Cézanne and Vincent van Gogh were beginning to trouble the artistic conventions of the nineteenth century before the arrival of Matisse and Picasso.

"But to return to the pictures" (9). With this minilesson in portraiture in mind, we look at the responses to Picasso's portrait of Stein and to Matisse's portrait of his wife. The first three chapters of the *Autobiography* revolve around these two paintings. The second chapter begins (in Steinian fashion) with the end of the story of Stein's portrait by Picasso: "Picasso had just finished his portrait of her which nobody at that time liked except the painter and the painted and which is now so famous" (6). After viewing the paintings by Watts, Sargent, and Whistler, students can now see how Picasso was both inhabiting and breaking conventions in his portrait of Stein. They notice, for example, that it returns to the palette of the nineteenth-century realists but that Picasso's disproportionate representation of Stein's eyes and his flattening of the background signal the emergence of cubist efforts to capture multiple perspectives on a flat visual plane.

Students next apply this new way of seeing to Matisse's *La femme au chapeau*. They quickly understand why it is described in the *Autobiography* as "very strange in its colour and in its anatomy," why the broad strokes and distortions of shape and color in Matisse's portrait produced the responses that Stein describes: "It infuriated the public, they tried to scratch off the paint" (34). But "the picture seemed to [Stein] perfectly natural." Stein notes that the crowd's response to the painting parallels the public's (and my students' initial) response to her writing: "It bothered her and angered her because she did not understand why because to her it was so alright, just as later she did not understand why since the writing was all so clear and natural they mocked at and were enraged by her work" (35). This sentence provides the reader with a verbal version of Picasso's cubism. All viewers are focused on the same portrait, whether visual or verbal, but each sees something different; what the public finds infuriating Stein finds authentic. Stein's writing is inaccessible to many but "clear and natural" to the author.

The narrative demonstrates that something new may be unsettling at first but becomes meaningful with more engagement. Toklas is at first "confused" by the atelier, but becomes "accustomed" to it to the point where she must look at "snap shots" to remind herself of her former response. Picasso's portrait of Stein was liked by "nobody at that time . . . except the painter and the painted," but later it became famous. The reception of Matisse's portrait followed a similar trajectory, as did the reception of Stein's work. Stein explains it to Toklas in the following way: "[A]s Pablo once remarked, when you make a thing, it is so complicated making it that it is bound to be ugly, but those that do it after you they don't have to worry about making it and they can make it pretty, and so everybody can like it when the others make it" (23). Thus a text that continues to unsettle its audience and destabilize convention becomes more appreciated over time.

Stein's anecdotes in the *Autobiography* create a collage of figures, events, and reactions that verbally echo the collage of images that drew viewers to 27 rue de Fleurus in the early twentieth century. Students begin to appreciate that Stein was producing in prose what her friends were producing in paint, namely, "portraits of practically everybody she has known . . . in all manners and in all styles" (114). This recognition can yield any number of assignments and research projects. Students can explore the paintings in the Steins' collection and the figures in the Steins' milieu and can compare the two. Analyses of the style of Stein and the paintings she describes yield interesting insights into her strategy of narration, whether through studies of collages (by Georges Braque and Picasso) or of repetition with variation (by Marcel Duchamp). For example, the repeated characterization of Fernande Olivier with her forefinger in the air (19, 96, 106) or of Fernande as a lover of hats (14, 26, 103, 110) accumulates throughout the *Autobiography* to create a sense of character that is both static and dynamic, established and evolving, much like the figure in *Nude Descending a*

Staircase, which Stein describes (210). The multiplication of identity inheres in the narrative, as Stein (as Toklas) records Picasso's response to Toklas's praise: "I murmured to Picasso that I liked his portrait of Gertrude Stein. Yes, he said, everybody says that she does not look like it but that does not make any difference, she will, he said" (12). This exchange reveals several different planes of appreciation that shape the viewing of a portrait: a portrait can please the viewer (as it does Toklas), it can accurately depict the subject (or not, as Picasso responds), and it can shape future perceptions of the subject. Students who are interested in portraiture can examine the many representations of Stein—by Man Ray or Cecil Beaton (photography), by Jo Davidson (sculpture), and by Francis Picabia or Félix Vallotton (painting).

Another way to encourage students to engage with the *Autobiography* is to ask them to practice life writing themselves. At the beginning of the course, I ask students to present themselves with a constrained version of life writing, such as an obituary, a personal ad, or a graduate school application. This exercise calls attention to the limitations imposed by the conventions of autobiography. After students read Franklin's and Douglass's autobiographies, they must write a piece in which the story of their life and the story of their society intersect—their experience of September 11, a presidential election, a tragedy in their hometown—which shows them how the choice of occasion shapes their selection and arrangement of autobiographical detail. I then ask them to tell a personal anecdote as a graphic narrative and to think about how the combination of word and text presents opportunities and challenges to life writing. After we discuss the *Autobiography*, I ask them to describe a single episode of their lives from an autobiographical perspective and a biographical one. Their attempt to mimic Stein's approach leads to fascinating discussions on the limits of one's self-perception and of historical writing. It has also led us directly into some of the controversies about Stein's book.

Some students wish to study the accuracy of the narrative and how the narrative was received by Stein's contemporaries. Here, responses to her work that were published in *Transition*, studies of her celebrity, and texts like *Everybody's Autobiography* are useful supplements. Other students are interested in feminist approaches to the *Autobiography*, which leads them to compare feminist celebrations of Stein's relational autobiography with the criticism that her book uncomfortably mimics patriarchal conventions. Still others prefer to use the *Autobiography* as a launching point into Stein's other writing, comparing the prose narrative of the Stein-Toklas relationship with the poetic *Stanzas in Meditation*. Phoebe Stein Davis ("Subjectivity") and Georgia Johnston provide useful overviews of the text's reception.

The *Autobiography* is a versatile text that yields great discussions, produces deeply thoughtful writing, and opens up many avenues for continued research, not only on Stein the person but also on her time, place, contemporaries, and work. Positioning that work in a broader culture of experimentation and innovation affords many opportunities for continued exploration.

Student to Student: Stein and Crimes of Convention

Lee Rumbarger

As an undergraduate in Radcliffe College's English A course, Gertrude Stein begrudgingly wrote daily themes. The theme was a contradictory genre: though its name seems to indicate an informality of topic—an invitation to shape the personal and everyday into prose—it appears instead to have been a constraint of discipline on the everyday rather than an invitation to bring the everyday into the academy. Stein wrote on 16 November 1894, "Avaunt thou valeful spectre! What! Shall I submit to losing all my joy in living? Can I endure having all pleasure blasted by that eternal refrain 'Wouldn't it make a good Daily?' Never" (R. Miller 115). On 20 February 1895, she wrote, "Not many years ago, my self-analysis ended in heroics, but now it simply turns into mild meditation, with a flavor of cynicism, and contents itself with inventing wise saws to garnish a daily theme" (130).

My lower-division literature and writing students enjoy meeting Stein the student and getting a glimpse of her resisting her homework and occasionally outwitting her professor with oblique critiques of his pedagogy. Indeed, her student essays, reprinted alongside faculty feedback in Rosalind Miller's *Gertrude Stein: Form and Intelligibility* (1949), offer an easy-to-relate-to example of the disciplining of one's writing voice as a pernicious process. When I have taught Stein without her student essays, some of my students rejected her stylistic experimentation out of hand, but the student pieces as introductory material seem to subtly draw them to her side. Perhaps the Radcliffe freshman with the wily pen was onto something. For instructors who seek ways to teach the conventions of academic discourse while at the same time allowing students to disrupt those conventions in the service of their own ideas and the creation of new knowledge, Stein's work is full of possibility.[1]

I have taught Stein's student essays paired with her longer works in college composition courses, a writing-tutor-training course, and, most successfully, in the detective-fiction-themed Introduction to Fiction course at the University of Oregon.[2] At Oregon I distribute a handout that includes quotations from several daily themes by Stein and her peers, along with their professors' feedback, as an interactive coda to a short, introductory presentation on Stein's life and work.[3] This session prepares them to read her murder mystery *Blood on the Dining-Room Floor* (1933), which breaks genre convention by refusing a traditional restoration of order and gestures toward a different, demanding way of seeing the home and conventionality itself as outright dangerous, especially for women. Stein's story is a collage of true crimes that touched her life during the summer of 1933, in Bilignin, including the violent deaths of two women in her social circle, the mysterious appearance of dust scattered over her desk and blood on her dining room floor, and the discovery of her and a guest's cars tampered with and of her phone lines cut—crimes perpetrated against women in the home and shrugged off by authorities. The text offers so many details and so few answers that everything is colored in violent cast, and the reader is taxed to remember clues that never add up. "How confused you all are but I, I am not confused," Stein taunts. "It really is not confusing. How many houses and families do you know about now. One two three four five. And how many crimes. One two three. And how many possible crimes. Six" (33).

We begin the course with Arthur Conan Doyle's Sherlock Holmes stories, then read Raymond Chandler's *The Big Sleep* (1939) and watch Christopher Nolan's film *Memento* (2000). Stein's *Blood* and Tim O'Brien's pick-your-own-solution mystery *In the Lake of the Woods* (1994) complete the ten-week term by pushing readers to consider just who gets to be a detective and what solutions are ethically acceptable. As my syllabus describes the course:

> We will look at several detective stories, turning first to texts that authorize a single character as master detective. Then, as we become sharper critical readers, we will take the detective's place, considering texts that make radical demands on us to interpret evidence for ourselves, pushing us to seek solutions to crimes when none are forthcoming in the text.

I want to encourage novice writers by linking deeply attentive reading to the popular appeal of detective stories. Moreover, with O'Brien and particularly Stein, I assign texts that blur the boundary between fiction and life, insisting on the wide relevance of such reading as a skill. I suggest that, unlike the detective, the detecting reader's role is not necessarily to restore social order (the detective solves the case; the criminal is removed) but to question the conventional assumptions on which social order rests. Finally, I endeavor to take this critical approach to convention seriously as my students work on their writing: I try to make them aware of—and to create an opening for them to consider alternatives to—norms of written academic discourse.

I offer here my own reading of several entries in the Radcliffe manuscripts and of Stein's detective story. I then detail a writing assignment I have developed that, through freewriting and templates, makes apparent to students the ways they can master—and strategically resist—convention in their own work.

Uncontrollable Voice

In "Controlling Voices: The Legacy of English A at Radcliffe College, 1883–1917," JoAnne Campbell describes papers in the Radcliffe archives that were routinely criticized for femininity.[4] She offers selected professor comments: "You write 'with a good deal of sentiment.' . . . 'Avoid the strained exaggeration of the feminine style'; 'Your tone of personal injury detracts a little, possibly, from the success of your work.'" To the student Annie Winsor Allen, he responds, "Your reasoning, if you will permit me to say so, is charmingly feminine. That is, you base it upon the notion of the world which exists in a well-brought up feminine mind, and not upon the world as it is. . . . Finally, I hate to dispel illusion, but your argument from family examples is a terribly weak kind of thing" (479). Campbell also recounts the paper-topic troubles of Dorothea Crawford Seidler, who—having been told that her writings "about the importance of mothers in a girl's college education, a first love, and short fiction about a mother in France who came to America to stay with her son were simply 'weak' and 'no good'"—decides to compare the relative merits of electricity and gas for lighting because it is a topic she has heard men dispute. "For the instructor such public topics may have been familiar, easier to engage, more comfortable to grade, but the message was that the student's experience and ideas had no place in the academy and were not legitimate sites of knowledge," Campbell concludes (479–80). Her interpretation is one that my Introduction to Fiction students come to instantly when they see excerpts of Radcliffe student writing and faculty feedback. For many of them, it is not the first time they have encountered a disconnect between what matters to them personally and what seems to matter to the institution, but it is almost always the first time that they have been invited to comment in class on this disconnect.

It is therefore not surprising that Allen and Seidler's contemporary, Gertrude Stein, rhetorically distanced herself from the feminine in some of her own daily writings for English A. In "Woman," a theme dated 20 November 1894, Stein wrote:

> Never again will I try to reason with a woman. She immediately gets hysterical and thinks she is calm. She acknowledges that you are right half a dozen times and then deliberately repeats the statement thinking she has got hold of a new point of view. At last in despair you either smile or frown according to your temperament and she goes home convinced of her rhetorical powers. The eternal feminine is nice to be sure but it's painfully illogical. (R. Miller 115)

Her professor remarks, "Point of view nobly remote." Stein forestalls the patronizing sexism of Allen's professor, usurping the power to assess with either a smile or frown. (Here, she and her professor cohabit "you.") Apparently unprepared to find irony in a freshman woman's writing, Stein's professor does not register her barb. A week later he responds with only a question mark when Stein writes in "A Conference":

> English Prof. "Yes that is a very good stroke. Twittering birds always remind me of spring. Ah but let me see your description is of autumn, yes birds do twitter in autumn too not so much perhaps."
>
> Meek girl student. "But excuse me sir my description is mid-summer."

> Professor undaunted. "Mid-summer, why yes, yes of course birds always twitter in mid-summer." (116)

The professor's assessment that spring and autumn birdsong—correction, midsummer birdsong—serves as a good scene-setting detail reveals his painfully hasty reading. His expert advice, the value of his conferencing time, and, implicitly, even the scope of his curriculum are reduced to useless observations on the seasonal twittering patterns of birds. One wonders what in fact would make a compelling daily theme for English A when women students' personal experiences and daily lives were off-limits topics. But, again, Stein's professor takes no offense—surely a "meek girl student" is not purposefully criticizing his pedagogy.

Several months later, Stein uses a daily theme to insist that she has virtuously applied herself to the anodyne observation required by its genre instead of indulging in the vibrant, engaged intellectual life she leads outside class: "Argument is to me as the air I breathe. Given any proposition I cannot help believing the other side and defending it. But I would be virtuous and would rather make a dismal failure of a description than revel in argument. The one I get all the time; the other in English 22" (130). If Stein loves a good fight, here she shows herself capable of feints and quick jabs. These student papers give us a glimpse of a woman being pushed toward conventionality at the level of topic and sentence.[5] My students and I observe Stein's pushing back. That the teacher-student relationship and the larger project of becoming college-educated should be in service of students' own developing voices and intellectual pursuits is simply not the assumed position of many of my students. It might not occur to them that instructor comments—and pedagogy more generally—can and in fact should be read critically. Opening classroom space to discuss the values animating Radcliffe student writing and faculty feedback—genres experienced by my own students in their writing lives as individual and ephemeral but now scrutinized as material of literary and historical interest—is one small way to invite them to consider what they value, what the institution seems to value, and how those values both converge and diverge.

Blood on the Dining-Room Floor

Stein's detective novel is a slender volume of fewer than seventy-five pages—an easy read, at first glance. But the text's opening crime and its too-convenient resolution—the crime is that discomfiting vandalism has interrupted a seemingly quiet day at a country house; the resolution is that the servants are sacked—suggest that the violence at the heart of a home is not easily purged. "The man servant served the lunch very well and then he and his wife were sent away. The garage man said send them away and forget about them and this was done" (*Blood* 14). But no evidence indicates that these servants, powerless outsiders, had any hand in the crime. They are gone but not quite forgotten. The story ends eerily: "No one is amiss after servants are changed. Are they" (81).

In its denial of closure and refusal to convincingly individualize guilt, Stein's text dismantles the genre conventions that Franco Moretti critiques in "Clues," a chapter in *Signs Taken for Wonders* (1983) that we read early in the term. Though Moretti's text is challenging in an introductory course for nonmajors, it has the virtue of making a strong, high-stakes argument that surprises my students and with which they tend to disagree, that detective fiction is bad because it encourages passivity in readers by having the detective do their thinking for them. Worse still, by pinning the blame for a crime on individuals, Moretti argues, the detective ushers in a return of the social status quo and relieves the need for anyone to consider how guilt might be more widely dispersed and collectively shared. "Innocence is conformity; individuality, guilt," he writes (135). In other words, typical detective fiction implies safety in conventionality; the individual or nonconformist is the criminal or victim.

In our first class meeting after students have read Stein's *Blood*, I ask them to do a five-to-ten-minute freewrite about what they noticed in the work, especially its stylistic features and the affective experience of reading it. I want to capture some of their first impressions and give them a way to vent frustration. I lead a short discussion of their experience of reading the novel, asking for their ideas about why it might have been important for Stein to write her detective story the way she did. I ask what crimes the students noticed. When we move into group work, the students discuss such issues as the narrator's insistent, direct address to the reader; how Stein describes trouble behind closed doors; the wide-scale disowning of knowledge by neighbors; and how clichés seem to close down conversations that clearly are helping the characters gather and exchange mystery-busting information. I might give students a quotation or two on a slip of paper and ask them to mingle with their peers, comparing quotations and self-selecting into groups. Or I might ask each group to develop a topic from a sample quotation. Here are four examples:

> *The Country House*
>
> The more you see the country the more you do not wonder why they shut the door. (38)
>
> *Women's Experiences of Heterosexual Married Life*
>
> She would know about clean linen, about peaches and little cakes, as few as possible of each, and yet always enough. She would oversee the maids at work, she would push them gently forward to do what there was to do and there was always all of that to do. For them and for her. All day and every day. She was always very near perfect when she stood. She never sat. (9)
>
> *Clichés and Common Knowledge*
>
> Everybody knows, and they need not say. That is why everybody talks and nobody says, because everybody sees, and everybody says they do. Not by and by, there are no secrets about what everybody knows and still they do

complain. Why if why not why do they not complain. Not here not in not choice not and not we. We like ate and late not we. (71)

Narrative Voice

Listen carefully. (5)
Do you see what I mean. (7)
Do you really understand. (9)
Think of all that. (9)
What did you say. (12)
Do any of you know a disease that makes complete black rings all around the eyes as if the rings were made with shoe black. (16)
I feel I do not know anything if I cry. (17)
Read the beginning again. (18)
I am sure I do not know. (21)
Please remember everybody's name. (27)
Do you remember. (73)

We also complete a mini writing assignment, "*Blood on the Dining-Room Floor* Paper Templates: The Paper You'll Never Actually Write."[6] I have created templates to simulate the strategies of analysis and the density of evidence that work in a literature course. (Students are welcome to modify these templates to suit the ideas they are developing.) This template activity is good practice for the students' next formal essay, but students do not write one at this time. Removing the shadow of the professor's assessment gives them an opportunity to be open and curious in approaching Stein's work; feeling like they need to instantly get it enough to write a full essay is a recipe for frustration. Indeed, this suite of activities—reading the Radcliffe materials, reading *Blood on the Dining-Room Floor* and capturing through freewrites some of the affective experience (students often recapture the scenes of their reading, including the responses of family and friends when they read *Blood* aloud to them), spending time with quotations, filling in templates, comparing freewrites and templates as engines of response and preparation—signals to students that something a little different is happening in class, outside the norms of the regular essay cycle.[7] They read and write while talking about reading and writing, and they develop some measure of intellectual autonomy.

Thesis Statements

(a) Though ____ [pick a stylistic feature] may tend to ____ [confuse, frustrate: pick one or use your own word] readers, ultimately it serves to ____. And that's important because ____.

(b) ____ serves to pique readers' curiosity and invite their active engagement with the text. That participatory reading is important because ____.

(c) Though Stein may have intended to ____, ultimately her experiment fails because ____.

Body Paragraphs

(a) The reader of Stein's *Blood on the Dining-Room Floor* quickly realizes ____. For example, "[quote]," Stein writes ([page]). What's intriguing about this is that ____. In other words, _____. Similarly, she writes, "[quote]" ([page]). Again, it's clear that ____. She builds on or complicates this idea by ____. She writes, "[quote]" ([page]).

(b) Perhaps the biggest success / failing of Stein's project is ____. The reader gets an early indication of this when we notice ____. For example, "[quote]," Stein writes ([page]). That's disconcerting / disappointing / provocative because ____. Later, she writes, "[quote]" ([page]). Though it may seem that _____, what she's really implying here is ____. She builds on / complicates this idea by ____. She writes, "[quote]" ([page)].

(c) Though some readers might argue with or object to ____, Stein pushes them to accept / acknowledge ____. Her project is clearest when ____. For example, "[quote]," she writes ([page]). Here, she simultaneously ____ and ____. Moreover, she writes, "[quote]" ([page]). Again, readers are put in the position of ____. Later, things seem to change when Stein ____.

A key part of this template assignment is the freewrite students have completed, because not only do I want novice students to become familiar with the academic conventions, I also want them to imagine their own power as writers and producers of new knowledge. Once they have completed their templates, we discuss what could not fit into them—the feelings, ideas, and words that would seem out of place in academic writing. Like Stein's work, this assignment allows us think about, name, and problematize conventional forms. And like student Stein herself, students begin to learn not only how to be heard but also how to wield a wily pen.

NOTES

[1] Kenneth Bruffee has put the challenge to instructors thus: "We must teach practical rhetoric and critical analysis in such a way that, when necessary, students can turn to abnormal discourse. . . . We must teach these tools in such a way that students *can* set them aside, if only momentarily, for the purpose of generating new knowledge, for the purpose, that is, of reconstituting knowledge communities in a more satisfactory way" (648).

[2] I was inspired to use detective fiction by John Cyril Barton, Douglas Higbee, and Andre Hulet's thoughtful essay "Reading Detectives." In it, they argue that detecting is a useful "heuristic analogue . . . for analysis en route to an interpretation" (Barton et al. 176). Though they ultimately seek to make visible more than disrupt the conventions of academic writing, they teach a compelling list of revisionary detective fiction (by Paul Auster, Walter Mosley, Sara Paretsky).

[3] JoAnn Campbell's "Controlling Voices" captures the written voices of some of Stein's fellow students.

[4] For more on reading Stein's undergraduate writing in the context of the Radcliffe archives, see my 2006 dissertation "We Moderns: Women Modernists Writing on War and Home." In its fourth chapter, I write about Stein and Virginia Woolf as students.

[5] Stein's professor critiques and corrects stylistic and grammatical features of her work. For example, "Your sentences are sometimes incoherent, and often awkwardly phrased. . . . You are careless too about punctuation and do not always express yourself clearly. . . . Your paragraphing is uncertain—particularly with reference to dialogue. It will pay you to review those parts of the textbook which treat of sentences and paragraphs. / Rewrite" (R. Miller 113).

[6] Gerald Graff and Cathy Birkenstein similarly offer templates designed to demystify the rhetorical gestures common to academic argumentation.

[7] I'm grateful to my former Vassar College Writing Center students Lila Teeters and Aaron Colton, who helped develop the pedagogical approach of contrasting freewrites with templates.

Narration and American Identity in Stein's Later Prose Works

Rebecca Walsh

"America is my country, but Paris is my hometown" (Stein, "American" 61). Stein's often quoted phrase encapsulates her expatriate status and her flair for the intriguing, well-turned epigram. It also signals an abiding interest in the meanings of American identity in a global setting, an issue that our students care about and often have to navigate themselves. In recent years I have assigned Stein's *The Geographical History of America* (1936) and her World War II dialogue *Brewsie and Willie* (1946) in my twentieth-century American literature and transnational modernism courses to address issues of national identity, geopolitics, and race. Taking Americanness as a focal point without taking it for granted as a privileged, monolithic, or isolated category, I assign these texts to model the ways that Stein's experiments with form and genre offer complex commentaries about a changing America affected by economic and geopolitical upheaval. Her late works pay attention to spatiality and American identity (Boyd 199) and open up valuable discussions about America's democratic promise and the relation of that promise to literary form and artistic genius.

Meeting wild success with *The Autobiography of Alice B. Toklas*, Stein embarked on a lecture tour across America from October 1934 through May 1935. For students who might doubt that an experimental writer could receive such public notice, I point out that there was tea at the White House with Eleanor Roosevelt (Burns and Dydo, *Letters* 344) and Hollywood parties with Charlie Chaplin and Dashiell Hammett (Stein, *Everybody's Autobiography* 2–3). This tour helps frame her new engagement with an American reading public in the last third of her career and her fresh need to come to terms with genius, celebrity, and popular circulations of her writing. She wrote *The Geographical History of America*, a text that defines or redefines American culture along with the nonliterary discipline of historical geography, almost immediately after her return to France. The last few years of her career focus on war and American soldier life, reflecting her experiences weathering World War II in France, as in *Wars I Have Seen* (1945), and touring American army bases in Germany in June 1945, which led to an August 1945 *Life* magazine article, "Off We All Went to See Germany." In *Brewsie and Willie,* Stein then turns to the topic of what soldiers do when war is over; the text is set in an ambiguous location that comes to be marked as France. Despite their generic and topical differences, both *Geographical History* and *Brewsie and Willie* explore roadblocks to the realization of America's democratic promise and chart new alternatives. Both books demonstrate Stein's global, comparative negotiations of national identity.

I open discussion with a handout of excerpts defining American exceptionalism, wherein invocations of America as a singular form of democracy rely on international comparisons and can also shade into justifications of imperialism. The work of Amy Kaplan and other American studies scholars can show students that American exceptionalism extends beyond the nation's unique origins as a Puritan experiment in religious freedom and individual liberty, that America's sense of its own "exceptional nature lies in its exemplary status as the apotheosis of the nation-form itself and as a model for the rest of the world" (Kaplan 16). The question I pose as we move into our analysis is how much Stein supports or skirts this exceptionalist logic in her exploration of American identity.

The Geographical History of America opens with an evocation of innovative American leadership synonymous with America's democratic ideals. The text proceeds through dizzying philosophical distinctions that celebrate the human mind (associated with fluidity, democracy, and genius) in contrast to human nature (associated with fixity, temporality, and history), but students can find a thematic anchor for their reading in the first line: "In the month of February were born Washington Lincoln and I" (367). Stein includes herself in the group of national heroes and liberators (Washington liberated America from the English, Lincoln liberated African Americans from slavery and liberated America from this failure of its democratic promise), registering the book's overall aim to free Americans of the limitations of the nation as usual and of literature as usual.

I highlight a tendency in Stein to privilege "nomadism or textual wandering" (Berry 154) as a strategy that frees her from obsolete or oppressive structures, and I ask students to consider how this strategy derives from her Americanness, her freedom to move across lines of convention. I ask them to consider the generic expectations she sets up and thwarts for her readers. Students identify and classify as many of the genres she engages as they can: prose poem, political treatise, philosophical proposition, autobiography, detective story, puppet play, dialogue with Thornton Wilder (who supplied an introduction for the publication of her *Geographical History*), advertisement for her own genius. The genre of geographic history, in the discipline of geography, deals with how physical features like topography, climate, and hydrology of the past have shaped present human circumstances in a given region. Stein's textual wandering disrupts the epistemological certainty offered by this genre, which would define America in definite ways.

Narrative order is also disrupted. *Geographical History* does not have a traditional beginning-middle-end structure that advances cause-and-effect logic, or conventional linear markers. More than one chapter 1 appears, Roman and Arabic numerals are mixed up, and the text's concluding sentence resists closure with a double negative: "I am not sure that is not the end" (488). Students can see these formal features as more than aesthetic experimentation for its own sake when they map the topographic descriptors in the text. One of my brief informal writing assignments has them track Stein's many connections between "flat" and "wandering." This exercise allows them to uncover the text's equation of the spatial qualities of America—relatively flat, internally borderless and large, and freely and easily roamed—with America's potential for democratic openness. "Wandering around a country has something to do with the geographical history of that country and the way one piece of it is not separate from any other one," she says, which makes wandering "a mission and an everything" (392). When students see how flatness promotes wandering, they are poised to grasp that both are linked to the privileged fluidity of the human mind: "[W]andering has something to do with the human mind," and "[t]he land has something to do with the human mind" (392, 407). These conditions invite a timeless form of writing: "[T]he mind that writes what any human mind years after or years before can read, thousand of years or no years it makes no difference" (406–07). Unconstrained by history or identity, the wandering human mind in this borderless landscape will take in and invent everything all at once.

After charting these linkages among the human mind, flat fluidity, and open form, students can grasp this landscape as a democratic environment conducive to both Stein's genius and the reader's freedom. Out of that environment come masterpieces: "[I]n a flat country it must have content but not form and that may make a master-piece" (467). Most geographic histories advance a sequential argument about the influence of particular features of the land from the past on present human arrangements. But in this textual landscape, with its accretive, repetitive, circular style, Stein's genius can proliferate and students can themselves wander suggestively over the sprawling text.

Although Stein's formulation of a democratically fluid, flat America might seem reductive or problematic because of its essentialism, it is not alone; the early-twentieth-century development of environmental determinism in the field of geography puts her maneuvers in a cultural context. I introduce my students to the work of Ellen Churchill Semple, whose *Influences of Geographic Environment* (1911) was widely read on both sides of the Atlantic (Keighren 46–91). Semple's *American History and Its Geographic Conditions* (1903) is another prime example of the geographic history genre; it was revised and republished in 1933 to widespread public notice in the months that led up to Stein's American lecture tour. Articulating a determinist paradigm in these books, Semple argues that environmental factors shape human society more than human endeavors.[1] Her *American History* posits (as Stein does) the exploratory, migratory, open, free qualities of the American people as a product of America's geography:

> Mere space, unconstrained existence, a buffalo hunt, or an Indian fray was pleasure enough. In the large, fresh environment of the American continent the English race had been born again and now was animated with the irrepressible vigor of a youthful people. A constant change of environment had given them the adaptability of youth; vast opportunity had bred the spirit of adventure and enterprise. Nothing seemed impossible and therefore little was impossible. (231–32)

Semple's attention to spatial enlargement, adaptability, and fluidity resonates with Stein's approach (Berman, *Modernist Fiction* 176–83; Walsh 96–123).

Yet students can also debate the degree to which Stein's *Geographical History* complicates, in the end, any straightforward application of environmental determinism. At times Stein emphasizes America's unique largeness and flatness, but I guide students to other moments in the text where she erodes the differences between America and France, the "little country" with which America is repeatedly contrasted (392); she undercuts the seemingly unique association between wandering and America's size and flatness. "Is there any difference between flat land and an ocean a big country and a little one," she asks (475). The topographic distinctions on which the text depends lose their specificity when largeness and flatness are no longer special conditions for wandering: "But really wandering has something to do with the human mind. A big or little country. Wandering in a big or little country," and "can it only be a big country that can be like that or even a little one" (392). *Geographical History* offers students a complex take on Americanness, since it both reflects and undermines the idea that specific American geographic features are linked to America's cultural, social, and intellectual freedoms, exploiting and refuting determinist cause-and-effect logic along the way. The ultimate question I pose to students is how much Stein sustains American exceptionalist dynamics if America's land is not always distinguishable from France's or if her ideas of America draw on French sources.[2]

Brewsie and Willie is more forward-looking than *Geographical History* in its hopeful construction of an America inclusive of gendered, cultural, economic, and racial difference, especially compelling just after the depredations and destruction of World War II. Its transnational crucible for ideas about America—from the perspective of American soldiers in Europe—reflects the nation's widening geopolitical engagements in the twentieth century.

The first part of my classroom strategy with *Brewsie and Willie* involves helping students recognize how the work confounds the conventions of war literature. War literature tends to privilege the battlefield memoir or lyric, whereas Stein presents dialogue among American soldiers in limbo in France after the war has ended. I ask students to consider questions of authority: What does it mean for her to write about war as a woman and a civilian, without firsthand military experience? Once students see her decision to write war's aftermath as a purposeful alternative to the battlefield narrative, I have them pinpoint places where authority might be subtly claimed, as in the epilogue, "To Americans," the only portion written in her voice: "I was always in my way a Civil War veteran" (778). She portrays herself here as a fellow comrade, likening her own successful battle against nineteenth-century literature to the soldiers' completed, successful mission (Bergen 217).

The ethical danger in representing war events—overgeneralizing, romanticizing, or overreaching the limits of one's knowledge or experience—is offset by a dialogue form that generates a nonauthoritarian response to war and its aftermath. Offering a different form of textual wandering than *Geographical History*, the meandering, polyvocal exchanges among Brewsie and Willie and their companions give the text an open-ended quality that students can link to America's democratic promise. Although the contemplative character of Brewsie may be considered a stand-in for Stein, other characters also question, postulate, disagree, interrupt, demur, defer, or circle back to previous topics. Given that the characters constantly speculate about what America will be like and what they will do when they get back, I ask students what values or qualities the text suggests might be beneficial for America's future. In the open-endedness of the text we see a commitment to democratic exchange and process that the soldiers can take home with them, much needed after a world war fought against authoritarian regimes. As Dana Watson has argued, Stein wanted this style of "playful conversation" to function as "an integral step toward improving the world's sociopolitical future" (171). Willie says to Brewsie, "[Y]ou're no leader, Brewsie, you just talk" (*Brewsie* 726); but this kind of contrarian talk is what America needs. In contrast to the top-down structure of European Axis regimes, the open dialogue of the American soldiers, facilitated by Brewsie's perspective but not dictated by it, highlights America's potential as a global leader.

My classes also address the text's focus on the military's policies for troop behavior, particularly sexual fraternization. Brewsie declares at the opening of the text that the whole military is "funny, pretty funny" about "this fraternization business" (715). I ask students to interpret this statement in relation to excerpts I provide from the work of military historians and literary critics. As Paul Fussell has noted, for unbombed America the meaning of the war seemed hard to process (*Wartime* 268), and the over two million American soldiers shipped overseas to fight the Axis powers had little knowledge of France or French culture (*Boys' Crusade* x, 39). Mary Louise Roberts's *What Soldiers Do: Sex and the American GI in World War II France* illuminates American military leaders' packaging of the Normandy campaign as "an erotic adventure" or mission of "sexual romance" designed to save Frenchwomen from the Nazis, motivating GIs to fight in a country in which they were not invested (8). In Brewsie's hands, this topic leads to larger questions about whether Americans are "isolationists" or are "isolated" (722) and invites the other soldiers and Stein's readers to confront sexual double standards as well as fears about national, cultural, and racial mixing. I turn students' attention to Willie's declarations that he will "sleep with any German wench who'll sleep with me and they all will" and that he would never want an American woman to sleep with a foreign soldier were America to be invaded. Indeed, his commitment to preventing future wars ("[T]here aint going to be any more war not if I can help it") seems to be about protecting not only his nation but also the ethnic purity of American women. Students are quick to note the hypocrisy of his position and find their own responses mirrored in Brewsie's comments, which are variations on "[A]ll your fathers and mothers were lousy foreigners" (715). These soldiers will take such ideas back home with them, and the text overall anticipates the multicultural world with which students are familiar. By this point in our classroom discussion, students can debate whether the text presents America as a country that likes and is like other countries or grants America an exceptionalist status.

I then ask students to track how America's pioneering appears throughout the text, with *pioneering* defined as being "ready to break down what has been built up" (760). It is characterized partly through the many indictments of its opposite in the text, industrialism, which is like chewing gum for having "taste . . . but no substance" (745). For Brewsie this economic system threatens to "use up all our raw material" and "make us all poor" (732, 747). If England's industrialism lay behind its exploitation of colonies for both raw materials and for new markets, America's industrialism has exploited its "outside market right at home" in the form of immigrant populations (733). For Stein, industrialism categorically turns people into "job men" with no agency and creates the conditions for an indentured servitude; such people—inevitably the working class, racial minorities, and immigrants—chase the purchase of unnecessary goods of low quality (756). But students can locate evidence for an exceptionalist logic in the text's argument that America's pioneering mentality makes America uniquely poised to avoid becoming "poor as England and other industrial countries" (778), a "city upon a hill" for the globe, to quote John Winthrop's founding ideal (150).

Discussing the relation between pioneering and American exceptionalism also sets the stage for turning to the text's positive portrayals of African American identity. Although white soldiers display racist behavior, Jimmie, a southerner and presumably white soldier, declares that African Americans back home are the only ones "doing the only real pioneering there is in America these days" of the sort that the characters unquestioningly praise (750). If *pioneering* is defined as breaking down old structures to form new ones, the soldier community Stein depicts is doing exactly that where race is concerned. As M. Lynn Weiss has discussed, Stein was aware of the Jim Crow structure of the United States Army, having seen it firsthand during her visit with United States troops in Germany, and she challenges this disenfranchisement in *Brewsie and Willie* with an empathetic counternarrative of dignified African American soldiers (136). A black major names racism as the reason he has no children: "Is this America any place to make born a Negro child" (720). A black soldier kneels like a "cavalier" before a French mother and child, a picture of courtly politeness and deference (728). In many respects, Stein's text counters military and social disenfranchisement of African Americans with a more inclusive America forged by war experience and a spatially distanced perspective. Her framing of race invites students to interrogate the American social structures that took shape in the aftermath of World War II.

Stein's later prose works offer an exciting opportunity to expose students to what experimental writing can do to reflect and reform democratic ideals. Approaching constructions of American identity in a historical context can provide students with a palpable way to navigate the books' wandering forms. Both *Geographical History* and *Brewsie and Willie* can be used in the classroom to make visible the nation's evolving sense of itself in the years of the Great Depression and World War II and to introduce students to Stein's complex approaches to American exceptionalism, isolationism, and social justice.

NOTES

[1] To demonstrate how entrenched these ideas were, instructors may wish to lay excerpts from Semple's *American History* alongside Frederick Jackson Turner's 1893 "Frontier Thesis" (in *History, Frontier, and Section: Three Essays*), whose equations between the expansiveness of the landscape and the vaunted character of the American people were an influence for Semple.

[2] The French geographer Paul Vidal de la Blache's model of possibilism, which attributed more agency to the human side of the human-land relation, is compatible with the textual agency Stein claims over America (Walsh 121–23).

Engaging Gertrude Stein's *Wars I Have Seen* as Secondary Witnesses

Elisabeth Hedrick-Moser

Gertrude Stein's *Wars I Have Seen*, composed from 1943 until the liberation of France in 1944, portrays the survival of Stein and Alice B. Toklas in German-occupied France during the Second World War. This portrait of wartime life garnered starkly contrasting appraisals when it was published in 1945. The composer Virgil Thomson hailed it as "the most charming and the most realistic picture imaginable" ("Gertrude Stein's France" 271). On the other hand, the French philosopher Jean Wahl, interned as a Jew at the Drancy camp in Paris, thought it "beautiful and very moving in parts" but also called one of Stein's comments on Marshal Pétain "unbelievable in its naïveté" (83, 84). Controversy over her political sympathies during the war years has lately been rekindled. A spate of articles accusing Stein of collaborationist sympathies followed the publication of Barbara Will's *Unlikely Collaboration* (2011), which explores her relation to Vichy politics. Defenders of Stein advance reasons not to denounce her as a collaborator. Edward Burns argues that members of the French Resistance admired her work and published it during the war ("Gertrude Stein"). Charles Bernstein advocates reading "Stein's war years as a survivor's tale. Jewish, female, homosexual, elderly . . . Stein and Toklas successfully escaped extermination" (Preface). I use the questions raised by the controversy surrounding this text to help students consider how cultural context and autobiographical perspective may shape the representation of historical violence. Instead of attempting to unravel the web of historical and political uncertainty that this work is tangled in—a task that literary scholars have struggled with for years—I encourage students to reflect on their own knowledge of violence and lead them to think about the interrelation between the survival of self and the response to violence experienced by others.

The question of how violence interacts with literary texts composed during war drives Civilian Literature of the Second World War, an upper-level literature course in which I teach *Wars I Have Seen*. The texts we study describe the impact of the war on civilians at varying proximities to its physical violence, from Primo Levi's firsthand experience of Auschwitz to Flannery O'Connor's view from across the Atlantic.[1] Our analyses of the effects of war on the human person are informed by the science and theory of trauma. Both historically and currently, the concept of proximity has drawn the boundary of trauma's reach.[2] Stein's memoir, having a peripheral relation to the violence of the war, offers insight into how war violence blurs the boundary that purports to contain it.

I ask students to think about how, in our position as readers, we are witnesses to the violence of the Second World War at a greater remove than Stein's. Dominick LaCapra's conception of the role of the historian as a "secondary witness" to historical trauma helps us think through this position (37). As secondary witnesses, historians gather information about traumatic events but also respond to them affectively and ask questions that resonate with present concerns. LaCapra calls for empathy in historical study existing "tensely" alongside objectivity (35). As a reading practice, secondary witnessing takes into account how our relation to current violence interacts with our response to literary representations of historical violence.

My focus on secondary witnessing is informed by the values of liberal education, the "cultivation of the whole human being for the functions of citizenship and life generally" (Nussbaum 9). Academic scholarship, Catharine MacKinnon argues, is often believed to be "disengaged . . . meaning from no preconceived position . . . making no judgments of value." Engaged scholarship, on the other hand, "centers on having and affirming direct involvement with the subject matter" (194). Through reflection on our own context and exposure to current violence in news media, I hope to make visible to my students the complex range of factors that drive the ways we interpret and respond to violence.

The course covers *Wars I Have Seen* in two weeks, over four class periods. I begin with an introduction into Stein's situation in occupied France. Because France signed the armistice with Nazi Germany only six weeks after the Battle for France began, the violence in that country was not primarily the violence of the battlefield but the oppression of the Jews, a violation of human dignity that led to the death camps after Jews were deported.[3] After the liberation of France in August 1944, the great majority of its citizens claimed to have supported the Resistance against Germany. Recent historical studies, however, have recognized that support of the collaborationist Vichy government was widespread, that French persecution of the Jews was homegrown in addition to being implanted by Germany, and that political ambiguity was common. Stein's memoir—sent off to be published directly after the liberation of France and before the "purges," when collaborators were shot in the streets (Jackson 577)—provides insight into the ambiguity of personal responses in the face of violence against others.

I briefly introduce students to Stein's support of Marshal Philippe Pétain, the collaborationist leader of the wartime Vichy government. At the outset of the war, Pétain was widely popular, as was his National Revolution to strengthen the country through a renewal of "*travail, famille, patrie* [work, family, fatherland]" (Paxton 37). After the war, Pétain was convicted for treason and sentenced to death, though this sentence was "commuted to imprisonment" because of his advanced age (Jackson 588). I draw from Stein's "Introduction to the Speeches of Maréchal Pétain" to consider with students her reasons for supporting Pétain, including her rationale that the United States was more likely to understand the need for a strong leader after it experienced the national trauma of the attack on Pearl Harbor (93). It is troubling that Stein continued her translations of Pétain's speeches until January 1943, "long after the United States had entered the war against the fascist forces that Stein was promoting to her fellow Americans" (Will 138). Yet her promotion of Pétain, even in 1943, when Jews were being deported by tens of thousands, does not necessarily mean that she supported anti-Semitism, as "little of the regime's propaganda targeted the Jews [and] no speech by Pétain directly mentioned the Jews" (Jackson 354). I caution students that *Wars I Have Seen* does not offer a clear articulation of her political beliefs—one claim seems to be contradicted by another. She argues, for example, that "naturalisation is foolishness completely" (131), which may be in part a reference to naturalized French Jews; she makes fun of those who are outed as collaborators (132); and she lauds the brilliance of the *maquis* Resistance fighters (198–99). My intention with this brief introduction is not to explain away the controversy surrounding the work but to awaken students to the text's attention to the complexity of representing the self in relation to violence against the other.

Students come prepared with a journal in which they analyze and respond to readings for each class day. The first day, I ask them to attend to how the autobiographical I filters the experience of the war.[4] Students may notice that Stein often describes the reality of war as unreal or dreamlike. Receiving news that "forty thousand people" were "sent out of their homes in Marseille," she remarks, "it is so real to me that it is a dream, not that I know any of them" (11). Specific news of violence that reaches the narrating I can register in the text as failing to register: "However near a war is it is always not very near. Even when it is here. It is funny that but it is true" (9).[5] The sensation of unreality also comes through in narration of encounters with the machinery of war. We turn to a paragraph on pages 46–47 in which Stein describes witnessing a train with human cargo in Aix-les-Bains. As she waited for her train to come, another train passed slowly by, and among "tanks and trucks . . . seated anywhere were Germans all naked except a little trouser nothing on their heads" (47). As Stein saw it, "all the French people were as if they were at a theatre that was not interesting" (47). She describes the community's response more than her own.[6]

I then ask students to write reflectively about a violent event in our time. Because I teach in St. Louis, the August 2014 shooting of Michael Brown, a young black man, by a white police officer and the ensuing protests and police response is a compelling example. This event may have been experienced as threatening, as justified, or with apathy, depending on how students identified racially, culturally, and politically. But any violent event in the media can be an avenue to speculate about how one's position in the culture affects how one interprets violence. We come up with a list of factors that affect one's perception of safety in regard to police violence and in protests or riots. Students note how Stein represents her own and her community's response to the violence and violation of war and how that representation relates to her ethnicity, her views about political power in France, and her perception of her own safety. Students' engaging personally with the questions we are asking of Stein's memoir is important both for teaching the transferability of reading skills and for creating motivation to explore the text. Personal reflection does not efface the importance of historical context; rather, it enables students to think through the necessity and difficulty of reckoning with ambiguous context and perspective.

For the next class, students come prepared to discuss how the style of Stein's text evokes an experience of war. In the 1946 "Transatlantic Interview," Stein explains that in *Wars I Have Seen* "I described something momentous happening under my eyes and I was able to do it without a great sense of time. There should not be a sense of time, but an existence suspended in time" (20). The class puzzles over how this statement relates to the book's narrative. One possibility is that the narrating I does not interpret the context for readers but instead conveys the experience of living through the war as it is perceived successively. I ask students to consider reading Stein's narration as a study in perception, especially the perception of indirect violence.

To illustrate this mode of reading, we turn again to the passing German military train, this time including the paragraph's surrounding text in our discussion. Stein's narrative moves associatively. The I is narrating in the present, "end of June 1943" (46). After describing the crowd watching the passing train, Stein relates, "[N]obody had noticed the train full of Germans except four young Frenchmen from the camp de Jeunesse and they like all young fellows of that age laughed, which reminded me of the dough boys in the San Francisco public. Which ones. Those Germans" (47). The statement that "nobody had noticed" raises the question, What should we notice? We are told that Germans with scant clothing are being transported on a train along with military equipment and that for "the French people" it was "not interesting." Stein turns the attention of her I from the train to the crowd.

The one group that does notice, the young men from the "camp de Jeunesse," a Vichy initiative that "put every French young man in a rural work camp . . . for eight months of his twenty-first year" (Paxton 165), attend to the passing Germans by laughing. Stein seems to rationalize this behavior with her qualifying statement "like all young fellows of that age." As we read this passage, at first it seems that these young Frenchmen remind her of "the dough boys," American GIs of the 1898 Spanish-American War, in the midst of the "San Francisco public," leaving for the Philippines—both were conscripted to service for their country. However, "Which ones. Those Germans," shifts the comparison; now it is the Germans on the train who remind her of the doughboys forty-five years earlier. The narrating I questions herself, her train of associations, and her memories: "Which ones." Her answer, "Those Germans," causes readers to question whether the comparison is between the Frenchmen and the doughboys or between the Germans and the doughboys. This ambiguity conflates all three groups of young male conscripts. Or the question and answer may rise from a different, untold place in the narrating consciousness.

Stein muses in the paragraph immediately following, "It is funny funny in the sense of strange and peculiar and unrealisable, the fact that so many are prisoners, prisoners, prisoners every where" (47). She recalls various people who have been arrested and narrates an event that happened in "February 1943," jumping back four months (48). Not only were she and Toklas forced to leave their house in Bilignin and find a new one in Culoz, but also her lawyer informed her that a government official warned that they should "leave at once for Switzerland . . . otherwise they will be put into a concentration camp." (They lived fifty miles from Geneva.) Stein relates that she "felt very funny, quite completely funny." They decide not to take the advice, asserting, "[I]t is better to go regularly where we are sent than to go irregularly where nobody can help us if we are in trouble" (50). Read in the continuous present, this recollection takes place in June 1943, in the immediate context of encountering the Germans on the train. The threat implicit in witnessing the German machinery of war had been set aside in the previous paragraph, only to rise associatively in the next.

To explore the connections between Stein's associational style and the workings of perception and responses to violence, I play a short newsclip describing a current violent event and then have students sit in silence for two minutes. Next I ask them to try to trace in writing the meanderings of their minds and assure them they will not turn this writing in. Afterward I ask them if this exercise gives them a sense of Stein's way of narrating experience, which shows perception operating moment to moment, interweaving present and past, and both expressing and repressing the knowledge of violence. In the context of this introspective, intuitive work, we think about the significance of Stein's and the community's turning away from the presence of the Germans.

For the third class day, students write in their journals about other ways the French populace responds to violence. They may notice how connection with the natural world sustains the French. Stein says that the French have a word for this connection: "[A]ll French people are terrien as they call themselves people who think and act and work in the ground, it is because of that that they can so well resist the disasters of war" (185). They root themselves in the earth's permanence in a time of extreme impermanence. Stein includes herself in the French rural community, as she and Toklas also are living off their vegetable garden. The practice of cultivation strengthens resilience; because farmers are used to living through the change of seasons and with the anxiety over whether they will have feast or famine, they are better equipped to take war in stride.

In our final class, we discuss the epilogue, in which Stein writes that the news that the Gestapo raided her Paris apartment led her "to have what you might call a posthumous fear." She relates that while "the Germans were here [in Culoz] we were so busy trying to live through each day that except once in a while when something happened you did not know about being frightened," but after being liberated by American soldiers and "hearing what had been happening to others, of course one knew it but now one had time to feel it and so I was quite frightened" (255). This description may reveal a posttraumatic reaction, as Barbara Will (145) and Julie Goodspeed-Chadwick (130) have argued. Stein waffles between saying that she did and did not know "what had been happening to others" and between being afraid and not having "time to feel" fear. The class discusses how attending to daily survival may have enabled her not to feel the horror of the war.

The mental ambiguity that Stein portrays sheds light on our responses today when we are confronted with peripheral violence. Do we have the responsibility or the ability to help people outside our personal lives who suffer violence? The introspective writing and thinking that students have done in their journals comes to a conclusion in a project in which they respond to a current violent event outside their direct experience, in a style imitating one of the works we have read. They must draw connections between their relation to that violence and representations of past violence and are asked how thinking consciously about narrative style influenced what they wrote.

Stein's attention to modes of survival during the Second World War illuminates the ambiguities that may be present in a person's perception of violence during war. In *Wars* she writes, "The one thing that is sure and certain is that history does not teach, that is to say, it always says let it be a lesson to you but is it." It "does not teach" because "circumstances always alter cases and so although history does repeat itself . . . nobody wants to learn either by their own or anybody else's experience, nobody does" (122). Although I acknowledge the validity of Stein's doubt and admit that we are witnesses at a second remove from a war that Stein described, I have found that *Wars I Have Seen* teaches us to interrogate how we perceive violence today and how our relation to past violence informs that perception.

NOTES

[1] Besides Stein's *Wars*, the course's required texts are T. S. Eliot's *Four Quartets*, Virginia Woolf's "Sketch of the Past," Simone de Beauvoir's *The Blood of Others*, Ezra Pound's *Pisan Cantos*, Primo Levi's *Survival in Auschwitz*, John Hersey's *Hiroshima*, and Flannery O'Connor's "The Displaced Person."

[2] For a discussion of how the psychological definition of trauma developed in tandem with the need to place and contain blame for railway accidents, see Luckhurst 21–29. For the current definition of psychological trauma, which limits the criteria for experiencing an event as traumatic to direct contact with the life-threatening event or with the accidental or violent death of a loved one, see "Trauma- and Stressor-Related Disorders." The *Diagnostic and Statistical Manual of Mental Disorders* also stipulates that witnessing an event through media, even if that witnessing is repeated or prolonged, does not qualify as exposure to a traumatic event ("Trauma-").

[3] "75,000 Jews from France perished in Auschwitz; 30,000 French civilians were shot as hostages or members of the Resistance; another 60,000 were deported to German concentration camps" (Jackson 1).

[4] Sidonie Smith and Julia Watson's discussion of the "four I's" of autobiography, which "differentiate" between "the 'real' or historical 'I,'" "the narrating 'I,'" "the narrated 'I,'" and "the ideological 'I,'" is a helpful resource (72).

[5] In the next two sentences Stein argues that gender makes no difference in this regard: "Perhaps if one were a boy it would be different but I do not think so. I think even when men are in a war actually in a war it is not very near" (9).

[6] We compare this passage with another on pages 172–73, where Stein describes seeing "thirty young fellows" at the Aix-les-Bains train station. The men were "going into freight cars and that is usually only done with soldiers"; they had been "rounded up in Annecy and were being taken well somewhere." The German soldiers there "are not real said one woman to us they are phantoms."

Teaching Diversity to Undergraduates via Gertrude Stein's *Tender Buttons* and Other Texts from *Selected Writings*

Julie Goodspeed-Chadwick

I teach Gertrude Stein's writing in a 200-level gateway course for my institution's undergraduate major and minor in English, though it is open to all undergraduates. As this course counts toward a diversity requirement, we focus on literary representations of diverse people and beliefs and investigate perspectives that are informed by gender, race, ethnicity, socioeconomic class, and sexual orientation. My students, by considering ideas and issues that may not resonate with them personally, become more knowledgeable about many different people, concepts, and situations.

Specific Reading Suggestions

To frame our encounter with Stein, I assign a novel that treats female embodiment overtly (Thomas Hardy's *Tess of the D'Urbervilles* is my favorite) and texts that treat race, ethnicity, and social class (the range of genres in Sondra Wilson's The Crisis *Reader* works well, and I have also used Mark Twain's *The Adventures of Huckleberry Finn*). Such texts allow students to practice identifying, analyzing, synthesizing, and, finally, addressing and interpreting diversity in relation to identity politics. I save Stein's writing until they have gained experience—and perhaps confidence—in interpreting other texts, so they can see that they need to be able to draw on the text and ground their reading in it, while being cognizant of historical and critical contexts, if they are to convince their reader to accept their interpretations or arguments. We approach Stein's texts attuned to diversity and ready to seek it out while engaging in close reading.

We spend six weeks on various pieces included in *Selected Writings of Gertrude Stein*, focusing mostly on gender and sexual orientation (to a lesser extent on socioeconomic class, race, and ethnicity), devoting most of that time—four and a half weeks—to *Tender Buttons*. I begin by walking students through generally accepted readings of Stein's work, offering multiple interpretations of the same passage or text, but I structure the unit so that students are expected increasingly to take more ownership of building an interpretation. I intentionally assign texts that speak to one another in terms of theme or style, but I also allow the students more and more freedom in choosing which poems we study from *Tender Buttons* and in directing the conversation when we are explicating them.

In all my classes, I promote responsible close readings, *responsible* meaning that students should read a document attentively, sensibly, and ethically: the text, in other words, cannot mean anything they want it to mean. A search online for explications of *Tender Buttons* by non-Stein scholars will show that it is very easy to map a reading onto a poem when the reading is only loosely connected to what is actually on the page. In class we talk through examples of unconvincing readings of Stein's poems (e.g., idiosyncratic and non-peer-reviewed interpretations on blogs and Web sites) along with grounded-in-the-text interpretations of them (published in peer-reviewed books and journal articles). Because this is a course in which students learn how to close-read, it is imperative that they see that interpretations should not be fabricated out of what is unreasonable or unsubstantiated, that close readings should be evidence-based.

Regardless of what Stein's position would have been in regard to contemporary identity politics, her work in *Selected Writings* allows us to interrogate and grapple with a range of issues involving diversity, even though her literary output is so different in its aims and voice from that of Hardy or the collective authors of *The Crisis*. The students view Hardy and *The Crisis* authors as progressive, and Stein, while not progressive in her personal political views, appears progressive in her aesthetics, specifically in her experimentation with language and form. The students and I do not spend a lot of time on her politics, but I do introduce them to the recent, impassioned discussions that have taken place about them (Goodspeed-Chadwick 102–35; Will; Bernstein, *Gertrude Stein's War Years*). We then consider how Stein's aesthetics, as manifested in her experimental language and literary forms, create a new direction in representation, and we acknowledge our tendency to expect that her personal political views must be radical or progressive to match that experimentation. It is important to give students this caveat: Stein and her work might not be consistent with her political positioning. Her texts may not make the statements we think they will.

Beginning with texts that are more conventional than *Tender Buttons* builds students' close reading skills. When students learn that they can and should discuss issues of identity and representation and learn to do so in a respectful manner, it paves the way for their study of work that appears to be less socially and politically charged. With readings from *The Crisis*, for instance, they are immersed in texts that address social justice issues from a politically radical viewpoint, and the style is often didactic. Although Stein is very different, *The Crisis* and her *Selected Writings* both respond to the world; in both anthologies, race matters, gender matters, class status matters, and sexual orientation matters—in the world of the book and in the world outside the book.

We begin our six weeks on Stein with "A Message from Gertrude Stein," "Three Portraits of Painters," and F. W. Dupee's introduction to the volume. From "A Message," students see that Stein was a literary celebrity in her lifetime and that she can be funny and serious at the same time. Dupee reflects on her canonical status and links her to cubism, providing contextual background to her portraits of Matisse (1909 or 1910), Picasso (1909 or 1910), and Cézanne (1923). Close-reading these texts prepares us for the more abbreviated portraits of objects, food, and rooms in *Tender Buttons*. I invite students to read passages out loud, a student for each paragraph, and the different voices help them see that these portraits are cubist representations of the famous painters, a modernist writer translating to her own medium what the modernist painters were doing. We also listen to Stein read "How She Bowed to Her Brother" (1931)—the recording is available at *PennSound* online. Because the poem is relatively easy, students can see Stein's experimental style and hear the conversational tone simultaneously. It has been my experience that when they hear Stein read and have the written text in front of them, she becomes more accessible. My goal in teaching "How She Bowed to Her Brother" is precisely to show them that they can grasp what she is saying.

"Miss Furr and Miss Skeene" (1911), a double portrait, gives us the opportunity to closely examine lesbian identities and gender along with socioeconomic status. We focus on how it holds open sometimes complementary and sometimes competing meanings of *gay*. (According to the *Oxford English Dictionary*, the most common meanings have been "happy," "carefree," and "homosexual." The *OED* cites "Miss Furr and Miss Skeene" as the text that coined the definition of *gay* as we use it now.) This piece asks us to read creatively, to keep different meanings at play on a signifying string. Students will accept some possibilities and reject others as they marshal their evidence from the text and build their interpretations. Reading creatively means to look for what is not obvious, not literal, not one-dimensional. "Miss Furr and Miss Skeene" comes before *Tender Buttons* in my class because it helps students become more comfortable with discussing homosexuality. When the piece is read aloud, we are taken by the audacity of its repeated use of "gay" and by the way words can be both transparent and opaque.

Reading Carl Van Vechten's "A Stein Song" and Stein's "Composition as Explanation" for our next class meeting foregrounds the difficulty of the avant-garde. We discuss Van Vechten's quotation from André Maurois: "Gertrude Stein is believed to be a difficult writer. This is false. There is not a single phrase in this book that cannot be comprehended by a schoolgirl of sixteen years" (xx). In "Composition as Explanation," I highlight Stein's observation that "each generation has something different at which they are all looking. . . . The only thing that is different from one time to another is what is seen and what is seen depends upon how everybody is doing everything" (*Selected Writings* 513). Stein positions artists as the ones "looking" first, the general population of her day following suit, but students understand that they will read her from their generation's perspective, which is informed by twenty-first-century norms and perceptions threaded with an awareness of cultural diversity that was not manifested in the same way for Stein's generation. The more perspectives we have in play, the richer our study of Stein and diversity is. Having made its way through these readings, the class is ready to approach *Tender Buttons.*

Discussion Strategies for Teaching Tender Buttons

We spend a good deal of time on gender and lesbian identity in *Tender Buttons*, considering the conventional expectations and meanings. "A Petticoat" asks us to think about color (whiteness and rosiness), honor and disgrace, women's bodies and clothing (undergarments and the supposed need for them), and what is charming and what is not. The phrase "an ink spot" can start a discussion not only on Stein but also on the status of women writers and their writing generally. The phrase is metaphorically straitjacketed between "a disgrace" on the one hand and "a rosy charm" on the other (471). Why are these words and ideas ordered in this way? For "A Little Called Pauline," I ask students to tell me what they know about Pauline, using evidence from the poem. In my reading, a young, good girl is depicted within the gendered conventions of a fairy tale (473–74). But the poem ends with the directive that we break out of the heteronormative script for women. The students and I see whether this reading can be substantiated.

"In Between" foregrounds sexuality. Its language hints at socially dictated values (reminiscent of *Tess*) in connection with female (curvy) bodies: "A virgin a whole virgin is judged made and so between curves and outlines and real seasons and more out glasses and a perfectly unprecedented arrangement between old ladies and mild colds there is no satin wood shining" (472–73). What does it mean to be "in between"? In "Sugar," what leads us to believe that the phrase the "teasing is tender and trying and thoughtful" is about lesbian identities, bodies, and intimacy—and about Stein's aesthetics?

Teaching diversity in relation to gender and sexuality is my concentration, but instructors and students can also locate socioeconomic class and race concerns. In "A Time to Eat," students can work with the denotations and connotations of "pleasant," "simple," "habitual," "tyrannical," "authorised," "educated," and "articulate separation" (472). They can explore the poem's couching of multiple subject positions in its short lines, primarily from bourgeois and proletarian perspectives. Mealtime ("a time to eat") means different things to those who have servants and to the servants themselves. "Dinner" has a racial slur embedded in it ("nigger" [494]), and instructors might want to discuss the ugly histories that attend racial slurs to this day. The puzzling final sentence of "Dinner," "All to be not a white old chat churner," might suggest that new ways of being, thinking, and doing need to occur or are occurring.

An entire class session (more time than that, if possible) is devoted to "Rooms," because it is an undifferentiated section full of everything we have studied up to this point. After discussing truth, disturbance, and doubleness, we consider possible references to lesbian identity, such as, "The sister was not a mister. Was this a surprise. It was" (499). Here is an opportunity to entertain multiple readings and demonstrate to students that uncertainty can exist even in a responsible reading. Stein herself was not a "mister," yet in her romantic relationship with Toklas she assumed many of the traditional male roles, even calling herself Toklas's husband. The text suggests that a lesbian identity was a "surprise" to heteronormative society. Another reading of this passage undoes a center: a statement of fact is given (the woman was not a man), but the following lines—the ambiguous modifier "this," the impersonal or unisex pronoun "it"—suggest uncertainty. Rarely do my students balk at multiple or competing interpretations; they are eager to see how they can ground convincing interpretive readings in the text.

A few pages later, we encounter a provocative passage on sexual and identity politics: "All along the tendency to deplore the absence of more has not been authorised. It comes to mean that with burning there is that pleasant state of stupefication. Then there is a way of earning a living. Who is a man" (501). Perhaps one of the most resonant lines in terms of diversity and plurality or multiplicity is placed in "Rooms": "[W]hy is not disturbing a centre no virtue" (506). Students will learn that recovering the marginal and reframing it while decentering the privileged is one agenda of *Tender Buttons*. The last line of "Rooms"—"The care with which there is incredible justice and likeness, all this makes a magnificent asparagus, and also a fountain" (509)—speaks to the "care" taken in the "justice" and "likeness" of the representations found in the collection. All three terms should describe our own close reading practices of Stein.

Writing Assignment

I conclude the unit on Stein by requiring students to produce a thoughtful and convincing interpretation, from three to five pages, of one or more poems from *Tender Buttons*. They respond to the following prompts: What is this poem about? What do you view as the most important issue (gender, race, ethnicity, economics and class, sexuality and sexual orientation, cultural history, and biography) at stake in the literary text or in the criticism? How is the issue manifest in the text and criticism, and why is it important to our understanding of the text and of our lives or of the lives of others outside the book? I encourage students to select an aspect of identity politics in *Tender Buttons* that interests them and that resonates with what they have learned in the course.

In teaching diversity in connection with *Tender Buttons*, we make the "poem[s] *a live issue*," in the words of Gerald Graff (49); we make *Tender Buttons* relevant, interesting, and maybe inviting. Approaching Stein with a focus on diversity presents students with the opportunity to learn that language and concepts can be denaturalized or decentered; that identities can be performed, deconstructed, or represented in new or different ways, ways that are not always stable or pinned down; that literature does not have to be transparent to be meaningful, important, and enjoyable; that responsible close readings allow us to become intimate with a text and produce convincing interpretations of it; and that literature can teach us about ourselves and about different people and perspectives.

The Tender Buttons of Avant-Garde Self-Assertion: Teaching Gertrude Stein's Feminism

Kimberly Lamm

She wrote, both cryptically and frankly, about lesbian sexuality, and many of her most famous texts tell stories about women attempting to emancipate themselves from their fixed placement in patriarchal families. Her work inspired—and continues to inspire—a wide array of experimental writings by women. She saw herself as a genius, equal to Pablo Picasso, and she composed an opera about Susan B. Anthony, an icon of the American suffrage movement, identifying her as *The Mother of Us All* (1945–46).

These aspects of Gertrude Stein's work and life have shaped an argument that runs through much of Stein scholarship: namely, that Stein and her work have strong affinities with feminism. But, as many scholars engaging with Stein's oeuvre have noted, such affinities are difficult to reconcile with the indications of her political conservatism. These indications have served as convenient targets for her detractors but are also alluded to by scholars, such as Juliana Spahr, who want to be honest about the fact that "Stein's politics make little consistent sense" (Afterword 111). For example, early in her career Stein drew from Otto Weininger's tract *Sex and Character* (1903), a text rife with sexist and anti-Semitic arguments, but she did so to imagine the breakdown of strict gender identities. This is to say that the relations among Stein, her work, and feminism are complicated and therefore, I argue, enormously productive for feminist pedagogy.

The complications involved in Stein's relation to feminism have helped me meet one of the most interesting challenges in teaching undergraduate women's studies courses: encouraging students to allow their understandings of feminism to loosen and expand. I have found that many students who identify as feminists rely on inert and narrow ideas about what feminism is and how it should appear. Often these ideas are implicitly informed by a definition of feminism as a mode of political intervention with certain goals—such as obtaining equality and leaving the domestic sphere for the workplace—that are unequivocally moral and measured through clear signs of progress. Because students most often circulate in worlds that are either hostile or indifferent to feminism, it can be easy for them to see less obvious articulations of feminism as capitulations. Stein's literary experimentations serve as rich resources for teaching undergraduates about feminism's nuanced manifestations, which can then open their perceptions of feminism to difficulty and uncertainty.

Exemplars of the link between Stein's literary experimentation and her feminist leanings, "Ada" (written in 1910, published in 1922) and *Tender Buttons* (written in 1912, published in 1914) can go a long way toward this pedagogical intervention. "Ada" tells how Alice B. Toklas unhinged herself from the expectation that she devote her life to domestic work. Composed just two years after "Ada," the cubist-inspired *Tender Buttons* imaginatively renders the details of everyday life in domestic interiors and becomes a radical meditation on reproductive labor (the work of sustaining households) and affective labor (the work of creating and sustaining affective bonds). To different degrees, the aesthetic experimentation of "Ada" and *Tender Buttons* manifests what the historian Nancy Cott identifies as the "avant-garde self-assertion" of early-twentieth-century Euro-American feminism (49). "Avant-garde self-assertion" offered women the possibility of detaching from the patriarchal family and participating in the opportunities modernity offered to imaginatively experiment with the self as an aesthetic form.

To teach "Ada" and *Tender Buttons* as texts that enact this feminist possibility, I assign them along with the first chapter of Cott's *The Grounding of Modern Feminism*. I focus on Cott's argument that in the first decades of the twentieth century there was a turn away from the clear "political action and argumentation" of the nineteenth-century women's movement into what came to be called feminism (49). Indeed, the word *feminism* marks this turn. Although before 1910 it was a "rare quirk," by 1913 it was "almost unremarkable" (13). While Cott shows that the women's movement of the nineteenth century encompassed an array of (sometimes competing) arguments and interventions, it announced itself through clear and unified political goals. However, as the twentieth century got under way, the women's movement became more explicitly heterogeneous. This shift hinged on religion and sexuality: the ties between the women's movement and Christianity were "severed," and the "stance of moral superiority" was "abandoned" (36, 42). Coincident with a new emphasis on sexual freedom, feminists sought release from what Jane Addams identified as the "family claim" and the still pervasive assumption that women are (or should be) "dutiful daughters, wives, and mothers" (qtd. in Cott 40). Cott is careful not to make the distinctions between the centuries too clear-cut—there were obviously overlaps and continuities—but she does stress that in early decades of the twentieth century, feminism expanded into a "multifaceted constitution" that made "avant-garde self-assertion" part of feminism's political project (49).

An early literary portrait, "Ada" is one of Stein's explorations of "avant-garde self-assertion" and a clear argument against women's naturalized ties to reproductive and affective labor. A love poem, it transcribes the arc of Toklas's life from daughter to family caretaker to lover "happier in living than anyone else who ever could" (103). This transformation manifests through a subtle change in Stein's writing style that students can see without too much difficulty. At the level of both form and content, "Ada" enacts the feminist possibility that women's relationships to each other, realized outside the frame of the patriarchal family, can be freeing and imaginatively generative.

The language of "Ada" is so spare and simple it is difficult, and students respond to it with bewildered amusement. But the simplicity of the language helps them identify the first part of "Ada" as a fairly conventional family narrative, and I guide the class to identify the basics of the story and the slow emergence of a feminist aesthetic. The beginning focuses on Ada's brother, Barnes Colhard, son of Mr. Abram Colhard, and what seems to be his confused entrance into masculinity through the rites of marriage and the acquisition of money. The only appearance of Ada in the opening paragraphs is through a letter in which she encourages her brother to marry. As Stein begins to tell Ada's story, Barnes fades into the background: "He had a sister who also was successful enough in being one being living" (101).

The feminism of "Ada" emerges through the act of storytelling and portraying the relationships among women. Stein emphasizes that Ada was close to her mother and that their intimacy is realized through "pretty stories": "She and her mother had always told very pretty stories to each other" (101–02). This storytelling foresees the attention to intersubjectivity realized more fully later in the portrait. However, not all Ada's stories were received well by her mother: "When her mother later was sicker the daughter knew that there were some stories she could tell her that would not please her mother." This sense of propriety, which may have to do with lesbian sexuality, will factor into the expressions of freedom on the text's horizons. With her mother's death, Ada becomes the primary caretaker for her family: "The daughter then kept house for her father and took care of her brother. There were many relations who lived with them." Ada is expected to care for and sustain her family for the duration of her life. If students are going to understand the feminist implications of "Ada," this expectation has to be highlighted, and the power of the "family claim" has to be reiterated. At this point, they should be introduced to the concepts of affective and reproductive labor and the Marxist-feminist argument that the devaluation of women and the devaluation of domestic work often reinforce each other. These concepts and arguments help students register the feminism of Ada's resistance to the idea that she must give her life to a fixed and subservient role: "The daughter did not like them [relatives] to live with them and she did not like them to die with them."

Leaving the Colhard family is invigorating: "She came to be happier than anybody else who was living then. It is easy to believe this thing" (102). Stein describes how Ada revisits the storytelling that she enjoyed with her mother, but the joyous repetition conveys the possibility that all stories—and, by extension, Toklas's lesbian relationship with Stein and the fullness of Stein's aesthetic experimentations—can now be divulged: "Ada was then one and all her living then one completely telling stories that were charming, completely listening to stories that were charming, completely listening to stories that having a beginning and a middle and an ending. Trembling was all living, living was all loving, some one was then the other one." Here the story of Ada becomes more explicitly poetic, and as students respond to Stein's lyrical composition, it is important to keep the text's feminism at the forefront of the discussion. The ring of the gerunds lightens the text, and the portrait both expands and circles in on itself: storytelling leads to the excitement of trembling that is living; living is linked to loving, which links back to storytelling. This happy encirclement evokes a transformative becoming and a blurring of boundaries between people: "some one was then the other one" (103). As with many of Stein's subsequent portraits, the pronoun "one" has a flexible anonymity that allows for multiple identifications. Indeed, in "Ada," subjectivity becomes manifest through literary reciprocity. All Stein's work warrants reading out loud, but I make sure the students vocalize the later half of "Ada" so they can better hear how the gerunds ring in repetition so that telling, loving, and listening echo and become interchangeable:

> She was telling some one, who was loving every story that was charming. Some one who was living was almost always listening. Some one who was loving was almost always listening. That one who was loving was almost always listening. That one was loving was telling about being one then listening. (102–03)

What enables this relation between talking and listening is the act of writing, which Stein's work represents as dialogic. In this sense, "Ada" is not a depiction of one individual but instead a moving portrayal of the intersubjective relationship between Stein and Toklas, which became an inspirational and supportive foundation for Stein's literary innovations.

To highlight the feminist dimensions of Stein's portrayal of intersubjectivity, I introduce students to Ulla Dydo's argument that "Ada" is intimately connected to the multiple forms of support Toklas gave to Stein's work, all of which were crucial for its flourishing. As Dydo argues, "Endless telling and listening to stories is the perfect writer's situation and the perfect lovers' situation, each enabling the other. 'Ada' is in a sense about audience—finding a you who listens to me" (Introduction 101). It makes sense, then, that Stein's definition of genius is "one who is at the same time talking and listening" ("Portraits" 170). Before introducing her definition, I ask students how they define the word. That their ideas usually point to individual gifts and distinctions helps show that Stein's definition of genius—talking and listening simultaneously—is premised on an engagement with others and does not transcend history but is embedded in it. Cyrena N. Pondrom has argued that " 'talking and listening at the same time' " is "a metaphor for the ability to register the full dimensions of one's era" (xxiii). Since "Ada" tells the story of a woman detaching herself from the patriarchal family and stresses the presence of another woman for inspiring and sustaining Stein's writing, turning to Cott's argument about the transformation of the women's movement at the onset of the twentieth century allows me to argue that one of those dimensions of the era is feminism.

I reiterate that Stein is engaging not with a feminism of clear political goals but with the feminism of avant-garde self-assertion, a phrase that needs to be thoughtfully explored and defined. Since the phrase is part of Cott's charting of feminism's Euro-American history, "self-assertion" is obvious—students are likely to link it to the strength associated with political agency and cultural visibility. To explain the aesthetic challenge that "avant-garde" names, I show Picasso's 1905–06 portrait of Stein, and we discuss how the self as a form that can become fixed through habitual perceptions can also be experimented with, reshaped, and rewritten by drawing on the creative imagination. This is precisely what women in the early decades of the twentieth century were doing with the material of their lives: asserting their right to imaginatively experiment with the habitual forms through which woman had been perceived. Stein's "Ada" and its enactment of "talking and listening simultaneously" show that collaborations among women were crucial to these avant-garde self-assertions.

But how would a character like Ada, whose story is defined more by convention than by resistance, align herself with avant-garde self-assertion? Put another way, if feminism is not only a form of "political action and argumentation," how does it reach people and encourage them to reshape their lives? Stein's work and the avant-garde self-assertion it advances demand a different understanding of feminism, a feminism that is not necessarily an identity or a political stance, that is more inside history than outside it. In "Portraits and Repetition," which I often include in this unit, Stein offers a theory of cultural influence that moves toward this expanded definition of feminism. Part of her *Lectures in America* (1935), this essay reflects on her work's relation to cinema. She claims that in writing her epic *The Making of Americans* (1903–11) and in composing her early portraits, she was "doing what the cinema was doing," in that she was "making a continuous succession of the statement of what that person was" (176). What is most interesting about the cinematic forms manifesting in her work is that she did not know that her writing was tapping into and indirectly revealing the signature features of cinema. She explains:

> I of course did not think of it in terms of the cinema, in fact I doubt whether at that time I had ever seen a cinema, but and I cannot repeat this too often any one is of one's period and this our period was undoubtedly the period of the cinema and series production. And each of us in our own way are bound to express what the world in which we are living is doing. (177)

In other words, without conscious awareness, one is enmeshed in and influenced by aesthetic and cultural practices that characterize the time period in which one lives. This insight applies to the relation between Stein's work and feminism and can be used to suggest to students that one may be influenced by and even engage with feminism without consciously identifying with its politics. As a frame for interpreting and historicizing texts such as "Ada," Stein's argument in "Portraits and Repetition" encourages students to move away from an insistence on positivistic definitions of *feminism* and toward seeing feminism's subtle influences and imaginative reverberations.

Turning to the kaleidoscopic *Tender Buttons* is a great way to underscore feminism's less discernible appearances. Stein's title evokes the tender care involved in sewing and dressing; it also links to small, cute, sentimental objects. Drawing out the poetic dimensions of this care and the implicitly feminized aesthetic categories with which they are associated, *Tender Buttons* brings avant-garde self-assertion to the objects and practices associated with the domestic sphere, thereby making the reproductive and affective labor performed there a composite imaginative enterprise.

Domestic labor is expressed through the dense texture of words, which represent a surplus of domestic objects. In the first section of *Tender Buttons,* "Objects," Stein renders a richly crowded bourgeois interior that includes a piano, a new cup and saucer, a drawing, clothes (a long dress, a red hat, a blue coat), as well as books, chairs, and umbrellas. Next, her portraits of foodstuffs—roastbeef, mutton, sugar, milk, cranberries, along with rhubarb, cake, and custard—together evoke a busy kitchen in which the making involved in cooking is always taking place. She names these foods, but in reading the passages that follow from the titles, it is clear that she is defamiliarizing them. She writes from the noun that represents the object as though it is a point from which to imaginatively jump, and the connection between the object and the description can seem completely arbitrary to students (and therefore pointless). Linking to the experimentation of avant-garde self-assertion, I argue that Stein writes from inside a process in which objects are perceived, used, and arranged, then ask students to speculate why she chose to write this way. Here it is helpful to remind students of Ada's resistance to the expectation that she will care for her family in perpetuity. Recalling Ada's rejection of the "family claim" opens the possibility that Stein's choice to portray domestic spaces and the objects in them with such imaginative richness is actually a subtle feminist argument that allows things as well as selves to become reshaped and rewritten.

In *Tender Buttons,* Stein reshapes things by making them part of processes and transformations associated with the domestic sphere. In "Plate," she depicts the buying and washing of a plate and then the celebration associated with the presentation of food: "An occasion for a plate, an occasional resource is in buying and how soon does washing enable a selection of the same thing neater. If the party is small a clever song is in order" (17). In "Apple," she creates an associative list that moves far away from an apple but then comes back to it when someone asks (in a tenderly playful and polite way) for what might be a piece of apple pie: "Apple plum, carpet steak, seed clam, colored wine, calm seen, cold cream, best shake, potatoe, potatoe and no no gold work with pet, a green seed is called bake and change sweet is bready, a little piece a little piece please" (48). Letting the passage spill into the poetry of a polite request represents the reciprocal dimensions of everyday life. And since there is only a hint of baking amid a list of things that seem randomly aligned, baking becomes one part of an imaginative practice that dissolves expectations of sense and coherence.

Just as Ada cannot be limited to the patriarchal family's definition of daughters, the prose poems of *Tender Buttons* cannot be pinned down to one meaning. As Rachel Blau DuPlessis writes, Stein's descriptions are "[b]right with tasty and spectacular signifiers that almost signal something but don't quite" ("Woolfenstein" 38). Though Stein resists composing a clear signal, one can present students with the possibility of seeing these passages as evoking the imaginative dimensions—the poetics—of making and sustaining a comfortable home dense with pleasures. I encourage them to see *Tender Buttons* as woven with traces of the subjective investments and care that domesticity entails, which works against the assumption (one that many students hold) that the domestic is a realm that feminists should transcend. In the last sentence of *Tender Buttons*' last section, "Rooms," Stein emphasizes care as a vehicle for equality and recognition, but she also links it to imaginative splendor, thereby bestowing affective and reproductive labor with the aesthetic value and importance associated with the avant-garde: "The care with which there is incredible justice and likeness, all this makes a magnificent asparagus and also a fountain" (76).

Tender Buttons provokes a desire to decipher—to make the text have a clear and discernible meaning—that it does not satisfy. Students will no doubt find this frustrating. I have responded to their frustration by posing the following questions: What if making sense is not Stein's point? What if *Tender Buttons* asks us to read, think, and see without a clearly defined picture emerging from that process? When framed by Stein's complicated relation to feminism, engaging with the difficulties of her literary experimentation can be immensely productive for eroding the almost unquestioned impulse to define *feminism* in recognizable and certain terms. Students who identify with feminism deserve this difficulty.

Teaching a Compositional Approach to Gertrude Stein's Portraiture

Linda Voris

> I began to think about portraits of any one.
> If they are themselves inside them what are they and what has it to do with what they do.
> And does it make any difference what they do or how they do it, does it make any difference what they say or how they say it. (Stein, "Portraits" 171)

Gertrude Stein's verbal portraits are appealing to teach because they are short texts, often lively and melodic, and many portray well-known subjects. However, the portraits present particular challenges for teaching, not the least of which is their varied styles. Stein wrote portraits over the course of her career, and she developed distinctive styles in each period, from the portraits in 1909–10 of Pablo Picasso, Henri Matisse, and Alice Toklas, to the breakthrough in 1912 of *Tender Buttons*, to the many portraits of the 1920s, which included second portraits of a few of her initial subjects, written in a style marked by heightened musicality and fewer references to their subjects, to a late period (ending around 1933) characterized by an even more hermetic, nonreferential style.[1] Much as cubist portraits display their nonresemblance to the subject, Stein's portraits confound most readers' expectations of representation, because they generally do not summarize and describe characteristic aspects of a subject's personality, behavior, occupation, or interests. Seeking a likeness or biographical material, we risk reading past the remarkable styles of her portraits. For Stein, this writing involved the question of how language use conditions our concepts of knowledge and identity, and I have found that most students can be engaged by the stakes of her project even if initially the reading is daunting.

I begin by asking students to imagine writing a portrait of a close friend and to consider whether the friend's occupation, interests, or habits are adequately particularizing and evocative of their experience of him or her. Descriptions such as "kind," "generous," or "intelligent" reveal at least two limitations that result from the iterability of words: language simplifies and reduces the experience of a particular person when the same adjective may be used to describe different subjects; the iteration of words fixes characteristics that may vary considerably over time, depending on circumstances, perspectives, or context.

We may expect that a verbal portrait will present a likeness and therefore will rely on the activity of looking, but in her earliest portraits Stein identified "the trouble with including looking" ("Portraits" 188). Looking, she reasoned, meant looking for resemblance, which entailed comparison of the person with other people or with the same person at other times, thereby introducing memory. An attribute is deemed characteristic because it repeats over time, but Stein theorized that experience and knowledge transpire with a quality of immediacy that does not involve repetition. As she explained, "there is no repetition in hearing and saying the things he hears and says when he is hearing and saying them" (178). Even when we engage in repeated actions, Stein contended that "each time the emphasis is different just as the cinema has each time a slightly different thing to make it all be moving" (179). She makes the philosophical claim that memory introduces repetition but that in the present moment the experience of living is not an experience of repetition. In her portraiture, she sought a strategy to convey the "intensity of anybody's existence" as it unfolds with contingency in the present (182).

Depending on time constraints, an instructor may discuss portraits of the same period, such as "Picasso" and "Matisse" (both 1909 or 1910), or compare portraits of a subject written in significantly different styles, such as "Picasso" and "If I Told Him A Completed Portrait of Picasso" (1923). I ask students to identify what they find baffling about Stein's portraiture so that we can use their resistance to begin discussion. Formal properties that seem a barrier when we try to read for conventional portraiture are expressive, and what they express are the problems of representation that Stein addresses.

I remind my students that while we cannot forget what we know about the eventual success of Matisse and Picasso, they were disruptive outsiders, not established artists, when Stein wrote her portraits. Perhaps she later exaggerated the outraged response to Matisse's *Woman with a Hat* (1905) by viewers who, she wrote, "tried to scratch off the paint," but this painting, like those of the other artists dubbed fauves ("wild beasts"), posed a radical challenge (*Autobiography* 34). Indeed, Stein and her brother Leo returned to look at *Woman with a Hat* again and again for five weeks before deciding on the purchase (Rabinow 32).[2] With this purchase, they signaled the boldness of their enterprise: to the French modern masters in their collection they added some of the most controversial paintings of the day, including Matisse's *Le bonheur de vivre* (1905–06; *The Joy of Life*) and *Blue Nude: Memory of Biskra* (1907), as well as Picasso's *Portrait of Gertrude Stein* (1906) and *Three Women* (1907–08). To convey the scope of the collection, I show images of the Stein studio at 27 rue de Fleurus in 1906, its walls covered with paintings by Paul Cézanne, Paul Gauguin, Pierre-Auguste Renoir, Henri de Toulouse-Lautrec, Matisse, and Picasso, among others.[3] The influence of their collection and Saturday evening salon before World War I has been widely acknowledged; certainly it heightened the influence of Cézanne, Matisse, and Picasso on contemporary artists (Rabinow 21, 28).[4]

Picasso, a frequent visitor of the Stein salon, must have seen the daring experiments in portraiture on display there, including Matisse's *Woman with a Hat* and Cézanne's *Madame Cézanne with a Fan* (1878–88). Art historians have speculated about how those experiments prompted Picasso to find a new approach, and some consider his *Gertrude Stein* a response: the painting does not offer a straightforward likeness of Stein, and this method of nonresemblance in portraiture signaled a major breakthrough for Picasso. Critics have noted various influences for the highly stylized and masklike face that Picasso painted when he returned to finish the portrait after a visit to Spain (Richardson 433–61; Antliff and Leighten 34–39). For Stein, whose portrait was painted often and by many artists, Picasso's remained the most representative: "[H]e painted in the head without having seen me again . . . and I was and I still am satisfied with my portrait, for me, it is I, and it is the only reproduction of me which is always I, for me" (*Picasso* 8). Both calm and intensely charged at once, the portrait vividly conveys Stein's presence. When she sat for her portrait, Stein was already engaged in *Three Lives*, an experiment with the nature of character and its portrayal, and surely her lively discussions with Picasso and his portrait of her must have contributed to her exploration of what would constitute modern portraiture in a verbal medium.

Comparing Portraits of the Same Period

When I read the opening passage of Stein's "Picasso," students typically protest that the style is repetitious and pointless:

> One whom some were certainly following was one who was completely charming. One whom some were certainly following was one who was charming. One whom some were following was one who was completely charming. One whom some were following was one who was certainly completely charming. ("Picasso" 142)

However, close reading teases out differences. I limit discussion to this passage, moving on only after students become adept at identifying the differences and debating their significance. In a method of repetition with variation, the meaning of recurrent terms such as "certainly" and "completely" changes depending on syntax. Does dropping the adjective "completely" in the second sentence render it a more or less positive statement of Picasso's charm? Does "completely charming" sound hyperbolic by comparison? The word "certainly" sounds various tones and conveys more than one meaning. Direct statement expresses certainty, but reiteration sounds more like a bid for reassurance and therefore conveys less certainty. Does dropping "certainly" in the third sentence press us to reconsider whether it is certain that "they" are following Picasso? They are less certain, or as readers we are less certain of their following, or both? What is the effect of bringing both adjectives together to bear at the end of the passage, "certainly completely charming"? Is it a ringing endorsement, or does the aggregation undercut the certainty of his charm?

Reading further, students observe that the meaning of words and phrases depends on their context and on their relation to other words and phrases. What seemed at first a cumbersome style proves remarkably subtle in conveying the dynamic and fluctuating assessments of Picasso's work, charm, following, and the reasons "some" have for following him. In place of fixing character, Stein conveys a complex, perspectival portrait that shifts from Picasso's perspective to that of "some who were following," suggesting that the assessment of his charm or of his "always working" is contingent and multiple. I ask students to describe the time sense that results when Stein combines different tenses of a verb ("This one was one who was working" and "This one always had been working" [142]) with gerunds conveying continuous states. Although these statements imply acquaintance with Picasso over time, no chronological narrative emerges, and no single statement concerning past action proves decisive. Instead, the method suspends and elaborates a compositional present by aggregating multiple time senses, combining past action, habitual action, present statement, and contradictory statements in what Stein would call the "continuous present" or the "prolonged present" (Dydo, *Stein Reader* 498). With this odd time sense Stein fulfills her ambition to convey "the intensity of anyone's existence," an impression that does not depend on memory but instead is consistent with the experience of the unfolding present ("Portraits" 182).

Students are now prepared to compare portraits written in the same style. If the repetition of the word "charming" in "Picasso" conveys lightness and ease, in the opening passages of "Matisse" we learn of the doubts that the artist suffered. Matisse comes to entertain certainty about his painting when he realizes that he cannot gainsay it, but this certainty is immediately complicated by the perspectives of others. In "Matisse," Stein tests knowledge claims without foreclosing possibilities, including the perspectives of "some," "anyone," and "everyone" as they debate Matisse's greatness and greatness in modern painting overall.

While we can detect in Stein's portrait some attributes commonly associated with Matisse—his doubt and personal suffering—its representation is not a summary likeness, but a complex and dynamic context in which his wish to be certain persists. Those who would follow Matisse's lead are uncertain whether he is "clearly expressing something" or "greatly expressing something being struggling" and which is the best tactic ("Matisse" 139). The portrait reveals that both certainty and greatness are constructions, that at some point the voices of "some" will be muted as "every one" comes to agree on greatness, forgetting that once it was a matter of perspective. Students often realize that "clearly expressing something" and "greatly expressing something being struggling" apply to Stein's portrait of Matisse. What should we make of this self-reflexive aspect of the text?

As literary critics have done, some students will describe Stein's method as cubist. For the visual analogy to prove useful, I discuss critical developments in representing both the human figure and landscape.[5] Using slides, I present Picasso, Braque, and Cézanne's innovations in open form and projective space in order to discuss whether these can be usefully compared to what Stein does. Open form is a reconfiguration of the relation of figure and ground that entails breaking open the closed figure to its surrounding space; in projective spaces, objects or figures seem to press or tumble forward toward the viewer. We consider how Picasso's *Three Women* uses a rhythmic repetition and simplification of the female body in a shallow space to create a new compositional unity that integrates the body with its surrounding space. We note the reiteration of the same graphic mark, "a curve, whose significance constantly changes, so that it represents an arm in one place, a thigh in a second, and a breast in a third" (Karmel 34). In its elaborate faceting, monochrome color, and "homogenous fields of geometric forms," Picasso's *Seated Female Nude* (1909–10) takes open form further still (71). Is the repetition with variation in Stein's portraiture a literary equivalent? Does Stein's method similarly thwart our ability to distinguish figure from ground?

In *Violin and Pitcher* (1910), Braque uses the same geometric faceting for objects as for the space around them, thereby fusing the two into a surface of simultaneously advancing and receding planes. This dynamic quality, the tension between surface and depth, or of space that seems to protrude rather than recede, reflects the influence of Cézanne's color modulation in a late landscape such as *Mont Sainte-Victoire* (1902–04, Philadelphia Museum of Art). In this painting, Cézanne exploits the relative impression of colors: warm colors seem to advance and cool colors seem to recede. His use of color puts three-dimensional effects into tension with the two-dimensionality of the uniform, discrete brushstrokes, and this technique imparts qualities of volume and movement that do not depend on conventional figuration (Shiff 111–23). Students recognize that meaning emerges and changes in Stein's earliest portraits similarly through dynamic relations and that her portraits thereby impart palpable expressive properties that resist paraphrase. The visual analogy is useful, not because it identifies influence but because it gives students compositional terms to describe the constitution of meaning through presentational force rather than mimetic representation.

After our class discussion I assign an imitation exercise to give students insight into Stein's method by learning firsthand how to modify a set of terms to convey complexity and contingency. I assign strict constraints: they must choose two adjectives to associate with the subject and add one assertion that can be either positive or negative. This is the first time that most students have tried to mine the resources of language, and they are often surprised, as one student reported, to discover "what the writing says."

Comparing Portraits of the Same Subject

When students compare Stein's first portrait of Picasso with her second, "If I Told Him A Completed Portrait of Picasso," written at the end of the summer of 1923 during or after a visit with Picasso and his family in Antibes on the French Riviera, they find that her portraiture method has changed dramatically. Stein experimented with what she called "landscape plays" during her stay in the south of France in 1922–23, and she carried over the spatial homology to physical landscape and landscape painting when she resumed writing portraits, including her second portraits of Picasso, Toklas, and Carl Van Vechten (Voris, "'Shutters'").[6] In contrast to the gerund-heavy first portraits, the second portraits are lighter and musical. (I recommend playing for students the recording of Stein's reading "If I Told Him," available online at *PennSound*.) The new style of portraiture reflects her effort to create the impression of spatial dimension and to impart qualities of immanence or movement that result not from representation but from compositional totality, when the particularity of elements is subsumed to an overall impression. Although these portraits contain some biographical details, they are splintered into fragments and punning associations. Nouns, combining with a dense iteration of coordinating conjunctions, articles, and prepositions, are swept up into a homogeneous surface and the strong rhythms of the portrait.

As an exercise in formal analysis, I help students identify elements in "If I Told Him" that seem referential, then ask them to analyze how these tokens are embedded in the text. An example is the allusion to Henry Wadsworth Longfellow's poem "Paul Revere's Ride" in the closing lines of the portrait: "One. / I land. / Two. / I land. / Three. / The land" (466). Stein's allusion to the warning signal "One if by land, and two if by sea" appears to be a broken signal, since "land" is repeated in place of "sea," until we hear the homonym for *island* in "I land." Add this to lines naming Napoleon, and surely we are reminded of Napoleon's exile to the island of Elba. On his fateful return to the mainland, Napoleon landed near Antibes, where Stein and Toklas visited the Picassos. The famous palindrome "Able was I ere I saw Elba" also comes to mind when we realize that "able" is very nearly spelled in the name Pablo. From Stein's monograph *Picasso* (1938) we learn that his "mother's family were silversmiths" (2), and we may speculate that this detail prompted the allusion to Paul Revere, who was an accomplished silversmith. Then in the name Paul Revere are Paul Picasso (as Picasso signed his early work) and Pablo's young son, Paulo; revere and revolution (Revere, Picasso, and Stein are all revolutionary figures); the Riviera; and perhaps even Pierre Reverdy, the poet and early enthusiast of cubism. Finally, the name Picasso generates the lines "As even say so" and "As a so" (466). Variations on this phrasing in the text structure a series of assertions that sound a range of affective tones without developing narrative or conveying likeness. Proper names and nouns that ordinarily establish signposts in a representational portrait instead become elements in an analysis of signs.

When we grasp both referential and denotative cues lightly, without expecting illusionism, much as we do when viewing a cubist painting, we can analyze Stein's critique of the practice of "exact resemblance" and her alternative.[7] Representation that strives for resemblance will never be exact, because it depends on comparison, as Stein reminds us: "the exact resemblance as exact as a resemblance, exactly as resembling" ("If" 464). In place of a likeness that is based on comparison, Stein blocks denotation and "exacts" differences—that is, repetition itself can exact difference. "If I Told Him" offers an intricate survey of the expressive range conveyed by words that imply connection, relation, and modality.

What kind of reading strategies do the different portrait styles demand, and what do these strategies reveal? In "Picasso" and "Matisse," Stein omitted or blunted references in a process of repetition and variation, but "If I Told Him" is chiefly composed by splintering references into a dense and complex grid. Students often conclude that the method for the early portraits suggests an epistemology that involves a knower and a known object or envisions a container or space in which knowing transpires, including the time sense of the prolonged present. The second portraits break with this fundamental premise and explore knowing as a dynamic event expressed through the articulation of multiple series in composition. Through this latter method, Stein proposes that making sense is making connections and yet further connections instead of forming comparisons or arriving at conclusions.

NOTES

[1] The dates given for the portraits are of composition, not publication. See Ulla Dydo for the dating of the early portraits (*Gertrude Stein* 30). Stein classified the periods of her portrait writing in "Portraits and Repetition" (200).

[2] After their purchase of Matisse's *Woman with a Hat*, Stein and Leo became acquainted with the painter, and they introduced Matisse to Picasso in the spring of 1906 (Baldassari et al. 41).

[3] Photographs identifying the paintings in the collection are available in *The Steins Collect* (Bishop et al. 360–76).

[4] According to Emily Braun, "It is no exaggeration to state that the Steins did more to support avant-garde painting than any other collectors or institutions anywhere in the first decade of the twentieth century" (49).

[5] To get a sense of the cubism on view when Stein wrote her Picasso portrait, see his *The Reservoir, Horta de Ebro* (1909) and *Head of A Woman* (1909), both of which the Steins purchased in 1909. I recommend T. J. Clark's discussion of the play of convexity against concavity involved in the innovation of reversible cubes (201–03). For examples of the cubist analogy and alternative visual analogies in Stein criticism, see Altieri 241–47; Perloff, "Poetry" and "Cessation"; and Steiner 143–49.

[6] Stein's second portrait of Toklas is "A Book Concluding with As a Wife Has a Cow A Love Story" (1923) and that of Van Vechten is "Van or Twenty Years After A Second Portrait of Carl Van Vechten" (1923). Dydo has grouped the three second portraits together in *A Stein Reader* with a useful headnote (451–66).

[7] A cubist analogy again proves useful in explaining how Stein's method emphasizes the difference between reference and meaning. Elements in her portrait, much like signs in a cubist painting, develop meanings that depend not on reference but on their placement in relation to other elements and to the composition as a whole. According to Neil Cox, cubist paintings make a practice of "*not* resembling" and reveal that resemblance in painting assumes a set of arbitrary conventions: "Braque and Picasso are relentless in their pursuit of inventing a basic set of Cubist signs and in overlaying them with signs drawn from other pre-established codes, proving repeatedly that neither words nor pictures have their meanings guaranteed by reference to 'real' things" (244).

"A Violent Kind of Delightfulness": Enjoying *Tender Buttons*

Roger Gilbert

Radically experimental and notoriously difficult, *Tender Buttons* might seem to find its natural home in the graduate seminar room, suitably garlanded with an array of critical and theoretical discourses. But for many years I have been including it in my introductory survey of modern poetry, a course aimed at freshmen and sophomores. I did so at first with some trepidation, assigning only a few excerpts from the "Objects" section as an extreme version of the thing-oriented poetics of early modernism. Once I took the plunge and began teaching the whole book, however, it quickly became an indispensable part of my syllabus. In fact I have come to realize that the aesthetic and interpretive challenges posed by *Tender Buttons* are in many ways less daunting to undergraduates than those of more canonical figures like Ezra Pound and T. S. Eliot, whose work flaunts the author's superior intelligence and erudition. The key point I try to impress on my students from the start is simply this: *Tender Buttons* is fun. The rewards of teaching it for me have everything to do with making the fun of the text, the diverse panoply of exhilarating pleasures it offers, fully available to students whose first response might be bewilderment.

I design my course to be as eclectic and inclusive as possible and do my best to give traditional and avant-garde strains of modern poetry equal play. We begin with William Butler Yeats and Robert Frost as exemplary practitioners of metrical verse, before turning to more formally innovative modernist poets. In the historical narrative I construct, *Tender Buttons* plays a crucial role, marking an early (and in many ways still unsurpassed) extreme of the experimental impulse. While I avoid polemical framings that would position Stein as a more adventurous and original poet than, say, Frost or Wallace Stevens, I try to offer students a detailed account of the specific character of her innovations. At the same time, I want them to see that for all its exuberant disruption of conventional form and meaning, *Tender Buttons* is a deeply satisfying book that offers some surprisingly traditional pleasures—including that most traditional of all pleasures, a happy ending. To make this point, I often begin by comparing the book with another seminal volume of modern poetry published in the same year, Frost's *North of Boston*. Frost's is formally the more conservative work by far, yet its portrayal of human relations, especially in the realms of marriage and domesticity, is unrelentingly bleak. Poems like "Home Burial" and "A Servant to Servants" reject the sentimental idealizations inherited from the nineteenth century, instead depicting marriage as a joyless struggle between incompatible species. For all its flouting of convention and continuity, *Tender Buttons* belongs to one of the most ancient poetic genres, the epithalamion or marriage song. That the marriage is between two women and therefore stands outside the social norms of its time allows the work to give off a transgressive energy while unabashedly celebrating the joys of domestic love and sexual fulfillment. One might go so far as to see the book's three divisions, "Objects," "Food," and "Rooms," as corresponding to the traditional accoutrements of a wedding: gifts, feast, and honeymoon.

I am presuming that some basic biographical information is a necessary context for reading and enjoying *Tender Buttons*, but that supposition is open to debate. One could certainly ask students to read the book without offering them any background on Stein's sexuality, her relationship with Alice Toklas, her apartment on the rue de Fleurus, and so on. But although we spend much of our time focusing on purely intrinsic features—verbal patterns, structural elements, et cetera—I am convinced that some extrinsic knowledge can greatly enhance readers' understanding and appreciation of the text. (The same can be said of other major modernist works, especially those that deal in queer sexuality. Knowing something of Eliot's relationship with Jean Verdenal or Hart Crane's with Emil Opffer adds layers of resonance to *The Waste Land* and "Voyages" that are impossible to dismiss.) In *Tender Buttons*, it is easy enough to provide students with the "story" behind the work. Pamela White Hadas's "Spreading the Difference: One Way to Read Gertrude Stein's *Tender Buttons*" gives the necessary background; I summarize its central argument and make this accessible essay available to students along with other biographical resources.[1] As Hadas points out, the story of the Stein-Toklas marriage is also the story of a divorce, the rupture between Stein and her brother Leo. All good marriage plots require a blocking agent or antagonist, and Leo ably fills that role: in his dismissal of Stein's literary experiments and his penchant for lecturing and classifying, he embodies the predilection for reason and order that his sister is intent on resisting.

Thus far I have been outlining a broadly narrative approach to *Tender Buttons* that highlights both celebration and struggle. But because those celebratory and agonistic energies manifest themselves at every level of Stein's language, in teaching the book it's equally important to dwell on its formal and stylistic particulars and to work through selected passages in detail. The most obvious place to begin is with the title, an instance of the kind of incongruous verbal juxtapositions found throughout the work. While it's worth reflecting on the title phrase in isolation, it can also be productive to link the phrase with the book's tripartite division, which furnishes another essential point of entry. Buttons belong to the realm of "Objects," tenderness to the realm of "Food"; when conjoined, they evoke the bodily eroticism most fully expressed in "Rooms."

I also draw attention to the formal anomalies that distinguish each section of the book from the other two. The titled subdivisions in "Objects" and "Food" give way to unsegmented prose in "Rooms," but "Food" is prefaced by a list (or menu) of its individual components, while "Objects" is not. These discrepancies prevent the book from assuming the stability of a triptych; instead each section establishes its own distinct shape and rhythm. Yet despite their structural differences, the three sections do form a larger trajectory, one that I would argue is fundamentally temporal and continuous rather than spatial and disjunctive. Could the pieces of the book be rearranged, either within a section or among the sections? My own view is that doing so would destroy the book's dramatic integrity, but the question is worth putting to students without prejudgment. While archival evidence indicates that Stein composed "Rooms" before the others and may even have contemplated placing it first in the published work, her adherence in subsequent printings to the order established in the first edition suggests that she regarded it as aesthetically preferable to the order in which the sections were written.[2]

Once we turn our attention to the short, titled pieces in "Objects" and "Food," issues of representation inevitably arise. The temptation to interpret individual segments as oblique renderings of their titular subjects is hard for students to resist. Stein herself encouraged such an understanding in her 1935 lecture "Poetry and Grammar" and in a 1946 interview with Robert Haas ("Transatlantic Interview"), excerpts from both of which should be given to students along with the usual caveat that the author's comments ought not to be taken as gospel. Stein's reflection in "Poetry and Grammar" on her effort to find "a way of naming things that would not invent names, but mean names without naming them" (236) deserves serious consideration despite the fact that the essay was composed more than twenty years after the book:

> And so in Tender Buttons and then on and on I struggled with the ridding myself of nouns, I knew nouns must go in poetry as they had gone in prose if anything that is everything was to go on meaning something.
>
> And so I went on with this exceeding struggle of knowing really knowing what a thing was really knowing it knowing anything I was seeing anything I was feeling so that its name could be something, by its name coming to be a thing in itself as it was but would not be anything just and only as a name. . . .
>
> I had to feel anything and everything that for me was existing so intensely that I could put it down in writing as a thing in itself without at all necessarily using its name. The name of a thing might be something in itself if it could come to be real enough but just as a name it was not enough something. (242–43)

One can easily indicate the gap between this theoretical retrospect and the actual texture of the book by pointing out that *Tender Buttons* is in fact full of nouns. Nevertheless the principle of capturing or evoking things (including, as Stein insists, emotions) without naming them directly can provide a crucial first perspective on the work's aesthetic procedures. Analogies with cubism and other painterly techniques are worth exploring, though their limits should also be stressed. More productive, especially in a general course on modern poetry, are comparisons with parallel strains of unnaming in poets like Walt Whitman, whom Stein credits with breaking the "rigid form of the noun" ("Poetry" 237); Emily Dickinson ("Tell all the truth but tell it slant" [poem 1263]); H.D. ("my patron said, 'name it'; // I said, I can not name it, / there is no name" [Doolittle 555]); and especially Stevens ("Throw away the lights, the definitions, / And say of what you see in the dark // That it is this or that it is that, / But do not use the rotted names" [*Collected Poetry* 150]). Elliptical, riddling, and catachrestic modes of indirect evocation constitute a central strain in modern poetry, of which *Tender Buttons* may be the purest specimen.

Certainly there are segments in "Objects" and "Food" that seem to obey a representational logic, seeking to evoke phenomena without relying on conventional descriptors. It is not hard, for example, to discern a relation between the subject of "Asparagus" and the two sentences that make up the text: "Asparagus in a lean in a lean to hot. This makes it art and it is wet wet weather wet weather wet" (52). (It helps to know that asparagus was traditionally steamed upright, leaning against the side of a narrow pot; such tidbits of culinary history may give students fuller access to "Food.") Some segments approach the status of poetic riddles, describing an object obliquely while challenging the reader to discover the circuitous links between text and title. Thus "A Handkerchief" is "A winning of all the blessings, a sample not a sample because there is no worry" (25). We can infer that the handkerchief wins or receives the product of sneezes, which prompt "blessings," and that it resembles a "sample" or swatch of fabric but is not one, thus removing any epistemological "worry" over the correspondence between part and whole. Such playful decodings offer one major source of fun in the book, and I encourage students to perform these kinds of interpretive maneuvers in their reading responses and essays, so long as they recognize that no solution is likely to be definitive.

The point that needs special emphasis for first-time readers of *Tender Buttons* is that Stein deploys language in many ways and for many effects. Verbal cubism is merely one of the book's modes, and attempting to read every piece as an eccentric word-painting will quickly lead to frustration. Donald Sutherland famously described the book as a kind of "Luna Park" or Coney Island, implying that it offers a wide variety of rides and diversions.[3] The Wittgensteinian notion of games as an essentially heterogeneous category may be a more apposite trope; the kind of language game being played in *Tender Buttons* is constantly changing, and the greatest challenge readers face is simply to keep up with those changes, adjusting their expectations and responses in accord with the text's shifting dynamics. Students do not need the references to Sutherland or Wittgenstein to appreciate the profoundly playful character of the book. In her ludic improvisations Stein activates every aspect of her verbal medium, from the graphic (in "Eye Glasses" she incorporates the unlikely word "saloon" because its double *o* serves as an embedded picture of the object [22]) to the acoustic (a section called "A Sound" is simply that [28]). Forms of semantic play range from puns—many of them interlingual (e.g., the much-noted "little sales ladies" [27], in which the French meaning of "sales" as "dirty" hovers)—to portmanteaus, anagrams, and malapropisms. Syntax can by turns be periodic, hypotactic, wildly run-on, or virtually nonexistent. Stein's manipulations of rhythm include passages in Blakean trochees ("all the joy in weak success, all the joyful tenderness, all the section and the tea, all the stouter symmetry" [37]), and a variety of repetitive effects from stately anaphora (a series of clauses in "Roastbeef" start with the word "considering" [36]) to frenetic stuttering ("A no, a no since, a no since when, a no since when since, a no since when since a no since when since" [59]). Language for Stein is an infinitely plastic substance to be plied and played with in every way imaginable, and spending time in class cataloging these modes of play is an excellent way to help students appreciate the work's technical virtuosity. Here I should note that I always devote at least two class sessions to the book (sometimes three or four), usually lecturing at first and then moving toward open discussion.

Yet while there are many passages in which the play of the signifier takes over, meaning is never far from the surface of the text, coalescing at times with startling clarity, only to withdraw from view a moment later. Students need to be reassured that this oscillation between lucidity and opacity is itself part of the book's radically variable nature and does not reflect their own shortcomings as readers. Despite its atomized form and its attention to concreteness, *Tender Buttons* is in fact a thoroughly thematic work. For the most part, however, themes are not articulated through direct statement but are instead encoded in patterns of verbal recurrence. Reading the book, one gradually notices a core vocabulary of key terms that keep getting obsessively recombined. Many of these terms possess strong moral or emotional valences: for example, "change," "difference," "dirt," "exchange," "pleasure," "substance," and "surprise" all seem to be positively inflected, while "authority," "centre," "costume," "cover," "custom," and "regularity" carry oppressive overtones. Choosing a handful of these words, tracing them through the text, and teasing out the thematic links that connect them can be a highly productive classroom exercise, one that lends itself especially well to small group work. While many occurrences of these theme words share in the book's general resistance to interpretation and paraphrase, they also appear in nodal passages of nearly aphoristic clarity: "The difference is spreading" (11); "Act so that there is no use in a centre" (63). Dismissing the possibility of thematic interpretation, as some critics do, seems to me a profound misreading of *Tender Buttons*, which at times exhibits a didactic force reminiscent of Ralph Waldo Emerson and Henry David Thoreau. Teaching the book as an instance of formal and stylistic innovation should not preclude consideration of its moral content, its profound commitment to an ethic founded on difference, desire, and freedom.

The book's interwoven thematic strands are closely related to its rich tonal dynamics. Tone is a difficult element to measure, but it plays an essential role. In the absence of explicit narrative or lyric signposts, affect is conveyed primarily through fluctuations in the grain and timbre of the speaker's voice. The book's mood is largely joyful, encompassing shades of amusement, affection, exhilaration, boastfulness, satisfaction, and pleasurable yearning ("Please be the beef" [39]). For all its celebratory impulses, however, *Tender Buttons* contains its share of darker tones, which often seem to be associated with masculinity. Thus in "A Cutlet" we learn that "A blind agitation is manly and uttermost" (23); a few pages later we are told that "A white hunter is nearly crazy" (29). These hints of violent male energy culminate in the last segment of "Objects," a nearly incoherent expostulation entitled "This Is This Dress, Aider," with a pun on "distress":

> Aider, why, aider why whow, whow stop touch, aider whow, aider stop the muncher, muncher munchers.
>
> A jack in kill her, a jack in, makes a meadowed king, makes a to let. (31)

Critics have discerned both sexual frenzy and homicidal rage in these sentences. Similar moments of incoherent stuttering occur near the end of "Food." Both sections move from measured, meditative openings to cacophonous conclusions.

Another tonal strain in the work deserves attention, because it represents a voice distinct from that of the primary speaker, encapsulating an oppressive normativity: in its pseudo-organization around domestic topics, *Tender Buttons* playfully evokes such Victorian manuals as *Mrs. Beeton's Book of Household Management* (1861).[4] The Martha Stewart of her day, Isabella Beeton epitomized social decorum and orthodoxy, issuing pronouncements like these:

> Cleanliness, punctuality, order, and method, are essentials in the character of a good housekeeper. . . . Order, again, is indispensable; for by it we wish to be understood that "there should be a place for everything, and everything in its place." Method, too, is most necessary; for when the work is properly contrived, and each part arranged in regular succession, it will be done more quickly and more effectually. (33)

We can hear Stein parodying this authoritarian voice in passages like "A Time to Eat" ("A pleasant simple habitual and tyrannical and authorised and educated and resumed and articulate separation. This is not tardy" [25]) or in remarks on entertaining like "If the party is small a clever song is in order" (17). By internalizing a voice that insists on propriety, containment, constraint, and other normative values, Stein allows her own anarchic and hedonistic impulses to push against their opposites. One way she does so is by celebrating the aesthetic possibilities of that bane of the good housekeeper, dirt, which to her heterodox eye intensifies rather than sullies what it touches: "Dirt and not copper makes a color darker" (14).

By the time we reach "Rooms," the oppressive Beetonian voice has been vanquished, and a new sense of ease and freedom takes over. Stein might easily have followed the template of the first two sections, creating titled subdivisions corresponding to various rooms. Instead she allows the book's final series of paragraphs to flow together unimpeded, in keeping with her insistence that "every room is open" (65). Reverting to the biographical narrative, we can surmise that the domestic space is no longer being shared with a disapproving male figure. Intimacy, love, and eros prevail, and closed doors and partitions are no longer needed. The expansive, fluid discourse and ebullient tone of "Rooms" have led some critics to dismiss it as a capitulation to the status quo; one editor omits it entirely from her selection of Stein's work.[5] For me "Rooms" is where the epithalamion achieves its fullest music, nowhere more gloriously than in the final paragraph:

> A light in the moon the only light is on Sunday. What was the sensible decision. The sensible decision was that notwithstanding many declarations and more music, not even notwithstanding the choice and a torch and a collection, notwithstanding the celebrating hat and a vacation and even more noise than cutting, notwithstanding Europe and Asia and being overbearing, not even notwithstanding an elephant and a strict occasion, not even withstanding more cultivation and some seasoning, not even with not drowning and with the ocean being encircling, not even with more likeness and any cloud, not even with terrific sacrifice of pedestrianism and a special resolution, not even more likely to be pleasing. The care with which the rain is wrong and the green is wrong and the white is wrong, the care with which there is a chair and plenty of breathing. The care with which there is incredible justice and likeness, all this makes a magnificent asparagus, and also a fountain. (76)

Nothing gives me more pleasure than to take students through a reading of this passage, which in its wonderfully contrary way celebrates a heterodox wedding of two women as the most sensible of decisions, one that could not be more pleasing were it accompanied by all the ritual trappings—formal vows ("a special resolution"), carriages ("terrific sacrifice of pedestrianism"), gifts, cake cutting, ceremonial animals, ocean voyages—lavished on more socially accepted unions.

One of the best ways to help students appreciate the book's heady mix of linguistic, thematic, and tonal ingredients is to invite them to imitate it. (Offering samples of poets' homages, like Harryette Mullen's wonderful *Trimmings* and *S*PeRM**K*T*, can prime the pump.) Here is an especially fine imitation, submitted to my class in 2006 by Willie Osterweil:

> WHAT IS THE CURRENT THAT MAKES MACHINERY, THAT MAKES IT CRACKLE
>
> *Tender Buttons* is about change and then if it is it is a strange thing. Themes there is much to say, noun and object and change all important, thusly. Nonsense is nonsense is sense is yes sense sense is sense. At first in we

> begin "all this and not ordinary, not unordered in not resembling." If misrepresentation is purposeful organized then where is the riddle. Determine the places she says. Find search maybe fruitless maybe fruitful maybe fruit is red and change is pin and cow is white. This is of an evolution we see in words from places. Vagaries, vagaries, curiouser and curiouser. Change is color we color that we change.
>
> A WOOLEN OBJECT GILDED
>
> Sometimes when the celebration is a gadfly, sometimes when the beauty is a handkerchief, but this can cause a whole thing to be a church. A church for things is *Tender Buttons*, this is a love. They nouns are they non-nouns. They are. A love out of a glove. A hope out of a pope. "There is no pope"; a whole thing is a church. It's common sense. Mundanity, insanity, calamity. The things are greater than the sum of parts, the parts are the sum, some parts are hard to chart, the heart was some part to start.
>
> THE TROUBLE IN BOTH EYES DOES NOT COME FROM THE SAME SYMMETRICAL CARPET, IT COMES FROM THERE BEING NO MORE DISTURBANCE THAN IN LITTLE PAPER.
>
> Small changes got it, colors got it, love got it, confusion not got not what got it. Things not simple not basic not used to difference, if spreading, change is coming watch out.

I cannot begin to note all the stylistic touches that Osterweil gets exactly right; I will simply point out that, like Stein herself, he artfully enfolds bits of commentary in his scintillating pastiche. Not all students will produce something this good, of course, but many can gain a keener sense of Stein's poetics from the exercise of imitation.

Near the beginning of *Tender Buttons* Stein poses a question that can be taken as a motto for the work as a whole: "What is the use of a violent kind of delightfulness if there is no pleasure in not getting tired of it" (12). The delights of *Tender Buttons* are indeed violent in their refusal of various modes of order and authority, but they are far from tiring or tiresome. As teachers we owe it to our students to help them discover the invigorating array of pleasures this book can offer, and to show them that difficulty and strangeness in no way preclude joy.

NOTES

[1] A more intimate sense of the Stein-Toklas household emerges from the collection *Baby Precious Always Shines: Selected Love Notes between Gertrude Stein and Alice B. Toklas*, edited by Kay Turner, which foregrounds the private lovers' vocabulary that frequently irrupts in *Tender Buttons* (the use of "cow" for orgasm or defecation, for instance [see 25–36]). Detailed accounts of the dynamics among Gertrude and

Leo Stein and Toklas can be found in both the Diana Souhami and Brenda Wineapple biographies.

[2] For a discussion of the archival evidence that "Rooms" was written first and was originally intended by Stein to precede the other sections, see Schuster. Logan Esdale has uncovered further manuscript evidence to support this view (private correspondence with the author).

[3] "*Tender Buttons* and a great deal of the work of Gertrude Stein can quite fairly be taken as a sort of Wonderland or Luna Park for anybody who is not too busy" (Sutherland, *Gertrude Stein* 83–84).

[4] This tonal affinity was first observed by Sandra Gilbert and Susan Gubar, who noted "the possibility that *Tender Buttons* is a demonic *Mrs. Beeton's*, a subversive conduct book that copes with traditionally female preoccupations—glamour tips, recipes, interior decorating—in a sibylline manner which ridicules social conventions even as it defies conventional interpretation" (356).

[5] Joan Retallack includes only "Objects" and "Food" in *Gertrude Stein: Selections.* Jonathan Monroe sees in the greater continuity of "Rooms" a "qualified acceptance and resignation to the status quo" (195).

Approaching *Tender Buttons* from Three Directions

Leonard Diepeveen

Tender Buttons is the only modernist text I teach that unfailingly delivers a rich educational experience: students, while not always pleased with it, are always engaged and always learn important things about affect, referentiality, the limits of meaning, and their own reading and interpretive processes. They never, in their end-of-year evaluations, ask that it be taken off the syllabus. I teach *Tender Buttons* in distinct units to third- and fourth-year students in Modern Poetry and American Modernism classes. The units are how the book's syntax and reference shape and resist meaning, the book's parodies, and the book's relation to the nonsense tradition. I begin with a short aside that explores the general background of the text, including Stein's biography, her composition process, how the text was advertised, and its reception. My major point here is that, for its readers, *Tender Buttons* was not just a text but also a social position and a symptom. A quick way to make this point is to show the images and text of the publisher's 1914 promotional brochure, which in part reads:

> Those who are avid for the literature of to-morrow will find great satisfaction in Gertrude Stein's *Tender Buttons.* It is one of the most unique books of the twentieth century. For several years Miss Stein has been the patron saint of the new artists—the Cubists and Futurists. Their work holds the centre of every art stage in civilization. It has affected and modified the other arts, as music and poetry. In the latter field Miss Stein unquestionably occupies the foremost position, and she is one of the most puzzling figures in the literary world, yet here-to-fore it has been practically impossible to obtain any of her books. . . . Her followers believe she has added a new dimension to literature; scoffers call her writings a mad meaningless jumble of words, and there are some who assert that with her tongue in her cheek she is having a sardonic joke at the expense of those who take her seriously. It is idle to attempt to pass judgement at the present moment. Time alone can give the verdict. For us it is merely that she is a real force to be reckoned with—she cannot be ignored. She is a ship that flies no flag and she is outside the law of art, but she descends on every port and leaves a memory of her visits.
>
> In *Tender Buttons* she goes even farther than ever before. Words are given greater freedom, but they are also charged with greater pregnancy. The last shackle is struck from context and collocation, and each unit of the sentence stands independent and has no commerce with its fellows. The effect produced on the first reading is something like terror, there

are no known precedents to cling to. It is a journey in unknown seas without a pilot. (*Claire Marie's New Books*)

Tender Buttons, we discover, was never just *Tender Buttons*: it stood in for other art movements; it was a scandal and possible hoax; revolutionary, it was an attack on meaning, a courageous foray into terror's territory.

Syntax and Reference

I ask students to prepare a passage to read aloud and have some read their passage in class. It's important that they work hard in their preparation: reading aloud helps them hear syntax, create intonation-based meaning, and discover moments of surprising pleasure. In short, it forces them to interpret the text. Students then comment on why they read their passage as they did, so they must articulate their interpretive decisions, explaining what was difficult in their preparation for reading, and why. We consider how Stein's passages half-promise and half-deliver meaning: through the anticipation of mimesis that the titles create, the conventions of closure that end many of these pieces, the use of periodic sentences to create suspense and climax, the overly confident pronouns that point back to unclear referents, and how metaphoric meanings are both encouraged and resisted. "Careless Water" exemplifies many of these characteristics—although one could profitably begin with virtually any passage:

> CARELESS WATER.
>
> No cup is broken in more places and mended, that is to say a plate is broken and mending does do that it shows that culture is Japanese. It shows the whole element of angels and orders. It does more to choosing and it does more to that ministering counting. It does, it does change in more water.
>
> Supposing a single piece is a hair supposing more of them are orderly, does that show that strength, does that show that joint, does that show that balloon famously. Does it. (23)

In *Tender Buttons*, the principles that one uses to create meanings shift as the reading unfolds. Consider the title and its relation to the first sentence. As it repeatedly does, *Tender Buttons* here employs bewildering, apparently unmotivated changes in direction, often by presenting a phrase that can be understood metaphorically to refer to something in an earlier, contiguous string of words (a broken cup may indicate, I suppose, that "careless water" was spilled). This interpretive chain is broken, however, by "that is to say a plate is broken and mending does do that." Despite the confidence with which this next phrase is introduced ("that is to say"), it is followed by a further, more startling change in categorical field and level of reference ("it shows that culture is Japanese").

Here, and elsewhere in Stein's book, meaning is enticingly offered through an apparent metaphor or metonymy that has a focus, but then that focus dissipates into nothing. Similarly, the syntactic repetitions (the use of "it does," for example) imply psychological emphasis and the stability of the reference, but the chanciness of the referents in this text makes it impossible to construct a stable purpose for those repetitions. Indeterminate, Stein's phrases suggest and close off different directions—directions that over the past century her critics have posited as specifically biographical (her life with Alice Toklas) or more generally as self-expression, as mimetic (considering, for example, how "A Seltzer Bottle" describes an actual seltzer bottle), as metacommentary, or as psychological research into the human mind.

Students also discover that for most of *Tender Buttons* they are immersed, primarily in the sound of syntax, the self-assured hum of logic going about its work. Stein's sentences, however baffling they are when one tries to relate clauses to each other, do things that sentences regularly do. They use repetition and periodic structure to create suspense and climax. Pronouns and other deictic markers display their usual confidence, although where they point is unclear. In many passages students can recognize the conventions of closure. *Tender Buttons*, with its sentences that exist as almost pure abstraction, presents neither propositions nor emotional expression but what one might think of as the personality of sentences. Through sentences that are aggressive, confident, or surprising, it shows us that syntax, untethered from stable reference, has an affect—which leads students to realize that both language and their interpretive abilities are much more nuanced than they thought.

Interspersed in this field of expressive syntactic abstraction is the punctuation of several kinds of discursive moment: an aphorism, a movement between particularity and generality that often results in the effects of bathos, a sound pattern, and a reference that points outside the text. Occasionally, in the flatness of the book's murmuring, sentences that sound like aphorisms rise to one's attention:

> If the party is small a clever song is in order. (17)

or

> A clatter is not a smell. (37)

or

> Startling a starving husband is not disagreeable. (66)

We discuss how these enigmatic phrases illustrate a particular kind of socially constructed information and how they work as instances of the unpredictability of what pleases us. *Tender Buttons* also occasions the surprise of stumbling on bathos in an apparently nonreferential text: "Out of kindness comes redness and out of rudeness comes rapid same question, out of an eye comes research, out of selection comes painful cattle" (13). These moments are produced by a movement from abstraction to specificity and back again, a movement that invites understanding the concrete terms as metaphorical. This back-and-forth, however, does not have to be bathetic: "A single climb to a line, a straight exchange to a cane, a desperate adventure and courage and a clock" (15). A similarly sharpened affective experience arises from those moments that suggest poetry's traditional aspects: rhyme and alliteration, as in this passage from "Roastbeef":

> Lovely snipe and tender turn, excellent vapor and slender butter, all the splinter and the trunk, all the poisonous darkning drunk, all the joy in weak success, all the joyful tenderness, all the section and the tea, all the stouter symmetry. (37)

Such aural pleasure works as a kind of punctuation. But then the text fades back into a murmur.

Finally, we look at how readers recognize phrases and words as having referential content. These have been a large presence in the history of reading Stein. It's not just about seeing that "A kind in glass and a cousin, a spectacle and nothing strange a single hurt color and an arrangement in a system to pointing" (11) could be a way of describing a carafe. There are also the surprising moments of names: "Mildred's Umbrella." There are puns: "alas" for Alice ("Alas, alas the pull alas the bell alas" [54]). There are sexually charged moments:

> THIS IS THIS DRESS, AIDER.
> Aider, why aider why whow, whow stop touch, aider whow, aider stop the muncher, muncher munchers. (31)

(Aider sounds like Ada, which Stein used for Alice in the 1910 "Ada" portrait.) There are also moments that invite being understood as metacommentary. From "A Carafe" comes a phrase that might well refer to the general project of *Tender Buttons*: "All this and not ordinary, not unordered in not resembling. The difference is spreading" (11).

These approaches to the text encourage students, who typically are intrigued but unsure at this point, to consider whether thinking about *Tender Buttons* as the experience of immersing oneself in the disrupted conventions of meaning changes what interpretation is. Critics have tended to anchor themselves in the practice of paraphrasing to point out what an opaque string of word refers to, what it asserts. *Tender Buttons* raises the question whether such interpretation is really all that important. The articulation of affect is itself a kind of interpretation, the purpose being not to get out of Stein's labyrinth but to reveal anxiety.

This immersion is restless, having no teleological direction. If *Tender Buttons* is inquiry into the nature of language, then, it probes not just the construction of meaning but also the experience of how meaning slides away from readers. (My optional writing assignment for *Tender Buttons* is not so much about interpreting an individual item as it is about describing, quite closely and phrase by phrase, the reading experience of that item. Few students take on this assignment, because they find it too difficult.)

To conclude this part of our look at *Tender Buttons*, I briefly introduce academia's dominant interpretive frames to students: readings that focus on biography, on the text's relation to feminism, on the nature of language (both queer and as inquiry), on the representation of domesticity, and on the text as a form of cubism. I point to Kirk Curnutt's *Critical Response to Gertrude Stein* and Michael Hoffman's *Critical Essays on Gertrude Stein*. We explore how different interpretive frames help with certain moments but not with others and accept that no one frame can ever hope to account for *Tender Buttons* as a whole.

Parody

In the second, shorter section of my lesson plan I turn to parodies of *Tender Buttons* (see Diepeveen), the early ones rather than the later ones, because they are more likely to look at the social context surrounding Stein and not limit themselves to a formalist takedown of the book. After showing some newspaper clippings from the Stein archive at Yale and pointing out that the response to *Tender Buttons* is the largest newspaper response to any modernist text, I linger over examples: an account of cubist fashion shows, Stein on the board of trade, Stein translated into the rules of polo, Alfred Kreymborg's account, or the dozens of responses by Don Marquis. (Examples of these and other parodic responses to Stein are available both in Curnutt's *Critical Response* and my *Mock Modernism*.) The following 1914 parody, from the *New York City Daily Trade Record*, is typical:

> Gertrude Stein, if she made a prose poem of our lines, might well say: Woolens, alas, alas, and again—the Northeast, warps, warps and no woof but sorrow. See far, far away the distant but unfeeling scope. A mill—a thing but not a person, all or none, but none so much as yesterday not tomorrow. A gum shoe—a feeling, but not pink—bitter. Worsteds, too—or worst. A thread but not spun. Cloakings—a riot, a dance, a minuet, a tango, but slow music, and hearts break in distant woe. What is a cloak? no wrap, but rainbows, not hosiery, no, not ever. But when? Ah! (Diepeveen 20)

For my students I define parody as citation with polemical discrepancy, then ask versions of the following questions: If parody is interpretation, what do these parodists perceive as the qualities of Stein's writing? What do they see as the social conditions that enabled such writing and the attention it garnered? Do these parodies discrepantly cite Stein's text, or do they try to replicate it? If to replicate, what kind of critique does that involve? What is the relation to ideology of a humorous replication or recontextualization? Students like to talk about how the parodies enact a mimesis- or pragmatics-based critique of Stein. They look at how the parodies argue that *Tender Buttons* is the result of madness, or of Stein's body, or of a social context that has spun out of control. They see that the parodies point to chance composition procedures and that many parodists experiment with bathos, the central tool of parody. But bathos, students discover, is hard to make visible, given the text's nonrepresentational nature.

We inevitably discuss what an individual parodist seemed to understand about Stein and what he or she missed. Parodists typically miss a lot, and we talk about why so many parodies of Stein are so bad. Consider, for example, the quotation above from the *New York City Daily Trade Record*: Stein doesn't use dashes or many words with emotive weight or exclamation or question marks. *Tender Buttons* is much more flat than the parody suggests. That flatness was a problem for early readers. Because of the structural uncertainties of the book, it was considered to have no movement, no features. Readers felt that an adequate evaluation of the work could be made by, as a *New York Evening Sun* reviewer said in 1914, "picking a few passages at random" (Curnutt, *Critical Response* 17). In one of his more awkward phrases, Wyndham Lewis described Stein's work generally as "a cold suet-roll of fabulously reptilian length. Cut it at any point, it is the same thing: the same heavy, sticky opaque mass all through, and all along" (77). The bad parodies of Stein's work, then, were no surprise: if you don't understand a work, you can't capture its features, then make them comic through exaggeration, recontextualization, and bathos.

Nonsense and Difficulty

Finally, we connect Stein to two related traditions: that of nonsense and that of difficulty. For a discussion of nonsense, I present Lewis Carroll's "Jabberwocky" and selections from John Cage's *Empty Words*. I ask how each of these works differs from the nonsense that is in Stein, and students find ways to talk about the relation to meaning in *Tender Buttons* one more time by comparing her nonsense with Carroll's mix of syntactic and grammatical clarity but lexical invention and with Cage's complete disruption of syntax and lexicality. I also relate *Tender Buttons* to a larger tradition of modernist difficulty, particularly to *The Waste Land*, and have students understand that the difficulties of Stein are not to be solved by looking things up or by using principles of collage or montage. I address the anxiety of the reading experience and show how it is part of a larger modernist examination and experience of aesthetic difficulty. Both anger and laughter were provoked by this anxiety.

Richly contextual and textual, my series of approaches to teaching Stein is flexible: what gets emphasized in a given year depends on the students in the class. I advocate not a single overt thesis about the meaning of Stein's work but an application of a multiplicity of topics and skills related to Stein, to modernism more generally, to aesthetic affect, and to the nature of interpretation. That multiplicity is itself an assertion about Stein's text, of course, about its richness and adaptability.

"What Is the Difference": Teaching Gender and Sexuality in "Patriarchal Poetry" through a Cultural Studies Approach

Jody Cardinal

Aptly described as "one of the great poems of the modern era" (Nelson 353), Gertrude Stein's forty-page prose poem "Patriarchal Poetry" offers a rich resource for introducing students to defining features of modernist literature and culture as well as to the complexity of Stein's experimental practice. Written from 1926 to 1927 (Dydo, *Gertrude Stein* 134–35), "Patriarchal Poetry" exhibits the subversion of conventional syntactic and narrative structures characteristic of Stein's writing and thus can familiarize students with some of her signature strategies and themes. It also provides a window into a particular moment of sexual modernity.

Though its length and difficulty preclude its full use in most introductory classes, "Patriarchal Poetry" has many points of entry and can enrich a wide array of advanced undergraduate and graduate courses, including those on modernism or modernist poetry, twentieth-century American literature or poetry, experimental writing, women's writing, lesbian and queer studies, and literary theory. Discussion might include Stein's language play, which draws attention to both the materiality of words and their referential function; her anticipation of poststructuralism; and her indictment of compulsory heterosexuality and rigid gender roles. Given that the poem uses constructions of female sexuality to reshape narrative and lyric forms, it pairs well with texts such as Mina Loy's "Songs to Joannes," the "Penelope" chapter of James Joyce's *Ulysses*, D. H. Lawrence's *Lady Chatterley's Lover*, Jean Toomer's *Cane*, and Nella Larsen's *Quicksand*.

This essay focuses on teaching "Patriarchal Poetry" through historicist and cultural studies methodologies. By 1926, Stein had achieved some publishing success yet continued to face difficulty getting her writing into print. Accordingly, her poem reflects on the persistent rejection of her writing by editors and the reading public ("Ought ought my prize" [567]), who responded with pleasure to the conventional literary forms she terms "patriarchal poetry" ("Patriarchal poetry left to renown" [603]). Stein employs interwar constructions of sexuality to differentiate her writing from these conventional forms and confer value on her aesthetic.[1]

In particular, the poem engages deeply with sexology, particularly that of Havelock Ellis, echoing and undermining constructions of gender and sexuality circulating in scientific discourse and popular depictions of companionate marriage. Courses focused on interdisciplinary studies of the modernist period might productively read the poem alongside, for instance, Ellis's chapter "The Art of Love," from *Sex in Relation to Society* (1910), and one of the many popular marriage manuals that disseminated his sexological model, such as Margaret Sanger's *Happiness in Marriage* (1926). While reading such texts in full will be impractical in most cases, even excerpts can effectively situate Stein's poem historically and help students appreciate literary texts as part of a larger social field.

The pedagogical strategy described here involves three steps: providing context for interwar constructions of the relationship between gender and sexuality,[2] modeling a reading practice attentive to both Stein's engagement with and resistance to denotative meaning, and juxtaposing specific passages from the poem with those from scientific and popular texts. Such juxtaposition allows students to read not only within but "*across* texts," a practice in line with the cultural studies perspective that "the political import of a text cannot be inferred from its internal form or logic, but derives from its position in a constellation of texts, practices, and interests" (Felski 512, 511). Students thus not only explore Stein's interventions in discourses of her time but also gain facility with cultural studies methodology.

Background on constructions of the mannish lesbian will be important, particularly if reading Stein's poem alongside contemporaneous depictions of lesbians, as in Radclyffe Hall's *The Well of Loneliness* (1928). Ironically, however, the poem seems to engage most directly with constructions of female sexuality circulating in the context of heterosexual marriage.

Stein wrote "Patriarchal Poetry" during a paradigm shift in constructions of female sexuality. By the 1920s, the Victorian belief that white middle- and upper-class women had a lesser degree of sexual desire than men had largely crumbled as women enjoyed increased opportunities for education and employment outside the home and as scientific discourses and popular media foregrounded female sexuality. The Victorian angel of the house became the flapper.

Yet in the transition from women's passionlessness to an equivalence of male and female sexual drives, conceptions of gender difference were not dismantled but reconstituted through various constructions of women's sexuality as different in type.[3] In Ellis's particularly influential version, women's sexual impulse differed from men's in seven specific ways (*Analysis* 256), including the slower development of orgasm (235–37), a greater capacity for multiple orgasms (247–49; *Sex* 522, 536–37), and more numerous erogenous zones (*Analysis* 249–50). To differentiate her writing from "patriarchal poetry," Stein identifies her aesthetic with the sexual characteristics attributed to women in the sexology of the period. For instance, she spreads eroticized passages throughout the poem to create multiple sexual-textual climaxes reflective of women's purportedly greater multiorgasmic capacity and widespread sexual sensitivity.

As women's sexual drives were more widely acknowledged, so was their right to sexual pleasure. The companionate marital ideal, emphasizing emotional and particularly sexual companionship as the basis for marriage, made women's sexual satisfaction a benchmark by which the success of a marriage might be judged. Ellis's construction of this ideal included several features adopted by marital advisers: a woman's right to sexual pleasure, a husband's responsibility to ensure his wife's gratification, and simultaneous orgasm. This emphasis on women's erotic rights proved useful to Stein in valuing her aesthetic. Coyly defining "patriarchal poetry" as a literature in which "one comes before the other" and in which "it was not expressed simultaneously" (589, 588), the poem associates conventional literary forms with selfish husbands who do not slow down to attend to their wives' pleasure. In contrast, she describes her aesthetic in a line whose delaying repetition enacts its meaning: "Everything described as in a way in a way in a way gradually" (592). Stein draws on erotic rights discourse to confer value on her aesthetic as more successful at producing and reproducing women's sexual-textual pleasure.

The poem's first paragraph provides a good opportunity for instructors to model an effective reading practice as it introduces an intertwined focus on aesthetics and erotics: "As long as it took fasten it back to a place where after all he would be carried away, he would be carried away as long as it took fasten it back to a place where he would be carried away as long as it took" (567). Stein implies a connection between conventional literary forms and the pattern of male sexual pleasure. With "carried away" suggesting both sexual and textual pleasure, the injunction "fasten it back so after all he would be carried away" signals both a cultural demand that male desire be satisfied and a facetious instruction to would-be writers of "patriarchal poetry" to "fasten" words back tightly to their signifieds so that readers receive textual pleasure. The notable absence of feminine pronouns implies that female sexual response has a different pattern.

Students should also note features that destabilize provisional meanings: the pronouns lack antecedents, and the sentence ends where it began, subverting linearity and implying that we are in a linguistic system that refers to itself more than any external reality. As students perform their own close readings, they can be encouraged to similarly explore the ways Stein's language both proliferates meanings and undermines referential meaning.

Students can then work independently or in groups to analyze passages from "Patriarchal Poetry" alongside excerpts from scientific and popular texts to consider the poem's varying responses to contemporaneous discourses of gender and sexuality. Following prompts like those below, students can practice what Rachel Blau DuPlessis calls "social philology," "an application of the techniques of close reading to reveal social discourses, subjectivities negotiated, and ideological debates in a poetic text" (*Genders* 12):

How is gender constructed in each passage? As an essential trait or a performance?

How is gender constructed in relation to sexuality? How are those constructions similar or different across texts?

Compare the tone, rhetorical purpose, and implied audiences of these passages.
Which passages use figurative language? To what effects?
What about Stein's text indicates its difference as experimental poetry?

Considering the texts side by side fosters comparisons that illuminate the poem's potential cultural work within a larger social field. Stein's meditation on "the difference between right away and a pearl" (583), for instance, can be read alongside excerpts from Ellis's sexology and Sanger's marriage manual that articulate differences in male and female sexual response patterns:

> Thus we see that a highly important practical result follows from the greater complexity of the sexual apparatus in women and the greater difficulty with which it is aroused. In coitus the orgasm tends to occur more slowly in women than in men. It may easily happen that the whole process of detumescence is completed in the man before it has begun in his partner, who is left either cold or unsatisfied. (Ellis, *Analysis* 236–37)

> First of all he must learn that the sexual nature of man differs profoundly from that of woman. Under stimulation the sexual nature of man asserts itself almost instantaneously ready for action. Due to tradition and by nature, physiologically as well as psychologically, the sex nature of woman is more deeply hidden in the mysterious recesses of her being. More deeply concealed, it is not so immediately susceptible to stimulation, is far slower in response and thus is not immediately ready for the act of love. (Sanger 127)

> What is the difference between right away and a pearl there is this difference between right away and a pearl a pearl is milk white and right away is at once. This is indeed an explanation.
> Patriarchal poetry or indeed an explanation. (Stein 583)

Reading across these passages, students can discuss the movement from Ellis's scientific detachment and deductive reasoning to Sanger's mixture of science and sentimental didacticism to the stark simplicity of Stein's diction. Together, the passages foreground the construction and reification of identity categories in discourse as each naturalizes a binary model of gender by connecting it to differentiated sexual functions. Even Stein reinforces—as she strategically echoes—these historically constructed differences in male and female sexual response patterns ("right away" vs. the slow development of a pearl) by associating her writing with female sexual response and differentiating it from the male patterns of patriarchal poetry ("Patriarchal poetry or indeed an explanation").

Stein's deceptively simple language, however, destabilizes this binary by turning our attention to the process of meaning making itself. As in other passages with the "what is the difference" motif, Stein articulates a structuralist view of meaning as constructed through differences within systems. "What is the difference between right away and a pearl" initiates a grammar lesson: "right away" is an adverb meaning "at once," while "a pearl" is a noun capable of modification by the adjective phrase "milk white." As units in a grammatical system, words are randomly assigned to denotations and differentiated roles that confer meaning. For Stein, "this is indeed an explanation," one that reveals there are no essential differences, only arbitrary relations within particular systems. Anticipating contemporary poststructuralist theory, she hints here at a parallel between linguistic and sexual difference: a binary model of sexual difference is not essential but meaningful only within a system like compulsory heterosexuality, which requires and naturalizes an opposition between man and woman. Stein's emphasis on difference as not inherent but produced within specific systems encourages us to doubt the essential nature of any difference, even the sexual differences on which the sexology—and her own passage—depend.

Stein also echoes interwar sexual discourse through her depiction of the "sexual blunderer," a character type that emerged as part of the companionate ideal to chasten men into gratifying their wives (Simmons 162). This figure of the husband who fails to satisfy his wife due to selfishness or "ignorance of women's sexual needs" appeared in a broad range of texts (163), including Stein's poem:

> If the wife is taught by instinct or experience she is apt to resent the awkwardness and helplessness of her husband in the art of love. Even if she is ignorant she may be permanently alienated and become chronically frigid, through the brutal inconsiderateness of her ignorant husband in carrying out what he conceives to be his marital duties. (Ellis, *Sex* 524)
>
> Many women have never experienced the supreme moment of the love drama because of the husband's extreme disregard for her and his ignorance of her emotional nature during coitus. He fails to control his own passions and is interested only in the immediate gratification of his own desire. His lack of consideration for the needs of his wife, who experiences no joy in the act, since she is merely the passive receptacle of her husband's passion, leads her to believe that she is "cold." (Sanger 170–71)
>
> It is very well and nicely done in Patriarchal Poetry which is begun to be begun and this was why if when if when when did they please themselves indeed. When he did not say leave it to that but rather indeed as if it might be that it was not expressed simultaneously was expressed to be no more as it is very well to trouble him. He will attend to it in time. Be very well accustomed to this in that and plan. There is not only no accounting for tastes but very well identified extra coming out very well identified as repeated verdure and so established as more than for it. (Stein 588)

Juxtaposition once again illuminates the resonances of Stein's diction as phrases like "they please themselves indeed" and "was not expressed simultaneously" repeat and resituate the emphasis in erotic rights discourse on male failure to please women sexually. Particularly interesting for students to explore in this grouping are issues of address and agency. Ellis and Sanger aim to inform men about female sexuality in order to prevent the trauma that inexperienced women might suffer on their wedding nights, yet at the same time, their rhetoric positions wives as passive victims. Indeed, the image of the sexual blunderer often aimed to shame men into taking charge of their wives' sexual experiences (Simmons 164, 169–70).

In contrast, Stein's version of the blunderer refigures the husband's failure as the need not for heightened male control but for greater female agency. Stein warns, "Be very well accustomed to this in that and plan," encouraging women to accept that heterosexual sex ("this in that") may not prioritize their pleasure and to "plan" alternative forms of gratification. She further implies that women's sexuality exists beyond the control or circumscription of male pleasure, even outside heterosexual parameters ("more than for it"), contingencies unimagined in the stock use of this figure. Stein thus repeats the sexual blunderer in order to reframe its implications for female sexuality.

Students can examine one of Stein's most complex subversions of interwar sexual discourse in a comparison of Ellis's construct of the female "invert" in *Sexual Inversion* (1901) with her constructions of gender and sexuality in the sonnet that appears toward the middle of the poem. While Ellis's invert lacks coherence between sex and gender (she is female in sex but male in gender), he naturalizes connections among gender, sexual object choice, and behavior: "[T]here are all sorts of instinctive gestures and habits which may suggest . . . that such a person 'ought to have been a man'" (250). His description of the invert, like his explanations of male and female sexual patterns, has the effect of shoring up gender by linking it to sexuality. By contrast, Stein's parody of Victorian gender constructions in the sonnet produces a variety of gender configurations:

> To the wife of my bosom.
> All happiness from everything
> And her husband.
> May he be good and considerate
> Gay and cheerful and restful.
> And make her the best wife
> In the world. (585)

The sonnet evokes the figure of the mannish lesbian in its address "To the wife of my bosom," cheekily implying the husband has a bosom (Stimpson 14), but goes further through complex language play to problematize both gender as a simple binary relation and gender as a biological imperative. On the one hand, the sonnet reveals gender to be a construction by suggesting the violence involved in molding individual women to a Victorian gender role: the husband will "make her [into] the best wife / In the world." On the other hand, the sonnet implies that the husband may be himself a wife: he will "make her [be for her] the best wife / In the world." If we read Stein as the implied speaker of the sonnet, the gender play is quite complex: the anatomical sex of the speaker—female—does not equal the gender marked by the pronoun, "he," which in turn does not equal the performance of the role of "wife." The gender play here and elsewhere in the poem shows much greater flexibility than that allowed for in sexological models of inversion and undermines even Stein's use of a gender binary to define her aesthetic. Stein invokes and transfigures sexology for strategic purpose even as her language play gestures toward its undoing.

A cultural studies approach to "Patriarchal Poetry" enables students to explore the poem's potential political work in context and examine how Stein intervened in an often misogynist and heteronormative interwar discourse of sexuality. With this approach, students witness modern identity construction in progress and can consider the potential for agency in repeating cultural constructs with a difference.

NOTES

[1] For an extended analysis of the relation between Stein's poem and interwar sexual discourse, see Cardinal, in which portions of this essay first appeared.

[2] Useful sources include Cott 41–50, 148–52, 156–62; D'Emilio and Freedman 171–274; Faderman 37–61, 89–92; Gordon; Inness; Newton; and Simmons.

[3] Poor and working-class women, women of color, and lesbians often continued to be associated with excessive sexual desire (D'Emilio and Freedman 57, 86–87).

"To Say Which of Two": Reading *Stanzas in Meditation* in the Undergraduate Classroom

Susannah Hollister and Emily Setina

Gertrude Stein's *Stanzas in Meditation,* written in 1932, is a masterwork of literary modernism. What Stein called "her real achievement of the commonplace" (*Autobiography* 225) has long helped shape literary experimentalism, influencing writers from a young John Ashbery forward. Nonetheless, as one of her most challenging texts and her longest poem, the five-part, book-length *Stanzas* rarely appears on undergraduate syllabi. It rewards teaching at the undergraduate level, though, not only for its distinctive poetics but also for the opportunity it provides to register the interpretive and aesthetic consequences of different reading practices. This essay describes exercises that we have used in our undergraduate classrooms to introduce students to *Stanzas* through the two major, seemingly divergent ways scholars have typically approached it. Reading and then rereading selections from *Stanzas in Meditation* by these two methods—one formal, one biographical—students gain familiarity with Stein's language and also discover how an alternate critical lens can transform a text's effects.

The two approaches we use run through Stein scholarship, dividing it, and have themselves been an object of recent studies (Ashton; Olson; Retallack, "On Not Not Reading"). The first is to read for the poem's patterns of language and uses of abstraction. This approach marked the poem's early reception—examples are Donald Sutherland's introduction to the first edition ("Turning Point"), published in 1956, and Ashbery's 1957 review for *Poetry* magazine. Both focus on vocabulary and internal dynamics, including the patterned, generic language (what Ashbery calls the poem's "colorless connecting words" ["Impossible" 50] and Sutherland its "frugality of imagery" [40]), the profusion of pronouns unanchored to antecedents ("For him and to him to him for me" [1.4.24]; "Just why they mean or if they mean" [4.12.1]; "Let them be mine therefor" [5.83.6]), and the concrete nouns and proper names that sporadically disrupt this flow ("Think birds and ways and frogs and grass and now" [1.11.44]; "It is a thought give a thought to Cuba" [3.18.59]). These features that distinguish *Stanzas* also contribute to its difficulty.

Ashbery meets that difficulty by turning to features of another genre, the novel. *Stanzas*, in his reading, "gives one the feeling of time passing, of things happening, of a 'plot,' though it would be difficult to say precisely what is going on" (51–52). In the poem's speculations about what "they" "should," "could," and "would" do, he finds stylistic echoes of the late novels of Henry James. But if *Stanzas* gestures toward elements of narrative, it demands reading strategies unlike those learned for prose or other narrative forms. Sutherland's and Ashbery's essays show how two early readers, lacking the contexts provided by later research, answered a question that faces any reader: How is the poem to be read? Both focus on the act of composition, Sutherland finding writing itself to be the poem's central topic, Ashbery formulating a poetics of generality he would later use to describe his own poetry.

A different answer to the question of how to read *Stanzas* was opened by the Yale archive. This approach reads *Stanzas* though Stein's biography, with reference to the romantic memory and jealousy that guided the poem's composition and revision. Uncovered by Ulla Dydo, this story involves the discovery by Alice Toklas, as she was preparing the typescript of *Stanzas*, of an early affair between Stein and a woman named May Bookstaver. That revelation came by means of another work, *Q. E. D.*, Stein's autobiographical novella based on the affair. Though written in 1903, *Q. E. D.* had been lost, and Toklas first read it when it resurfaced among Stein's papers in 1932. Then, rereading *Stanzas*, she found the poem suspiciously littered with the word "may," and she demanded substitutions. Most often "may" was altered to "can," though a variety of revisions were made. Some changes Stein entered in her manuscript notebooks, leaving visible cross-outs and rewriting on their pages; others she marked by hand on the second typescript Toklas prepared; still others Toklas incorporated directly into that second typescript. The second, heavily revised typescript, with "can" replacing "may" in many (though not all) instances, became the copy text for the 1956 edition of *Stanzas*, the only version that Sutherland, Ashbery, and other readers knew before Dydo's archival revelations. We recount the story of Toklas's objections and Stein's resulting alterations in *Stanzas in Meditation: The Corrected Edition* (2012), which restores Stein's unrevised manuscript as its reading text.[1] Dydo's work also informs Joan Retallack's introduction to the poem, written for this recent edition ("On Not Not Reading"). With Sutherland's and Ashbery's essays, which we reprint in the edition, these materials model and facilitate distinct ways of reading *Stanzas*.[2]

Class exercises and writing assignments oriented by these two major critical approaches help students experience *Stanzas* in multiple ways and prepare them to take a stance themselves on how to read the poem. These exercises, though adaptable to other contexts, are designed for undergraduate seminars on modernism or twentieth-century poetry. Although *Stanzas* stands out on a syllabus, never disappearing into the crowd, it also has meaningful continuities with other works we teach, and its stylistic features and poetic concerns make it recognizable, even indispensable, to varied literary histories. In courses that feature major modernists, such as T. S. Eliot and Virginia Woolf, aesthetic investment in impersonality and consciousness will resonate with the attention to interior life and mimesis of experience that Sutherland and Ashbery emphasize. In courses that feature poets from later movements, including confessionalism and Language poetry, the balance that Retallack describes between indeterminate language and autobiography makes the poem a useful foundational text, introducing questions about the relation between life and art, language and meaning. In any course, *Stanzas* guides students toward a more sophisticated understanding of how biography and aesthetics can work together. Students who have studied *Stanzas* are prepared to read confessional poetry not only for personal history but also for language and to approach modernism with the realization that formal experiment does not exclude selfhood.

To introduce *Stanzas*, we get students working with vocabulary and what Ernest Hemingway called the "valid and valuable" discovery of Stein's writing, its uses of repetition (*Moveable Feast* 27). We suggest starting with a single stanza, one that both Sutherland and Retallack reproduce in their introductions:

> I wish now to wish now that it is now
> That I will tell very well
> What I think not now but now
> Oh yes oh yes now.
> What do I think now
> I think very well of what now
> What is it now it is this now
> How do you do how do you do
> And now how do you do now.
> This which I think now is this. (5.8.1–10)

As a group, the class tallies up the repetitions of each word, finding that "now" appears twelve times in ten lines, "do" seven times, "I" six, "think" four. Only "very," making a single appearance, has more than one syllable. Having gathered initial observations about the poem's language, the students are ready to consider how the meanings of the repeated words and phrases change across iterations. "Now" comes to mark an increasingly instantaneous present. Within a single line and by a twist of syntax, a question, "What is it now," turns into a statement, "it is this now." The speaker "wish[es]," "think[s]," "will tell," and even begins a conversation ("How do you do"), but does not let "you" answer. If the stanza charts "the movement of thought," as Sutherland writes, what is that movement like? What are the rhythms and concerns of this particular mind? Retallack describes this stanza as a moment "[w]hen the crowd of Theys suddenly clears, the I achieves meditative clarity, is confident" ("On Not Not Reading" 25). For students, the language may not seem clear, but the strong voice will.

Working through one stanza together prepares students to read a selection on their own without balking at the poem's unfamiliarity. When they have read a number of stanzas (we recommend selections below), we have them choose, individually or in groups, a single stanza to study in depth. Their work on it will help them gain a sense of both the poem's composition history and the differences that variant word choices make. Using the textual notes in our 2012 edition, students reconstruct several versions of their chosen stanzas, one for each version of the poem recorded in our appendix D: revised manuscript; first typescript; second, revised typescript; early publications. An overview of these several texts is important at the start of this exercise. We direct students to the key introducing the notes (268) and talk through the notes' format. To model the work of reconstructing the texts of a stanza in full, part 1, stanza 13 ("She may count three little daisies very well"), works nicely. Stein revised five of the stanza's lines in manuscript, in each case crossing out "may" and writing in "can." All but one (the first) of these changes were typed directly into the second typescript by Toklas. The 1956 Yale edition follows the second typescript and introduces an additional, unique variant, substituting "may" for "make" in line 4. With the manuscript, revised manuscript, second typescript, and 1956 Yale edition, four different versions of this stanza exist.

When students have selected and reconstructed the various texts of their stanzas, we have them compare those versions. To structure their comparisons, they first identify aesthetic tendencies. They are likely, following the class reading of part 5, stanza 8, to point out repetition—of sounds, words, phases, even whole lines. Some repetitions follow patterns, such as the listing of rhymed nouns: "A weight a hate a plate or a date" (4.8.1). Others enact a process of revision, as when "May be I do but do I doubt it" (4.8.4) becomes, two lines later, "I will not may be I do but I doubt it" (6). Students may also notice Stein's use of the present tense, which predominates even when other tenses enter: "May be will may be" (7). Maintaining their focus on the texture of language, they choose one text of their stanza to perform before the class or record as an audio file. Working with sound and other features of performance helps them move beyond anxiety about meaning or its seeming absence and deepen their observation of the poem's distinctive style.

Only after students have entered into the language of *Stanzas* do we introduce the story of May Bookstaver. The story—compelling as it is and more readily grasped than Stein's language—risks overwhelming other aspects of the poem. Some may find their way to it earlier, but such discovery need not disrupt the sequence of the exercises we propose. Our goal is not to withhold the poem's history but rather to ensure that students have multiple ways to consider the poem. This sequence also has the advantage of conveying, in compressed form, the stages of the poem's critical reception. If students ask about Bookstaver or Toklas at the start, we promise to get to the story but redirect attention to the poem's internal dynamics. When later we present the story in full and discuss the circumstances of the poem's revisions, questions arise around how we define authorship. Given that Stein revised the poem at Toklas's insistence, can we say the resulting *cans* are Stein's? Or does Toklas become another author of the poem? Where artistic creation threatens personal relationships, or vice versa, how do writers balance their allegiances? In this case, Stein chose Toklas over her poem's original form. Every time we have taught *Stanzas*, this choice finds strong defenders and fierce critics.

These questions eventually lead us back to the issue of how to read the poem. Knowing the circumstances of its revision reveals some of the poem's consistent concerns: romantic partnership and professional ambition. Students are likely to notice themes of judgment and relationship more powerfully in the light of this history, focusing newly on pronouns and repeated words that signal preference and possession ("like," "mine"). Lines such as these from part 4, stanza 9, for example, readily support a thematic reading:

> I like it too to be one of one two
> One two or one or two
> One and one
> One mine (19–22)

or

> May be they like me
> I like it for which they may
> Not pay but say (28–30)

To explore these themes of the choice of a partner and the pursuit of an audience, students return to the stanzas they have been working on and experiment with replacing the ubiquitous pronouns and numbers with names and other specifics from Stein's biography. Lines 19 and 20 above, for example, might become: "I like it too to be Gertrude of Gertrude Alice / Gertrude Alice or May or Alice." Or: "I like it too to be the writer of autobiography poetry / Autobiography poetry or autobiography or poetry." Line 28 might become "May be May and Alice like me" or "May be readers like me," and, in the following line, "it" might become "love," "partnership," "this poem," "fame," or something else. This exercise has students follow Toklas as well as recent scholars in reading the poem for references beyond the few proper nouns it includes. (At this point, we often show images of pages 83 and 186 from the second typescript—reproduced in our edition [257–58]—where Toklas typed Stein's *mays* with capital *M*s and even turned "may be" to "May B.") The new text of the stanza each student or group creates stands in contrast to the poem's generic language but brings out its referential possibilities, typically focusing on romantic relationships and professional pursuits.

After reading their rewritten stanzas, students can return to the existing texts with a new perspective. We discuss the range of meanings Stein preserves by withholding or obscuring specifics. Where Toklas and Bookstaver might inhabit the same pronouns, the poem shows the memory of a past relationship persisting in the experience of a present one. Where the professional might be confused with the personal, the poem shows the two becoming indistinguishable, as they often were in the Stein-Toklas home. The unrevised text of part 2, stanza 7, for example, might voice a wish for the approval of partners as well as readers, "May they like me oh may they like me" (34), with "May" naming both past lover and current desire. Later in the same stanza, the first-person possessive that ends the line, "And therefor I like what is mine" (48), might claim partner or poem—or audience, ambition, affection. . . .

Short writing assignments can be coordinated with these exercises to have students compare the versions of the stanzas that they reconstruct, analyze a recording, and contrast their rewritten stanzas with the version of the poem that Ashbery, Sutherland, and a generation of readers knew from the 1956 Yale edition, before Dydo's revelation. In a concluding paper or class presentation, each student or group chooses among the several versions of the stanza they have now studied. We ask students to decide which text—of those they have read, reconstructed, and created—best conveys the features of the poem they consider most defining. Their papers or presentations justify their choice, discussing how it either draws on one of the two major critical approaches or combines them.

We offer below a selection of stanzas, including three groups of continuous stanzas (1.1–8, 4.4–14, 5.78–83) that have worked well in our classrooms. These stanzas lend themselves to close reading and provide varied points of entry to the whole work, conveying on a smaller scale the poem's linguistic texture and thematic concerns. We believe that the poem as a whole rewards sustained reading. However, our experience teaching it—even in a survey with just a day to devote to it—has shown that excerpts offer students excitement and discoveries.

Asterisks denote stanzas that—for their textual variants, patterns of language, and referential possibilities—suit the exercises described above. All of these demonstrate Stein and Toklas's extensive revisions of "may" to "can." Other kinds of revisions that make their way into the poem can raise interesting questions of intention, accident, and authority. For an advanced class with time to consider a broader range of textual variants, part 1, stanzas 5 and 8 (included in the list below) and their notes offer especially provocative examples.

Part 1: stanzas 1, 2, 3, 4, 5, 6*, 7, 8*, 15*
Part 2: stanzas 3*, 7*, 19*
Part 3: stanza 18
Part 4: stanzas 4, 5, 6, 7, 8, 9*, 10, 11, 12, 13, 14
Part 5: stanzas 1*, 8, 78*, 79, 80, 81, 82, 83*

NOTES

[1] *The Norton Anthology of Modern and Contemporary Poetry* (Ramazani) contains only the final stanza, in a text that follows the first typescript (the one Toklas prepared before reading *Q. E. D.*, the *mays* not yet altered). Dydo's *A Stein Reader* prints a selection of sixteen stanzas from parts 2, 3, 4, and 5, along with a clear overview of the poem's composition and revision. Dydo's *Reader*, like the reading text of our edition, follows the text of the unrevised manuscript, restoring Stein's original *mays*. The two complete texts of the poem currently in print are our 2012 Yale edition and the second volume (1932–46) of the 1998 Library of America edition of *Gertrude Stein: Writings*. The latter follows the first typescript and includes a brief description of Stein and Toklas's revisions in a discursive endnote.

[2] In an upper-level course, students might consult further critical treatments: Dydo reveals the poem's connections to Stein's biography but, like Neil Schmitz, emphasizes

the openness of its language (*Stein Reader*). Emily Setina and Heather Cass White ("How") both consider Stein's poetics as a source of selfhood and personality. Placing the poem in relation to *The Autobiography of Alice B. Toklas*, Susan Schultz and Elizabeth Winston both focus on tensions between audience and abstraction, while Jean Mills identifies *Stanzas* as a turning point in Stein's relation to her career and to language. Alison Rieke and Elizabeth Fifer both read the poem for its coding of sexuality. Lyn Hejinian ("Common") and Rebecca Ariel Porte find other kinds of salient content, including, respectively, daily life and landscape. Mary Loeffelholz considers the place of *Stanzas* in, and its exclusion from, histories of modernism.

PLAYS AND OPERAS

Exercises in Group Analysis: Sounding Out Stein's Plays

Adam Frank

More than a decade ago I ran a graduate seminar that offered an in-depth survey of Gertrude Stein's writing and its uptakes in later-twentieth-century poetry and musical composition. When the students found the experience of reading several of the plays especially frustrating, I suggested that imagining their staging might help us achieve critical perspective. One of the students took up this idea in a seminar paper that unfolded a staging of Stein's play *Identity*, then went on to complete an MA thesis that combined literary interpretation with theatrical performance of several scenes from *A Play Called Not and Now*. Her work sparked my critical sound project *Radio Free Stein* (www.radiofreestein.com) by demonstrating that the process of staging Stein's plays could help readers interpret, understand, and enjoy them.[1]

Consider the similarities and differences between the staging of Stein's plays and the usual staging of drama in the undergraduate classroom—scenes from Shakespeare, for instance. In both cases, the opportunity to read difficult poetic writing aloud leads students to notice, for example, Shakespeare's many puns, the extended resonance of a word or sound over the course of a scene or passage, or how dialogue may change its addressee over the course of a few lines. Stein's plays offer these challenges for reading along with additional ones (to put it mildly). A reader who aims to read any Stein play aloud needs to ask fundamental questions: How many voices are there? Are the voices characters, and if not, what are they? What is the play's setting? Does it have an act-and-scene structure or some other structure? Should you read aloud the act and scene titles? Is any given sentence of the play a line of dialogue or a stage direction? If dialogue, to whom is it addressed, and if stage direction, how is it interpreted? Asking and answering these and other questions require basic knowledge of theatrical form, and this knowledge must be made explicit. Like other reflexive modernist works, then, Stein's plays can be useful pedagogical tools for raising student awareness of form.

Answering these fundamental questions involves fruitful guesswork, a process of trial and error that resembles the intonational, rhythmic, and grammatical guesses readers make when they read almost any piece of Stein's writing aloud.[2] When we begin a Stein sentence, we tend to have one idea of its grammar, then encounter a knot or obstacle that requires us to start the phrase or sentence over in order to discover a different structure or intonation that lets the sentence make sense. Staging (or imagining staging) Stein's plays involves readers in an elaborated version of this iterative practice. Readers attend not only to grammatical but also to dramatic sense, a process that is most effective when undertaken by a small group.

A commitment to this process as critical and pedagogical technique distinguishes it from approaches to Stein's plays as linguistic experiments meant primarily for the page. While there is much to be gained from exploring the rivalry between language and performance in Stein's plays (as both Jane Palatini Bowers and Martin Puchner [*Stage Fright*] have done), sounding out the plays leads critics and teachers to explore the illocutionary and perlocutionary aspects of Stein's writing and its peculiar forms of intelligibility as speech. In this context the criterion of enjoyment becomes crucial. Recall Stein's reply to a radio interviewer's bemused question about the intelligibility of her speech relative to her writing: "Look here, being intelligible is not what it seems. . . . You mean by understanding that you can talk about it in the way that you have a habit of talking . . . putting it in other words . . . but I mean by understanding enjoyment. . . . If you enjoy it, you understand it" ("Gertrude Stein" 89). If Stein's writing, especially her plays, disables the masterly critical habits of explication, paraphrase, or "putting it in other words," it encourages us to invent other modes of reading. In order to get anywhere with Stein's work, readers first have to let themselves be immersed in, and to enjoy, the sheer flow of writing. Of course, this experience activates feelings other than and beside enjoyment, especially in the classroom, where students and teachers alike typically feel that they have so much to lose if they give up the fantasy of mastery that accompanies skilled reading. To read Stein at all, it seems, we need to return to the deskilled reading of childhood: reading slowly, confusedly, with a commitment to the inevitability of mistake and therefore of surprise.

Upper-level English majors, schooled in techniques of interpretation, do not find it easy to embrace such deskilled reading. They tend to encounter Stein's writing as either encrypted message or complete nonsense; in either case they feel defeated, frustrated, or offended by the text's recalcitrance to their interpretive strategies. Pedagogically, the challenge is at once emotional and cognitive: How can students be encouraged to tolerate their confusion, to read her plays slowly, multiply, with an open mind, and to enjoy and be surprised by the process of discovering their meanings? I find that creating a workshop environment gives students permission to try out ideas and make mistakes. I arrange students in small groups of four or five and ask them to read a play aloud. I begin with *An Exercise in Analysis* (1917) precisely because it utterly confounds first-time readers. It begins this way:

> A PLAY
> I have given up analysis.
>
> Act II
> Splendid profit.
>
> Act III
> I have paid my debt to humanity.
>
> Act III
> Hurry.
>
> Act IV
> Climb. In climbing do not be contented.
>
> Part II
> Run ahead.
> Run on ahead. (*Last Operas* 119)

The play goes on like this for many pages and consists entirely of act and part titles followed by one or more sentences. When I point out to students that the act and part titles can be read as names of four characters or voices (Act II, Act III, Act IV, and one whose name begins as A Play and becomes Part *x*, where *x* is a roman numeral from II to LX), the play suddenly becomes readable and amusing. The students read it aloud, and we approach it together as a skewed exercise in analysis of the competitive and collaborative relations among four voices. These voices slowly become characterized over the course of the play: Part *x* is assertive and sets the topic of conversation; Act II often one-ups Part *x* by correcting the assertion; Act III either comments ironically or initiates a new topic; and Act IV concludes these short, circular exchanges with something practical, petulant, or ditzy.

It turns out that such dynamic, emotionally charged group relations are precisely what Stein imagines her plays generally to be about. Her lecture "Plays" (1934) makes this clear:

> I had before I began writing plays written many portraits. I had been enormously interested all my life in finding out what made each one that one and so I had written a great many portraits.

> I came to think that since each one is that one and that there are a number of them each one being that one, the only way to express this thing each one being that one and there being a number of them knowing each other was in a play. (119)

I assign this key lecture to students (after they workshop a play) so that they can begin to understand Stein's landscape poetics and what motivated her play writing. The lecture's remarkable phenomenological exploration of the temporal, sensory, and affective dimensions of theatrical experience lets me introduce the important context of modernist psychology. I show how her discussion of "nervousness" ("Plays" 95) and emotional syncopation at the theater—what she describes as the audience's difficulty keeping time with the performance because of the inordinate claim that narrative makes on attention—is indebted to her early training in psychology with William James and Hugo Münsterberg. I introduce James's definition of emotion and his pragmatist orientation toward knowledge, which lets me locate Stein's portrait writing as part of a larger epistemic project of depicting the rhythms of persons and personalities.[3] Taking this context into account, the plays can be seen as reflexive attempts to depict not individuals or couples, as the portraits do, but aggregates of individuals in dynamic relations of mutual knowing. They are, I suggest, experiments in group psychology, contributions to the difficult project of trying to understand groups.

Workshopping the plays in the classroom may be thought of as an attempt to recreate the group dynamics that Stein wishes to depict. By carefully attending to their own affective responses while in the process of sounding out a given play, students may observe these dynamics as they emerge. This experimental perspective, in which students are at once scientists and guinea pigs, is often very involving. But while some students become excited by the possibility of discovering meaning in Stein's plays, their recreations raise a number of genuinely difficult questions: Is there some actual, historical group of people that a given Stein play is aiming to depict? Or are the relational dynamics that emerge from sounding out the play independent of the circumstances of its writing? More generally, how important is historical context for understanding the plays? How can we move between the moment of Stein's writing and the moment of our reading? When these difficult questions are posed, in some form or other, I feel that my basic pedagogical goal has been met: Stein's plays have come to be accessible to students insofar as they raise the kinds of questions that accompany the critical reading of any literary work. Practically, students now have interpretive material available for class discussion and techniques to develop a reading of a play in a written assignment.

Workshopping Stein's plays fits well with a pedagogical practice that I use in many of my lecture courses. At the beginning of the last class meeting of every week, after students have begun to process the readings and lectures, I arrange students in small groups of four or five and ask them to answer a set of discussion questions on a handout about that week's readings. After ten or fifteen minutes, they choose a representative to summarize each group's findings in general class discussion. These smaller and larger group discussions give them the opportunity to help one another work through course material and to compare their understandings with the rest of the class. The discussions also allow me to clarify the week's lectures and provide new contexts for understanding the readings. The handout does double duty: students write short critical responses (two or three per term) to their choice of discussion questions. Moving gradually from small-group discussion to classroom discussion to written assignment gives them time to develop their ideas slowly, carefully, and with greater sophistication.

When I teach Stein's plays, I inform students about *Radio Free Stein* and explain how workshops serve as a form of research in that project. I ask them to listen to several of the audio adaptations of the plays we are reading (in particular, those available through *Softpalate* and *Radio Free Stein*).[4] Audio, although immediately appealing to students, has its own set of challenges. Students may feel comfortable with a familiar medium accessible on their devices, but they can find it difficult to bring the critical vocabulary of the classroom to that medium. To address this challenge, I emphasize what Charles Bernstein calls "close listening," a poetic attention to the relations among sound, rhythm, and sense (*Close Listening*). Having sounded out Stein's plays in workshop, they have already encountered a version of close listening. I remind them to pay attention to form as well as affective response and to pose (again and again) the question of the relation between form and affect. Depending on the nature of the course and how much time we are spending with audio materials, I will assign or refer to critical, historical, and theoretical texts on listening and radio (Barthes; Benjamin; Adorno) to offer students vocabulary for understanding the peculiar intimacies of audio experience.

For instance, I have asked students to workshop *For the Country Entirely: A Play in Letters* (1916; in *Geography and Plays*) and then compare the *Softpalate* and *Radio Free Stein* adaptations. Stein wrote this play during her wartime year on Mallorca. It explores questions of patriotism and sexuality and especially the participation of women in war. The *Radio Free Stein* version is somber in mood; the *Softpalate* one is farcical—an interesting question is why Stein's plays often invite treatment by way of the genre of farce. The workshop experience and the openness of Stein's writing give students the authority to offer their own judgments and interpretations of the play. Indeed, it should be clear to them by now that *Radio Free Stein*'s sonic stagings are interpretations that can be argued with, that they are invitations to grapple with the complexities of Stein's plays.

I recommend that instructors wishing to use these sound resources in the classroom have students workshop Stein's plays before listening to them. In this way, what is interpretively distinctive about the audio stagings can emerge in the context of the students' grounded arguments for their own interpretive choices. Consider *He Said It: Monologue* (1915; *Geography and Plays*) which begins this way: "Spoken / In English. / Always spoken. / Between them" (267). The sentences that follow are liberally sprinkled with first- and second-person pronouns, immediately raising the question of how to reconcile the clearly dialogic nature of the play with its subtitle. At the *Radio Free Stein* workshop on this play, participants developed several different answers to this question before agreeing that *He Said It* could be heard as depicting two women trying to recall, discuss, and (at times) recreate a man's monologue. No doubt other workshops would arrive at another staging idea, one that would result in a very different interpretation (again, a comparison with the *Softpalate* recording is useful).

One goal of the *Radio Free Stein* project is to let students hear Stein's plays as "not a-referential but *multiply referential*" (Porte 83). How can we show students that her writings can be multiply interpreted not because they mean either nothing or anything but because their meanings emerge from her distinctive compositional methods as these intertwine the personal, literary, and historical in a complex weave? Consider *Photograph* (1920; in *Last Operas and Plays*), one of the audio adaptations I am currently working on. The play thematizes twins as bearing some analogical relation to photographic duplication ("Let me hear the story of the twin. So we begin. / Photograph." [152]), but it is not yet clear to me or my collaborators what this play is specifically doing with this idea. The next time I workshop the play in the classroom, I will need to decide how much historical and biographical research to bring to students. There is certainly an opportunity to discuss the history of photography in the United States, from its Civil War embedding in sentimental discourses of preservation and revelation to the changing meanings of photography in modernist revaluations around the First World War. One could also discuss Stein's personal relationships, especially with her brother Leo and with the family members of their parents' generation. These different strands might be woven together around a possible setting of this play: one or two people looking at an old photograph of a family on the verge of separation. This approach risks bringing too much detail into the classroom, but at the same time it could show students how the process of interpreting Stein's plays involves moving back and forth between conventional historical research methods (which they typically learn in their English courses) and more experimental approaches to reading (which the workshop experience provides).

I invite students to use whatever resources they can to read and think with Stein's plays inventively. Those who are particularly keen I give the option of creating their own audio adaptation, which will be linked to the *Radio Free Stein* Web site; sometimes I invite them to join my collaborators at one of our play workshops. Each of our audio adaptations is accompanied by an interpretive essay that asks, What can we say about the play now, from the perspective of having staged it sonically, that we could not say before? This question highlights the movement between creative-dramatic and critical-interpretive approaches. My specific goal is to find ways to make sense of Stein's plays; my general goal is to introduce students to the necessarily reciprocal relations between forms of experience they tend to place in opposition. Instead of setting the academic against the creative, I suggest that critical and epistemic energies may motivate theatrical works, and vice versa, that theatrical energies may motivate works of criticism and knowledge. Stein's plays offer the opportunity for students and teachers alike to consider the fundamental connections between theater and thinking.

NOTES

[1] *Radio Free Stein* plans to render at least ten of Gertrude Stein's plays into recorded dramatic and musical form. For more information and a link to a video recording of Heather Arvidson's MA thesis, see www.radiofreestein.com/info/.

[2] On the role of intonation in reading Stein, see Meyer 296–317; Pound.

[3] For more on Stein's relation to James's psychology and late-nineteenth-century science, see Meyer 209–40. Two James essays I recommend are "What Is an Emotion" (1884) and "The Place of Affectional Facts in a World of Pure Experience" (1905). For a reading of Stein's "Plays" vis-à-vis several theories of emotion and a fuller explication of the idea that Stein's plays are experiments in group psychology, see my *Transferential Poetics* (96–118).

[4] For the *Softpalate* project, see www.ubu.com/sound/softpalate_stein.html. Other resources on Stein and sound (such as the recording Stein made for Columbia in 1935) can be found on *UbuWeb* and at *PennSound*. See the bibliography on the *Radio Free Stein* Web site for an extensive list of online resources on Stein and sound.

Performing Stein, Inviting Affect

James Peck

Across her writing life, Gertrude Stein wrote seventy-seven plays. In her essay "Plays," written for her United States lecture tour of 1934–35, she insists that though she lacks practical knowledge of theater production, these works are not poems, fiction, or essays but plays. "I have written a great many plays," she asserts with wry self-assurance, "and I am quite sure that they are plays" (111). To a typical undergraduate, however, her plays are not plays. They do not meet student expectations for the genre of drama at all. Lines of dialogue almost never follow left-justified character names. She toys with the progression of acts and scenes, so that a play might have ten renderings of act 1, scene 2, scattered across its full length. If we look beyond such anomalies, we see that the plays elude the usual reading strategies associated with drama. Many of them lack identifiable characters, populated as they are less by people than by fragmentary, compound, or shifting personae. The lines, if they can be called that, are so erratically assigned to a fixed speaker that the conversational riposte of stage speech rarely emerges. Perhaps most critically, Stein's plays lack, at least by any usual definition, dramatic action. Since Aristotle, the sine qua non of writing for the theater in the West has been that plays embody events. Stein eschews this premise.

In the place of stories, she promotes what she calls landscapes: "What is the use of telling a story since there are so many and everybody knows so many and tells so many" (118–19). Instead, she creates glimmering tableaux vivants of people, speech, thoughts, objects, and activities. Her plays aim to capture the unique essence—what she calls the entity (Ryan 24–32)—of a particular scene. They extend her practice of writing portraits—short, closely observed character studies—to relationships. "I came to think," she explains, "that since each one is that one and there are a number of them each one being that one, the only way to express this thing each one being that one and there being a number of them knowing each other was in a play" ("Plays" 119). Instead of representing events between people, though, she decenters the plot. She rejects the linear accumulation of causal narratives, the "syncopated time" of dramatic anticipation, fulfillment, and release (93). She prioritizes the theater's spatial possibilities. Her plays do not tell a story. Rather, they move around and through a context of human interaction. Most often, they spring from simple scenarios of domestic life. Her text traverses the situation, depicting it from multiple vantage points in the manner of a cubist painting. That locale and those occurrences unfold in a series of carefully composed images that crystallize a figure or a gathering and then dissolve to give way to a next figure or gathering. Space eclipses time as the theater's paramount element: theater as social geography. "Of that relation I wanted to make a play and I did, a great number of plays" (125).

Of course, this displacement of narrative renders Stein a useful figure to introduce students to numerous strands of experimental performance in the twentieth and twenty-first centuries. Undergraduates in the United States typically imbibe a narrative of American theater history that privileges the formidable but aesthetically circumscribed achievements of poetic realism. Tracing the history of the American stage through Stein and her followers decenters that normative view and provides a diverse but surprisingly coherent array of alternative approaches. Stein influenced successive generations of innovators, particularly in the United States, many of whom have repurposed her precepts for their own ends. Among others, The Living Theater, the Judson Church Poets' Theater, Richard Foreman, Robert Wilson, Meredith Monk, The Wooster Group, Mac Wellman, Anne Bogart, David Greenspan, Erik Ehn, Suzan-Lori Parks, Target Margin, Nature Theater of Oklahoma, and Ripe Time all were or are explicitly in dialogue with Gertrude Stein. It is hard to imagine the work of Goat Island, Elevator Repair Service, Richard Maxwell, Young Jean Lee, or Half-Straddle without the precedents she established. As Bonnie Marranca writes in her introduction to the 1995 reissue of Stein's *Last Operas and Plays*, "If John Cage has been the father of the American avant-garde, surely Gertrude Stein has been its mother. Together the two of them are the progenitors of the last half-century of American avant-garde work" (xxiii).

A semester-long theater history class might productively trace Stein's influence in American experimental theater.[1] In this essay, I suggest some reasons why the study of Stein also benefits from performing segments of her plays, even in the context of classes oriented more toward literature than production. Having both directed her plays and taught her theater, I have come to believe that crafting stage pictures for her seemingly opaque playtexts reveals the radical potentials of her aesthetics. In particular, engaging students in the process of moving their bodies through time and space to illuminate each moment foregrounds the potent affective registers of her writing. In my experience, students readily warm to her formal brilliance and playful ebullience. She's fun from the get-go, and students relish her invitation to frolic. However, the intractable modernism of her texts, their refusal of a certain kind of clarity, often limits students' emotional engagement. But to miss the intensity of Stein's plays is to miss their point. The delicate, sometimes searing intimacy of the bonds that link and separate people is her abiding subject matter. "All her plays," writes Marc Robinson, "start from and return to feeling" (*Other American* 16). The pedagogical task of staging Stein, even small snippets of her, reveals the profound emotional intelligence undergirding her plays. More fundamentally, performing her provides students opportunities to see and feel anew the deeply felt, complexly socialized layers of their own lives.

Many of Stein's plays can serve to introduce students to her theater, but I especially recommend *Identity A Poem* (1935). I teach at a small liberal arts college with a large, well-regarded theater program, and my classes contain between ten and thirty students, mostly majors or prospective majors. I have taught this text at all levels, from first-year students to seniors, and used it both in courses devoted to theatrical practice and in courses with a more historical emphasis. Good supplementary readings are Stein's essay "Plays" and her 1935 essay "What Are Master-pieces and Why Are There So Few of Them." If time permits, the study of *Identity* amply prepares students to analyze one of her longer theatrical masterworks, perhaps *Listen to Me* (1936) or *Dr. Faustus Lights the Lights* (1938).

Identity is culled almost entirely from fragments of Stein's *The Geographical History of America or the Relation of Human Nature to the Human Mind* (1935). Stein assembled *Identity* in 1935 in response to a request from the American puppeteer Donald Vestal for a text to perform with his marionettes. It is a good classroom text in part because it is so short, just seven pages, and so less apt to flummox young adults still learning to mingle pleasure with confusion. It is brief and punchy enough that they do not much mind not getting it, and they can easily reread the whole thing when it becomes apparent that they will need to do so. More important, *Identity* packs in numerous literary stratagems that exemplify Stein's artistic practice, and it works through questions about the nature of human being that obsessed her throughout her writing life.

"I am I because my little dog knows me," *Identity* begins (588). As with most of Stein's plays, the characters are not neatly delineated. However, two central personae quickly emerge: Human Nature and Human Mind. In her thinking, Human Nature embodies the human compulsion toward habit, cleaving to stability and craving recognition. Human Nature's opening statement, "I am I because my little dog knows me," becomes its mantra, a proclamation of self repeated frequently in moments of crisis. Human Mind, on the other hand, seeks freedom from the boundaries staked out by Human Nature. It is unconcerned with consistency of identity over time and seeks no external affirmation. Unfettered by memory, it pulsates with potentiality. On first appearance, Human Mind trumpets the liberating capacity of play: "The human mind. The human mind does play. The human mind. Plays because it plays" (589). Over time, more figures join the fray. Human Nature's little dog crystallizes into a character. Eventually, two Choruses appear, one in league with Human Mind and another called Tears. Threaded throughout are directorial and authorial voices. Sometimes they chime in with stage directions, like, "The figure wanders on alone" (588). Often they query the process of writing itself, debating the ramifications of a particular artistic decision—for example, "So then the play has to be like this" (589).

Over its seven pages and, depending how it is staged, perhaps twenty-five minutes playing time, *Identity* probes the relations among identity, emotional ties, and creative work. A landscape takes shape that gives flesh to the joy, tussles, and ultimate solitude of becoming a self that makes art. The central conflict dramatizes one of Stein's recurrent themes—the difference between Human Nature and Human Mind. This distinction is a key conceptual framework of Stein's mature writing. Stein associates Human Nature with the lure of popular appreciation, Human Mind with the autonomous imagination. Ever the modernist, she deems Human Mind the necessary state of consciousness for the creative artist. *Identity* even includes an authorial voice aspiring to this realm: "And then to make a play with just the human mind. Let us try" (589).

The scenes accumulate around these themes, though more as an unfolding body of imagery than as a story. Here is a brief section to illustrate the play's nonlinear form:

> A PLAY
> I am I because my little dog knows me.
> Which is he.
> No which is he.
> Say it with tears, no which is he.
> I am I why.
> So there.
> I am I where.
>
> ACT I SCENE III
> I am I because my little dog knows me.
>
> ACT I SCENE
> Now this is the way I had played that play.
> But not at all not as one is one. (591)

The fragmented, seemingly helter-skelter quality of this pseudo-dialogue is typical of Stein's plays. Though it is not possible to arrive at a singular meaning for this text, a gathering of voices queries the sources of personal identity, registers the affective dimensions of identity, and considers, with disagreements, how best to show identity on the stage. The text resists a definitive and stable interpretation, but puzzling through possible meanings and ascriptions of each line is part of the fun. The process of glossing can never be definitive but provokes engagement with Stein's thinking on art, emotion, and the longing for external affirmation.

Identity makes concrete Stein's ideas about theater. For example, it enacts her theory of theatrical temporality: Stein aims to promulgate what she calls "the continuous present" ("Composition" 498). To a degree perhaps unmatched by any author before or since, she prioritizes the sensate intensity of the current moment. In her essay "Plays," she rejects narrative drama in large part because of the genre's propensity to project forward and hark back, to conjure an emotion out of step with that of the viewer. The "syncopated time" of traditional theater, she says, makes her "nervous" (95). The authorial voice of *Identity* similarly aspires to circumvent the troubling experience of syncopated time: "And so to make excitement and not nervousness into a play" (589). *Identity*'s scenic structure provides students a clear example of Stein's invitation to lay hold of the continuous present. The scenes seem to be randomly ordered. Part 4, for example, appears midway through the play without any prior reference to parts 1, 2, or 3. It contains multiple scene 1s, scene 2s, and scene 3s that do not appear in sequential order; for example, the first scene 3 precedes the first scene 1, and the fifth scene 1 follows the fourth scene 2. Though initially befuddled, students easily grasp and often find amusing Stein's conceit to subvert linear progression and pin audience members to the now. Each scene exists for itself; each moment offers its own insights and pleasures.

Identity amply illustrates many such characteristics of Stein's theater, and for that reason I find it pedagogically useful. But ultimately I am more impressed by the landscapes of feeling that the play constellates. Its geography of affect is informed by Stein's artistic and existential concerns. The play returns again and again to the question of identity. Where does identity come from? Is it necessarily bound up in others? "And how do you like what you are," says someone. "And how are you what you are. And has this to do with human mind" (592). Does identity facilitate creativity? Or, more probably, impede it? Can one have a sense of self separate from memory and identity? Might that sense be human mind? The play is not structured by the cause-and-effect logic of drama, but something does mysteriously transpire. Human Nature eventually hears, and perhaps accepts, that being someone does not depend on the warm affirmations of its dog: "The little dog knowing me does not really make me be I no not really because after all being I I am I has really nothing to do with the little dog knowing me, he is my audience, but an audience never does prove to you that you are you" (593). Human Mind maintains its independence, a sense of artistic personhood that does not require the flattery of a successful book tour or the applause of the theater.

One reading of *Identity* might emphasize the antagonism between Human Nature and Human Mind and locate the play's fundamental movement in the triumph of Human Mind. Stein's writings certainly support such an interpretation. In "What Are Master-pieces," for example, Stein neatly encapsulates what might be considered the thesis of *Identity*: "I am I because my little dog knows me, but creatively speaking the little dog knowing that you are you and you recognizing that he knows, that is what destroys creation" (355). But such a binary, agonistic approach to the text closes down the play's breathtaking emotional complexity. Performance recovers this richness.

Students might be asked to stage ten lines of the play, two contiguous scenes, or half a page. I suggest they work in teams of about five, each group on a different section. They will need to make many decisions: which characters to embody, how to cast the roles, who says what, how each character moves and speaks, how they relate to one another, what to wear, what else is onstage, where to put the audience, and on and on. It is important that they make these decisions with clarity and force. In the process, they will come up against the clunky materiality of the theater: it is an art form of bodies, speech, sets, costumes, and props. When they press against that solidity, they will discover what in the play they think matters.

Imagine they are staging the moment when the Chorus that supports Human Mind definitively declares, "[H]uman nature is not at all interesting" (593). On the page, the moment reads as a victory for Human Mind, and it is. But on the stage, the students will need to grapple with the consequences of the statement for Human Nature. Is the character present? What sort of person, in the world as we know it, does Human Nature evoke? How does he or she feel about being deemed uninteresting? How should that reaction be shown? And how does the dog feel? Does the moment bring Human Nature and the dog together or drive them apart? For whom or what is the Chorus of Tears crying? Are the tears tears of grief or rage? How about Human Mind? Is it happy for the support of a Chorus? It would seem that Human Mind should not care whether or not it has the support of others, being a consciousness independent of the desire for approval. But might not such affirmation be tempting? Does Human Mind stand with the Chorus? Is it moving or still?

The point is that such a moment becomes more nuanced, contradictory, and layered as the students begin to play it with their bodies. The cost of artistic autonomy needs to be dealt with. Students must wrestle with the consequences of every choice they make. They will encounter problems—practical problems of where to stand and what to wear and when to move and how to speak and whether to listen—that can be solved only by facing the bottomless questions of what it means and how it feels to be an artist in the company of others. The very openness and ambiguity of Stein's text authorize them to give a physical, temporal shape to their imagination. Because theater is a collective enterprise, they will test, temper, and perhaps transcend their sense of the possible in the evolving imagination of their group. They will have the opportunity to experience, in their own creative process, the pushes and pulls of belonging, creativity, competition, and autonomy that Stein's play so profoundly investigates. The exercise, if it goes well, will make for the sort of learning that, because it touches simultaneously on intellectual, emotional, and social registers, stays with them beyond semester's end.

Speaking of prose, Stein writes, "A long complicated sentence should force itself upon you, make you know yourself knowing it" ("Poetry" 221). This imperative applies also to staging her plays. In crafting each moment, people come to know themselves anew. Because theater is a collaborative art form, they discover themselves alongside others who are also coming to know themselves anew. As useful as it is to read and discuss Stein's plays, performing them is also a vitalizing pedagogical practice. Staging even brief fragments of her dramatic oeuvre makes it impossible to treat her playwriting as only a lively curiosity. When I teach her plays, I know that my students will enjoy her puzzles, wordplay, and gaiety, but I want them also to know her force, to experience her as a playwright who abides in feeling and in flesh. Bringing her words to their bodies makes this happen.

NOTE

[1] Besides Marranca's introduction, good critical resources are Ryan; Robinson, *American Play*; Bowers; and Bay-Cheng.

"To Know to Know to Love Her So": Teaching Gertrude Stein's Operas to First-Time Stein Readers

Michelle J. Brazier

One approach I use in teaching Gertrude Stein is to show how other artists have made sense of her work, and not only sense but also art of their own. A second approach is to introduce Stein to first-time readers by teaching them how to listen to her words, to read the way she wrote and not the way they are used to reading. Though students may not be convinced that she is for them, they cannot deny that the sound of her words is interesting, that her "sentences do get under their skin," as she claimed in *The Autobiography of Alice B. Toklas* (70). Hearing and performing her words make a difference in knowing what they mean.

The Gertrude Stein–Virgil Thomson operas, *Four Saints in Three Acts* (1934) and *The Mother of Us All* (1947), are among Stein's more accessible texts because other artists have already done the work of parsing meaning for performance: Thomson shaped her words and set them to music, and Maurice Grosser created the scenarios, or synopses, giving the operas their overarching plots so that they could be staged effectively. Teaching Stein's operas thus involves teaching how her text became the script for an opera and then a full opera production with a musical score, scenario, stage directions, set design, choreography, dancers, and singers. Artistic collaboration is at the heart of how I teach her operas to first-time readers. In this essay, I focus on the literary-musical-dramatic collaboration that produced *Four Saints*.[1]

In teaching the collaboration between Thomson and Stein that began in 1927 and produced the 1934 performance, I show students how Thomson made sound sense of Stein's words. By *sound sense* I mean that setting words to music can enhance their meaning by evoking images or intensifying emotions, as in film music or powerful ballads. Indeed, Thomson understood that Stein's words did not make "sense" in the usual way, noting that they could be "genuinely hermetic [and] virtually impenetrable" (Preface v). Of *Four Saints*, he wrote, "It is a text of great obscurity. Even so, when mated to music it works" (*Music* 52). Thomson's process of "musical declamation"—setting the words to rhythms and pitches—may not be understood by untrained listeners, but the marriage of the words and music can create a range of emotions in all listeners—pleasure, discomfort, sadness, joy. In his autobiography, Thomson explains:

> My theory was that if a text is set correctly for the sound of it, the meaning will take care of itself. And the Stein texts, for prosodizing in this way, were manna. With meanings already abstracted, or absent, or so multiplied that choice among them was impossible, there was no temptation towards tonal illustration, say, of birdie babbling by the brook or heavy

> heavy hangs my heart. You could make a setting for sound and syntax only, then add, if needed, an accompaniment equally functional. (*Virgil Thomson* 90)

For Thomson, meaning was manifest in the correct setting of words to music. My goal in teaching sound sense is to convince my students that they can understand Stein's words in the way that Thomson set them and early audiences heard them. As Carl Van Vechten wrote in the playbill for the New York production, "Miss Stein's words always sound better than they look and they sound especially well when projected through the sensitive medium of Virgil Thomson's music" (Program notes).

I devote two eighty-minute classes (at minimum) to a Stein opera in a survey course, and I always assign the full text.[2] In the first class we address the historical context of its creation and production, using Steven Watson's *Prepare for Saints* and archival materials; in the second we discuss both Stein's text and Thomson's adaptation and listen to the opera. When I have more time, I include her lecture "Plays" (1935), critical commentary beyond Watson's, and Thomson's opera score, and we stage informal student performances. The accessories of music, images, scenario, "Plays," and so on make *Four Saints*, a difficult text, more accessible and more pleasurable.[3]

Beginning with historical context, I assign Watson's prologue and chapters 15–18: these sections describe the collaboration and the debuts in Hartford and New York in 1934 and situate the opera's avant-garde production at the tail end of the Harlem Renaissance, which we have usually just covered in class as part of an American literature or modern drama curriculum. I distribute a handout to students: questions to help focus their reading of Watson and emphasize the collaboration.[4] Students answer them in preparation for the first class, in which I share primary materials I have gathered from the Stein archive at Yale's Beinecke Library: photographs of the debut productions, the 1934 playbill, performance reviews, and notes by the artists. (Watson's book reproduces some of these materials.) Other images of the debut are printed in the front matter of the Thomson complete vocal score with piano reduction (published in 1948 by Schirmer), both of which—images and score—I show to the class (Stein and Thomson).

I then distribute Grosser's scenario for the opera's four (not three, in fact) acts, and we walk through it together. Our study of it reveals the malleability of Stein's text. I highlight how Grosser managed to find his way in by extending in dramatic terms what Thomson did in musical declamation. Describing his artistic process and guiding future directors of the opera, Grosser wrote:

> One should not try to interpret too literally the words of this opera, nor should one fall into the opposite error of thinking that they mean nothing at all. On the contrary, they mean many things at once. The scenarist believes that any practicable interpretation of the text is legitimate and has

> allowed himself, in consequence, considerable liberty. He counsels equal freedom to stage directors and choreographers, in the hope that they will find in this deeply fanciful work stimulus to their own imagination. ("Scenario" iii)

Stein agreed with him, writing in *Everybody's Autobiography*, "[Grosser] had a way of knowing how it was possible to play the plays that I have written" (77). His guidance encourages students to approach her text with some confidence in their own reading.

We end the first class with my "How to Read Gertrude Stein" handout. I tell students about an encounter that Stein had with some reporters during her American lecture tour in 1934–35. When they asked her, "Why don't you write the way you talk?," she responded, "Why don't you read the way I write?" (Brinnin 334). To begin understanding her, we have to relearn how to read. These instructions are geared to the first-time Stein reader; they anticipate struggle.

How to Read Gertrude Stein

1. Commit *one hour*. Approach this reading homework as a time commitment rather than a comprehension goal. You may spend this hour all at once or over several sittings.
2. Read aloud. Get a feel for the *sound* of her writing, the rhythms and patterns. Think of *Four Saints* not only in terms of "reader as actor" (as if you were performing) but also of "writer as actor." Stein is performing.
3. Abandon mastery. Read every word. But do not expect to *understand* it in the way you would expect to "understand" Mark Twain's *Huckleberry Finn*, for instance. Stein's texts are less about plot than about process, less about dramatic conventions than about language.
4. Watch for puns & wordplay. For example, "four saints" / "for saints" or "scene" / "seen." Meaning may be found in a sound relation between words that seem disparate, and her humor may be a kind of inside joke that years of deciphering may, or may not, uncover.
5. Remember that you're reading an opera. It was envisioned as an opera, not a play or story; the text was written by Stein to be set to music by the American composer Virgil Thomson. Consider *how opera sounds when it is sung*. Even if you have never heard an opera, you have heard parodies of them (google "Bugs Bunny Opera"). The singers trade a phrase back and forth, embellishing it with pitch, tempo, emphasis, etc., even though the words on the page may look repetitious and monotonous. If a passage of an opera were written out word for word, it could read like a Stein text.
6. Read with a sense of humor and imagination. Stein can be very amusing if you pay attention.

First-time readers need to unhinge their analytic reading brain, the one that demands an explanation, for long enough to notice how Stein's writing is written and to seek out various meanings, not one, just as Thomson and Grosser did in handling her text.

On day 2, after some discussion about their first experience reading Stein—which invariably includes confusion and a few impassioned objections—I orient students to the relation between the texts they have been reading and the music they will be hearing. We use three sources in this class period: Grosser's scenario, Stein's *Four Saints*, and an abridged recording of the *Four Saints* opera, conducted by Thomson in 1947. The liner notes for the BMG-RCA (1996) release of the 1947 recording includes the (abridged) text of the Stein-Thomson libretto. Using these notes, I can show my students how Thomson adapted Stein's text for the stage. For example, here is a passage in Stein's text:

> Who settles a private life.
> Saint Therese. Who settles a private life.
> Saint Therese.
> Saint Therese. Who settles a private life. (587)

Thomson assigns every one of these lines to a singer or speaker in the opera, and he cleverly inserts nonvocal orchestral interpolation for the missing line of text following the second "Saint Therese." On the recording, we hear the text and musical line together, then hear the same line repeated by the orchestra alone. In Thomson's adaptation, that same passage is as follows (note the shift from Therese to Teresa):

COMPÈRE [spoken]:	Who settles a private life.[5]
ALL [spoken]:	Saint Teresa.
CHORUS I & II:	Who settles a private life.
COMPÈRE [spoken]:	Saint Teresa.
CHORUS I & II:	Who settles a private life.
COMPÈRE [spoken]:	Saint Teresa. (12)[6]

In contrast, observe the passage in Stein just preceding the aria "Pigeons on the Grass Alas," sung by Saint Ignatius:

> Scene II
> Saint Ignatius. Within it within it within it as a wedding for them in half of the time.
> Saint Ignatius. Particularly.
> Saint Ignatius. Call it a day.
> Saint Ignatius. With a wide water with within with drawn.
> Saint Ignatius. As if a fourth class. (604)

Here is Thomson's adaptation, with the first line, "Scene II," spoken by St. Teresa I:

> ST. TERESA I: *Scene two.*
> SAINT IGNATIUS: Within it within it within it as a wedding for them in half of the time. Particularly. Call it a day. With a wide water with within withdrawn. As if a fourth class. (25)[7]

I then give a demonstration of sound sense. For their listening, students receive a handout that ties together Stein's text, track numbers from the abridged 1947 recording, and the libretto in the notes for that recording, which gives the names of characters who are singing the lines. Each new musical motive, as it relates to the text, is numbered in the handout. Thomson used three conventional musical strategies to set Stein's unconventional text: standard key signatures (e.g., beginning in F major makes the music sound happy, whereas a minor key would make it sound sad), standard time signatures (3/4 time is like a waltz; 4/4 time is common in rock and folk music), and singable, lyrical lines. Each number corresponds both to a line of Stein's text (e.g., "St. Teresa in a storm at Avila" and to a musical motive in Thomson's score (e.g., a new melody introduced by a singer). Before I play tracks 1 and 2, I have the students number their text where the words appear; then, as we listen, I call out the numbers so that they can follow along, from one musical motive carrying Stein's text to the next.[8]

> The 1947 Recording of *Four Saints in Three Acts*
>
> Track 1: Prologue
> 1. "To know to know to love her so" (581). Chorus. Listen for orchestral "Oom-pah-pah" in 3/4 and 4/4 to emphasize the rhythms of Stein's text.
> 2. Cut to roll call of saints spoken by Commère and Compère (585). A garden at Avila in early spring. There is a wall and a tree. St. Teresa II is seated under the tree painting flowers on very large eggs.
>
> Track 2: Act 1 (Saint Teresa in a storm at Avila)
> 3. "St. Teresa in a storm at Avila" (586). First motive. Sung by Commère, mostly rhythmic, very little variation in notes and harmony.
> 4. "A pleasure April fool's day a pleasure" (586). Recitative transition by Commère.
> 5. "Not April fool's day a pleasure" (586). Second motive. Solo melodic line for St. Teresa I accompanied by a rhythmic chorus: "St. Teresa seated," "St. Teresa seated and not surrounded."
> 6. "There are a great many persons and places" (586). Listen for interwoven first and second motives, as well as individual solo voices and chorus; note the words being the music.

7. "How do you do" (587). Recitative between Teresas I and II, punctuated by St. Stephen singing "The garden inside and outside of the wall."
8. "Nobody visits more than they do visits them" (587). Recitative by Compère. Textual extension of first and second motives (same melody as "there are a great many persons").
9. "Who settles a private life" (587). Third motive. Spoken by Compère, sung by Chorus. Sounds like trumpet calls, punctuated by "St. Teresa" from chorus and soloists; this leads to the announcement of St. Ignatius, "Left to be."

I ask students to describe what they have heard, and I offer context and musical or textual explanation as needed. Thomson's music might be described as happy, uplifting, jocular, jaunty; it is harmonically consonant and rhythmic. The instrumentation is also mostly conventional: Thomson used standard orchestral scoring but, unusually, added an accordion and a melodeon, giving the orchestra a parlor or street feel rather than the atmosphere of a concert hall. His music was assembled as a collage, drawing from Spanish dance, African American spiritual, and chant and Renaissance styles exemplary of his formal training in sacred music. This collage technique is one of the few unconventional aspects of his composing that dovetail with the avant-garde elements of Stein's text: the apparently random ordering or repetition of scenes and acts, her juxtaposition of historical and fanciful saints in conversation. Music and text share this sensibility of collage.

We listen to the music again, and this time the students compare the Stein and Thomson versions, original and adaptation, reading Stein's while listening to Thomson's. This cross-textual work allows students to see the decisions Thomson made in setting Stein's words to music, how he made sense of her text. I distribute another handout like the one above, and we listen to track 15 from act 3, the best known of the arias: "Pigeons on the grass alas." (According to Grosser, Stein intended this aria to represent Saint Ignatius's vision of the Holy Ghost ["Scenario" v].) Students read and hear how Thomson's music offsets the expectation of nonsense from Stein's libretto, which was roundly ridiculed in the press at the time, especially this passage about pigeons on the grass. In these same newspaper reviews, the music is described as melodious and harmonic, not dissonant—everyone had expected dissonance, as if Stein's words could only inspire chaotic sound. His simple harmonies couch her abstruse meanings in a welcoming sound environment, thus disrupting—if we trust our ears—the tyrannical need to understand what her words mean in favor of experiencing how they sound.

When these words are delivered by singers with conviction and received by other singers as if they conveyed conventional meaning, our imagination allows us to believe that the scene before us makes sense. Grosser's scenario provides a conventional framework, and Thomson's setting of Stein's words propels that plot forward as musical narrative. In class we echo the task of the composer, director, or actor of taking these words and making them mean something. Using text, score, and performance history convinces students that that there is a payoff—a sense of intellectual accomplishment and enjoyment—in wading through such unfamiliar literary territory. They can indeed learn how "to know to know to love her so." My goal is to make them fall in love with Stein as I did, as her collaborators did.

NOTES

[1] Stein completed *Four Saints* in 1927 and first published it in the journal *Transition* in June 1929; it then appeared in *Operas and Plays* (1932), *Last Operas and Plays* (1949), and, more recently, the Library of America edition of her writings (1998). In 1934 an abridged version (for copyright reasons) was published as a stand-alone libretto (without the musical score) by Random House, with an introduction by Carl Van Vechten. This version then appeared in Van Vechten's *Selected Writings of Gertrude Stein* (1946); the reprint of that edition (Vintage, 1990) is what I assign in my classes. The libretto used for productions is Thomson's adaptation of Stein's text. He not only composed the opera's music but also transformed Stein's unconventional libretto to a traditional one, cutting passages and clearly indicating "who sings what" (Holbrook and Dilworth 219). For the Random House abridgement Stein used Thomson's cuts. Although it does not show "who sings what," it is, line by line, close to the libretto Thomson made for the stage. To an extent, then, the Random House edition was collaboratively produced. See Holbrook and Dilworth 214–21.

[2] I have taught Stein's operas in a variety of contexts at both undergraduate and graduate levels, including 200-level courses on American literature, on women in literature, and on modernist drama.

[3] I use a video made available by the Metropolitan Museum of Art: *Four Saints in Three Acts* (1934) features Stein answering questions about what understanding the opera means as well as film of the original production. There are many clips on *YouTube* of the Mark Morris production at BAM in 2006.

[4] Among the questions on the Watson handout are "Why did Virgil Thomson want to set Gertrude's Stein's words to music? Use a quote in your answer. When did Stein begin writing the libretto (the text of the opera)? When did Thomson begin writing the music? When did he finish? Who are some of the other important figures (people) mentioned in this chapter? Name three of them, who they are, what they do, and/or why they are important."

[5] The characters of the Compère and Commère were introduced by Thomson as musical vehicles for Stein's text, "non-saintly commentators or 'end men'" (*Virgil Thomson* 107). Background on this innovation can be found in the 2008 critical edition of the orchestral score (Hitchcock and Fussell).

[6] The two-CD recording (Elektra/Asylum/Nonesuch) of the 1982 production of *Four Saints*, conducted by Joel Thome, contains the Stein-Thomson libretto in its liner notes. Unlike the notes for the 1947 recording, these indicate when the lines are being sung or spoken. I have added that information here, in brackets. The 1982 notes include the Grosser scenario as well.

[7] Thomson explains, "I set all of Stein's text to music, every word of it, including the stage directions, which were so clearly a part of the poetic continuity that I did not think it proper to excise them" (*Virgil Thomson* 104). Yet during the writing process he did make musical decisions, especially in assigning lines to singers, that involved excising Stein's words—for example, the repetitions of "St. Ignatius" in this passage. This approach is documented in Hitchcock and Fussell's introduction to their edition of the opera's orchestral score. For Grosser's story of the writing process, see his "Visiting Gertude and Alice" (1986).

[8] The abridged recording opens with the first six lines of Stein's text and then cuts to the roll call of saints preceding the first "Act One" in Stein's text; this corresponds to "Act One" in the performed opera. Thus, in this abridged recording, most of the opera's prologue is cut.

A Seriously Playful Pedagogy for Gertrude Stein's Late, Great Opera, *The Mother of Us All*

Patricia A. Schechter

Gertrude Stein's opera *The Mother of Us All* can wake up language and thinking today as powerfully as it did at the dramatic close of World War II, when it was written. Playing up and playing on rituals of state, the opera stages a provocative dialogue between the United States Civil War and World War II. Why should today's students care for an opera, of all things, about either of these wars, in which the correct side won, bad things like slavery and Nazism were defeated, and both victories confirmed the best of American values? Because exploding such propagandistic readings of history is part of the Steinian project. In a class on literature, history, American studies, even political science, Stein's work can open up a discussion of Americanism. The ideology of Americanism valorizes the sovereign legitimacy of the secular, electoral state, defends rights-based individualism, and endorses scientific and material progress, often voiced as the American dream. William Gass has usefully reminded us that Stein never "argues" anything (23), but I suggest that this opera was a culminating intellectual statement for the author and carries an urgent thesis. It situates women's bodies, violence, and marriage at the center of the racist political economy of the liberal nation-state and makes a pointed comment on the United States and its place in the world that is as pertinent today, as campuses address movements such as Black Lives Matter, as it was in 1946.

Although I teach in a history department, and "the libretto can stand alone on its own terms" (Barlow 277), the pedagogy I advance here encourages instructors and students to play around with reenactments of Stein's text, in part because public and everyday rituals are the major concerns of the play and in part because such activities make for ready assignments that involve more than conventional papers. In Stein's handling, the quotidian (children's playground games and housework), the official (voting and marriage), and the epic (war and memorialization) all partake in nation making by embodying or enforcing racial boundary keeping. A pedagogy of playing around involves having students read aloud and experiment with performing lines in small-group exercises, presentations, and ministagings. Following Juliana Spahr, I recommend that we approach Stein's work with the general idea that reading is a form of "co-production" between author and audience (*Everybody's Autonomy* 6).

As well as suggesting reading-aloud exercises as a teaching tool, I advocate a focus on the libretto's rhetoric of black and white to highlight the opera's unmaking of racialization. Students conventionally understand the Civil War as being about slavery, but Stein directs our attention to World War II and its aftermath as another crisis of white (and male) supremacy by nesting the two wars and their aftermaths together in the opera. This nesting permits her to cast her opera with historical figures from the two eras, from politicians to stage stars, and allows her to unsettle a linear time line and notions of progress. The hub for these explorations is her grasp of racialization as a form of epistemic violence that entails or implies physical violence. Revolving around the character Susan B. Anthony are the opera's scenes of political debate, voting, celebrity activity, marital courtship, and memorialization.

Preparing to Teach the Libretto

The Mother of Us All is an opportunity to bring various historical narratives to life in the classroom, if not on the operatic stage. It illuminates topics like the politics of the suffrage movement, the intellectual legacies of the Civil War, and the post–World War II cultural moment. In an American studies vein, it can also open up the social function of memory and memorials. If the opera is scaled to an end-of-term project, students can be assigned scenes to investigate, rehearse, and stage, replete with imagined tussles between actors and directors and with reviews by critics. This kind of engagement both echoes and relies on the academic protocols of research, narration, causal explanation, and even peer review. Whether for only a week's assignment or for a culminating project, student groups can be productively tasked with critically important contextualization work: biography, event history, and official commemoration.

Biography. Details about the historical figures—like Anthony, Daniel Webster, John Adams—especially their relation to the politics of their day, their status (sex, race, class), and whether they knew one another or not, are well worth the trip to the library. *Wikipedia* entries can be a good starting point, since gauging characters' status in our own time speaks directly to Stein's themes of history, memory, and memorialization. The opera's allegorical characters—Jo the Loiterer, Angel More, Chris the Citizen—open up more room for engagement. Who can they possibly be? How shall they be played? Do their looks matter and, if so, why?

Event history. A second area of student research has to do with slavery, the 1860s constitutional amendments, the rise of Jim Crow, and the role of state and informal violence in each of them. The Civil War engendered a remaking of citizenship and the polity: the first Reconstruction brought three constitutional amendments (1865–69) that ended slavery (the thirteenth), established national citizenship as federal and male (the fourteenth), and removed race as a bar to voting (the fifteenth). The Nineteenth Amendment, ratified in 1920, established the right of women citizens to vote, though none of these changes to the Constitution adequately secured the rights of African Americans at the time or for decades afterward. Since Stein quotes the amendments directly, it is well worth bringing these texts into the classroom, along with excerpts from Rosalyn Terborg-Penn and Ellen Carol DuBois on the suffrage movement. Students should be fluent in answering questions like, "When did slavery end?" "Why could only male citizens vote?" "In what ways were slavery and racial segregation enforced through violence and the threat of violence?" "When did interracial marriage become legal?"

National Monuments. The culminating drama of the opera involves a statue, Adelaide Johnson's *Memorial to the Pioneers of the Woman's Suffrage Movement* (1921; see www.aoc.gov/capitol-hill/other-statues/portrait-monument). In an academic setting it can be easy to assume that most history lessons are between the covers of books, but memorials and historic sites are the primary way that people living in and visiting the United States connect with its history. The students' own stories can articulate in the classroom what are usually unstated rules of visits to memorials, stories that can be both didactic and packaged as fun. What is the personal etiquette or emotional choreography at memorials? What of the presence of guards; the paying of fees; the permanence, size, and location of memorials to the living or the dead; the protocols that concern touching, talking, photographs? Which figures or events are memorialized, and which are not?

An Interpretation for Today

Laws and rituals having to do with the body, from war to marriage, are literally how the nation-state constitutes and knows itself; and the politics of race and the state's claim on bodies are central to Stein's opera. Students can be asked to reflect on the ways that the state and other institutions sort and demarcate our bodies, as when we are asked to check a box on a government form, select a restroom, or produce a medical history. In the opera, the Anthony character resists such containment, and in Stein's hands she is a shape-shifting protagonist: saint, hero, virgin, mother, ghost. Her sage and oracular pronouncements, like, "I am but one all one, one and all one" (806), and the work's vague and vaguely pagan title alert us to Stein's mischievous treatment of the box mentality. Susan B. Anthony protested the coding of humanity by skin color, sex, and marital status—see, for instance, her petition "First Appeal of 1854," which is framed around "justice and perfect equality to every human being" (857). *The Mother of Us All* unpacks the binary structure of truth regimes, like the Law and the News, stereotypically written in black and white.

Scene by scene—depicting marriage courtship, a political rally, or daily housework—the body and its skin color are key elements for staging the opera's dramas. A turning point occurs in act 2, scene 2, when Susan B. confronts the politics of the Fifteenth Amendment and its prohibition on racial discrimination in voting rights. In the 1860s, Anthony opposed this amendment in favor of universal suffrage. Stein's Anthony mulls the false choice presented by lawmakers' color-coded rhetoric, language that defaulted to male and that she wanted to rewrite altogether: "I must choose colored or white white or colored I must choose" (795). As she delivers these lines, she is crowded by "all the men coming forward together" on stage, including the "V.I.P." characters of Senator Daniel Webster and President Andrew Johnson. Then Stein inflames the scene by having bystanders call out a playground chant, "Fight fight fight, between the nigger and the white. / And the women" (795). By conflating matters of state with a schoolyard scuffle, the scene dramatizes how anyone who even considers interfering with normative white male power becomes figuratively darkened ("nigger") and subject to punishment by a gang of elected officials. To stage the scene, one must ask, how is Susan B. being menaced? Will she be tarred and feathered? run out on a rail? lynched? raped? What is at stake in staging the violence of this scene? The tensions are ultimately not resolved but frozen, triggered by the word "Missouri" from the mouth of the character Virgil T.—Virgil Thomson, the opera's musical composer and a Missouri native.[1] The stage directions then state, "Everybody suddenly stricken dumb" (797). "Missouri" evokes the Missouri Compromise of 1820, which stayed but did not resolve the political conflict over slavery, as well as the Congressional gag order of 1836, which squelched debate on the issue.

The Daniel Webster character then introduces "a woman without a last name," Henrietta M., whom he describes as "rare delicious and troubling," while the other characters stand around staring (797). His presentation of Henrietta M. stops the scene-fight-show. Though several of Stein's well-known characters (Virgil T., etc.) sport initials in place of their surnames, Henrietta M. is a mysteriously generic figure, a kind of Anywoman. Does the absence of a surname tell us that she is free from a father's or husband's authority? Does the winner of the fight get the girl? What do students make of a social system that rewards male success in combat (or elsewhere) with access to female flesh? What of resistance or contestation? The ambiguity around Henrietta M. portends instability, for if women's bodies cease to be the marker and means for a husband's or father's or nation's dominion, they could then become subject to anyone or everyone's designs, a "troubling" prospect for some, a "delicious" prospect for others. In figuring out how to read or play Henrietta M., students have to take some stand on women's status in the past and present, in particular on the ways that female sexual and reproductive powers become implicated in warfare, nation building, and, of course, marriage—indeed, a refrain in the opera is "What is marriage." Assignments for students at this point include answering that question (marriage is a mechanism for reproducing racial difference, for establishing sexual hierarchy, for preserving male property rights, etc.) or writing a response to a staging that portrays Susan B.'s being trounced by a gang or mob, who are then distracted by Henrietta M.'s appearing on stage as a World War II pinup girl. What would Guerrilla Girls make of such a scene? What would Fox News make of it?

The frozen quality of the activist debate over the Reconstruction-era amendments is restaged in the very next scene, when an unnamed "negro man and negro woman" appear with Susan B. in a "snowy landscape" (799). They rehearse the dilemma of the Fourteenth Amendment, which makes being male a criterion for full citizenship rights. As was the case in the 1860s, the voice of the black woman in Stein's opera remains muffled; she uses her voice just once and then only in unison with the man's. How do the two black characters respond to Susan B.'s seeming indecisiveness? Susan B. whimpers, prays, or demands, "[M]ight, might, might there be what might be." The word "might" teeters between the auxiliary verb meaning "possibly" and the noun meaning "force." The black characters respond with, "All right Susan B. all right." Stein's word choice may indicate the white woman's power ("[you have] all [the] right") rather than the black characters' assent to it, placing pressure on interpretation and delivery. What do students make of this subtlety? What if the audience hears "all right" as a tactful withholding of approval rather than as acquiescence? The staging can suggest that the black characters are frozen out of the debate, "following" Susan B. into the cold white snow (798). They also lack the dignity of personal names; they remain racial types, without the allegorical qualities of the other dramatis personae. Do students think that Stein's libretto points up the sexual and racial economy of Anthony's time that unfairly reduced African American humanity to flat color type? Or does Stein simply repeat and thereby reinforce the political foibles and blind spots of the earlier era, including Anthony's limited responsiveness to black inclusion in the polity?

I suggest that by mixing and matching the dramas of nation building, citizenship, and marriage, Stein makes visible the normalized, unnamed coercions entailed by the rule of a nation-state. The libretto destabilizes the everyday ritualizations of the nation, calling into question what is worth voting for, fighting for, dying for, or marrying for and asks how we might engage authentically with social ritual rather than go dumbly through the motions or simply forget. The idea of a name, enunciated by the commonplace refrain in the libretto, "What's in a name," is a philosophical hub around which the historical events and figures all turn in the opera.

The final act of *The Mother of Us All* focuses on the role of art, statuary, and commemoration, allowing Stein to unpack whiteness in the opera's falling action. The last scene is set in Congressional Hall, in front of Adelaide Johnson's statue of the suffrage leaders Anthony, Elizabeth Cady Stanton, and Lucretia Mott. From behind the statue, a ghostly Susan B. addresses a mishmash of characters. They are unsure what to make of the statue and gather around sighing, bowing, frowning, curtseying. Students can be asked to view a photo of the statue and ponder whether it is a work of art, a gravestone, or an altarpiece. Henry B. asks, "Does it really mean that women are as white and cold as marble does it really mean that?" This question points to the old antisuffrage criticism that political participation would harden women, canceling out their sympathetic, comforting nature or role. It also alludes to the exclusionary whiteness that attended expanded citizenship rights in the United States: neither the Reconstruction amendments of the 1860s nor the so-called Anthony Amendment of 1920 effectively enfranchised African American citizens. As the characters puzzle over the statue, Andrew Johnson "shuffles in" and offers a despairing view: "I have no hope in black or white . . . no hope" (815). Since he supported neither "Negro suffrage" nor "woman suffrage," Stein here underscores and ironizes the bankruptcy of color-coding human bodies and individual rights, with a swipe at black letter law and the newsprint along the way.

The statue's color also has an obscuring, blinding effect. "I cannot see what is so white," states Constance Fletcher, who could represent someone Stein had written a portrait of in 1912, the writer Julia Constance Fletcher. The character Fletcher's "I am almost blind" (816) is ambiguous, pointing to a literal loss of eyesight (actual, in Julia's case) or to figurative deprivation and concealment. The statue occludes as much as it illuminates, forgets as much as it memorializes. It features three busts without feet, legs, hips, or hands; the women are rendered immobile, half people, and voting is symbolized as only half a victory for (some) women. Indeed, the statue went directly into storage in the capitol crypt when gifted by Johnson in 1921. No black activists are represented, an exclusion remarked on by the National Political Congress of Black Women in 1997, when the statue was installed in the rotunda, and again by First Lady Michelle Obama, when a bust of Sojourner Truth was unveiled in Independence Hall in 2009. In the opera, Susan B. speaks from behind the statue—and from the grave—and pronounces a sobering, haunting challenge to the characters on stage (and to us), who seem lost and in need of a script: "Do you know because I tell you so, or do you know do you know" (819).

As in many of her works, Stein's artistry casts into relief the politics of knowledge. Unlike the provocative terseness of her early plays, *The Mother of Us All* features an ample libretto, and the opera has been successfully staged many times (see samples on *YouTube*). Stuffed with facts and whimsy, it can stir a hunger for the past in the present. It thus offers a chance to know such hungers in ourselves more deeply by exploring the rituals—from voting to marrying to fighting to winning fame—that purport to satisfy them. The character Susan B. voices a hunger for emplotment in a grand narrative, and she struggles with the telescoping of her life's work into mere winning and the flattening of her memory into shallow celebrity.

An artist highly skeptical of fictions of closure and fixed meanings for words, Gertrude Stein ended her career with a work that dramatizes the many ways that sex and race imbricate with the work of the nation. In *The Mother of Us All* she keenly dissects the sexual politics of marriage and citizenship as constitutive of race and racial hierarchy, enforced by state violence. Before World War II, she played with race more flippantly than either serious white supremacists or committed antiwhite supremacists would have tolerated. But her last great work portrayed whiteness as a washout and racism as the clay feet of the nation.

NOTE

[1] For more on the collaboration between Stein and Thomson, see S. Watson; see also Holbrook and Dilworth.

A Rose Is a Rose Is a . . . Thesis Statement: Gertrude Stein in the First-Year Writing Classroom

Erica J. Kaufman

"Civilization begins with a rose. A rose is a rose is a rose is a rose. It continues with blooming and it fastens clearly upon excellent examples" (Stein, "As Fine" 262). Gertrude Stein's "rose" has much in common with the composing process. Her work, despite its initial strangeness to students and teachers, reverberates with many concerns of compositionists and beginning writers. In fact, her work comes up often in composition studies, specifically in the writing process movement,[1] which emphasizes the importance of learning through the act of writing. As Janet Emig points out, "according to Stein, writing is an act of discovery emanating 'out of the pen and out of you'" (*Web* 16; Stein, "Conversation" 188).

I use Stein's work in my composition courses when I feel that students are struggling with their academic prose. When I ask them what they think their essays are evaluated on, the reply always includes such things as organization, grammar and mechanics, and transition statements. Engaging with Stein's work helps them get outside this common rubric. It can provoke a transformation: they learn that the essay-writing process can be an act of discovery, that one can hear grammar and proofread by ear, and that the best writing is surprising (in form and content). One reason that using Stein can spark such changes is that her vocabulary is familiar: "If I told him would he like it. Would he like it if I told him," for instance ("If I Told Him" 464). Recognizable words makes the decoding of meaning a less daunting task for beginning writers and English-language learners who experience academic writing as a form of translation.

In this essay I give portraits of two class sessions in a writing-based and student-centered composition course at a large public, urban university. I include my own teaching notes as well as excerpts from student work to demonstrate the kind of writing with and through Stein that the course involves, as well as to give examples of the changes clearly visible in student writing when a student becomes willing to take risks.

"If I Told Him A Completed Portrait of Picasso": Class 1

It is October, and my students are struggling to craft essays that show instead of tell, essays that present detailed arguments with the requisite evidence (quotes and examples). They are working on their second essay of the semester, an assignment to imagine their ideal learning environment and then build it through words. I am surprised to read first drafts that assert little more than "my ideal learning environment is outside because nature helps me think." We spent weeks looking at essays that immerse readers in how and why arguments are constructed, supported, and developed.[2] I decide to begin the next class by asking students to write about the word *portrait*, and then we explore some of the common definitions of *portraiture* (visual, realistic, the focus on a person from the shoulders up). My hope is that examining our assumptions about a single word will move us toward a conversation on how to write a thesis-driven essay supported by evidence and analysis. We think about our definitions and compare them with those in the dictionary.

In "Portraits and Repetition" (1935), Stein describes her turn to portraiture as "creating in my writing by simply looking" (191).[3] For students, this statement underscores the value of detail and description in formal writing and speaks to the lack of engagement I found in their draft papers. Stein's idea of creating through "simply looking" asks that we trust what we see and hear and that those sights and sounds can be translated into writing; this approach forces students to avoid relying on research and the ideas of others. I want them to envision a way of writing that centers on their ability to "create something out of something without adding anything" ("Portraits" 180). Instead of summarizing the kinds of learning environments that others have described, I want my students to find value in the kinds of classrooms they desire and imagine. Linguistic portraiture pushes them to move beyond restating information, to really look in or with words, to trust in their own particular vocabulary and perspective.

I distribute Stein's "If I Told Him A Completed Portrait of Picasso" (1923), saying nothing to introduce it. We read the poem out loud together several times: one student reads the entire poem from start to finish; we alternate reading one line each; we listen to a recording of Stein reading the poem (available on *PennSound*); we read the poem backward and then again straight through.

> If I told him would he like it. Would he like it if I told him.
>
> Would he like it would Napoleon would Napoleon would would he like it.
>
> If Napoleon if I told him if I told him if Napoleon. Would he like it if I told him if I told him if Napoleon. Would he like it if Napoleon if Napoleon if I told him. If I told him if Napoleon if Napoleon if I told him. If I told him would he like it would he like it if I told him. (464)

We pause between each reading to jot down our first thoughts, anything we notice about the poem, including how it sounds and what the language is doing. We also pause to share some of these first thoughts, noting a trajectory of response from resistance and confusion to observations about the music or drone of the piece to some level of acceptance.

We then reevaluate our sense of a portrait. Who is Picasso? What do we need to make a portrait out of words? What is the goal of a portrait for Stein? for us? How does a "completed portrait" differ from a portrait? Stein's diction and use of repetition, the students note, create a sense of Picasso even if we do not see him. Can we write a portrait of the learning process, of what it means to write to discover? Stein: "Do you do you do you really understand" ("Portraits" 204).

"If I Told Him A Completed Portrait of Picasso": Class 2

In preparation for this next class period, students complete a response paper: no more than two pages about what Stein has taught them. It should be specific to their reading of "If I Told Him" but also represent their reading process, which might not involve Picasso at all. They should consider what Stein's lines, sentences, or phrases accomplish and why but also feel free to include whatever associations they have to Stein's piece. We begin class by hearing excerpts from these reader-response portraits and then discuss them. Here is one:

> I'm not sure what happened, but by the end of the day I honestly started thinking that I had done something wrong. It was almost as if I was making this kid's skin crawl. It was so painful just and awkward, I didn't think it was a good idea to ever hang out again. And then I think I started to go back and rethink EVERYTHING. "*Was there was there was there what was there was there what was there was there there was there.*" Was I mistaken from the beginning? Had I just thought so much that I made something that wasn't there, there? I mean, if you repeat something enough, you start to believe it. . . . This brings me to the connection between that and the poem for this response paper, "If I Told Him" by Gertrude Stein. See all the time that I was crushing on this guy, despite how often we spoke, in my head I thought carefully about everything I said.

> And I'd think about it more than once before saying it. This was a lot easier when we spoke online because I had time to think before I typed. So I'd just edit and reedit all the little words that I wanted to string together to hopefully make up the perfect sentence. Often it would sound like, which is also my favorite part of the poem, "If I told him would he like it would he like it if I told him. / Now. / Not now. / And now. / Now."[4]

Although this response has a confessional urgency to it, it asserts a perspective on or argument about Stein's poem, questioning the nature of time and interpersonal relationships and using direct quotes in an innovative manner. This paper is not written in a style typical of academic writing,[5] but the student definitely fulfills many of the learning goals privileged in a composition course: she identifies key ideas in Stein's text, recognizes the stylistic choices Stein makes, and analyzes these by way of crafting an imaginative argument—all while honoring, in a visceral way, Stein's repetition echoing in her own head. As Joan Retallack has said, "For Stein, to compose authentically out of one's contemporary situation is to live in the new time that one is taking part in making through the act of composition" (*Poethical Wager* 170). The student, composing through Stein's work, experienced "taking part in making" through the act of engaging the poem in writing. Stein's repetition and attention to daily speech were sparks to this student's composing process.[6]

Through the rest of the semester, this student's process writing[7] continued to demonstrate the influence that working with "If I Told Him" had on her writing in English. At some point I asked, "What gift did reading Stein give you?" The student observed, "It was like I was reading the way my voice sounds in my head. Then I understood how to fix the words on the paper." The sound of Stein's words empowered her to change her approach to essay writing: she stopped using dense, thesaurus-driven sentences in favor of clear analysis, and, when revising, she began to listen to her own ear instead of searching for the right grammatical rule.

What is it about "If I Told Him" and Stein's work generally that pushes students to enter into conversations not only with the writer but also with themselves and their peers? Why is it that Stein's compositions, which, as Sharon Kirsch notes, "rarely provid[e] pre-packaged meanings for readers to extract" ("How to Read" 109), prompt students to take risks in their own writing? I teach "If I Told Him" because it helps them become less resistant to thinking of essay writing as a chance to express their ideas in a way that others can enter into dialogue with.

In class 2, after hearing bits of these response papers and after reviewing some process writings, I ask students to work in pairs.[8] They have fifteen minutes to engage with Stein's poem as a real thing made of words, taking some of "If I Told Him" and transforming it into a grammatically correct paragraph. They cannot change or add words.[9] After rearranging them and adding punctuation as needed, each student does a short piece of process writing in response to the prompt "How did you approach this task?" The pairs then read their corrections out loud and share their individual process writing.

> If Napoleon if I told him if I told him if Napoleon. Would he like it if I told him if I told him if Napoleon. Would he like it if Napoleon if Napoleon if I told him. If I told him if Napoleon if Napoleon if I told him. If I told him would he like it would he like it if I told him.
>
> *Sample Correction:* "I told him he would like it. He liked it and I told him, Napoleon would like it. Now kings would like it for this exact resemblance."
>
> *Sample Process Response:* "We began by reading the beginning of the poem again. We underlined the parts of the poem that we knew did not make grammatical sense. We talked about what a sentence is supposed to do and then tried to make the words do it. Some of Stein's ideas seemed backwards, so we fixed them. We did not know what to do with Napoleon, so we decided to just include him as a neutral character."

Working with words as materials, the students played with syntax, repetition, and pattern, and they learned that even simple, basic words can be highly expressive. Their responses show that they discovered that they knew what makes and how to make grammatical sense. Because in a first-year writing course, grammar and mechanics tend to be what students worry most about, this discovery was reassuring to them. Stein offers a definition of writing that differs from what students typically encounter. The process I have described, one guided by working with Stein, helps them feel a new kind of pride in their writing and to move on to more complex academic tasks.

A central lesson that Stein can teach students is that everyone has "words that had to be written inside me" (*Everybody's Autobiography* 66) and that these words are valid even when learning to speak the language of the university.[10] Students seldom enter a freshman composition course as self-proclaimed writers, although they have likely written hundreds of pages of material (whether in classes, on their phones, or online). They know the sentiment that Stein often expressed: a divide exists between speech and composition, between talking and writing. In the classroom, writing has been valued over talking. Yet Peter Elbow, for one, advocates celebrating the repetitive and familiar "home voice" and admits, "[I]f the words that come naturally to our mouth or pen are labeled wrong, we feel ourselves to have a problem" (*Everyone* 324). In *Everybody's Autonomy*, Juliana Spahr too, in discussing readings of Stein that first-year writing students devise, has noted, "Stein's work serves as an empathic relation for second-language speakers. They see a reflection and validation of their sense that English is unusually structured" (45). In other words, Stein gives students permission to see their own language as full of potential to "[continue] with blooming." In the context of this specific course, she helped my students imagine their own ideal learning environments using language that was vivid and convincing.

NOTES

[1] Examples of this movement's philosophy are found in Emig, *Web* (see "The Relation of Thought and Language" and "The Uses of the Unconscious"); Elbow, *Writing* (see "Writing and Voice"); and Berthoff.

[2] Examples are Nicholas Carr's "Is Google Making Us Stupid?," Ralph Waldo Emerson's "Self-Reliance," and a variety of op-ed columns relating to economics by Paul Krugman.

[3] I use quotes from "Portraits and Repetition" in class but usually do not assign the essay.

[4] This student is an eighteen-year-old female college freshman. She is the first person in her family to attend college and wants to pursue a career in marketing. She is a non-native English speaker, originally from China, who has had difficulty with sentence structure and syntax all semester. She was vocal in class discussions but stymied by what she thought was correct formal English, an English that was actually jargon-laden and lacking the unique perspective I heard from her in class.

[5] I do not grade response papers, allowing students to write informally and without the fear of being wrong.

[6] Sondra Perl notes that repetition sets up "a particular kind of composing rhythm, one that was cumulative in nature and that set ideas in motion by its very repetitiveness" (324).

[7] Alfred Guy defines *process writing* as "a practice of using writing to step back from an activity to assess how that activity is going" (53). I assign process writing on a regular basis in class, both during an activity and after it has been completed.

[8] By this point in the semester, we have established a learning community in which reading aloud is a regular part of our in-class activities. If something feels too personal, however, a student is never forced to read it.

[9] This constraint is central to the activity. It would be easier for students if they were allowed to add words to turn fragments into sentences. This way, they must think more carefully about each individual word that Stein uses and what it does.

[10] David Bartholomae's seminal essay "Inventing the University" begins, "Every time a student sits down to write for us, he has to invent the university for the occasion" (60). It's also interesting to note that "Living with Style," the first essay in Bartholomae's *Writing on the Margins* collection, begins with a list of quotations from his "reading and teaching . . . moments of striking eloquence" (1). Two out of these six quotations are from Gertrude Stein ("Poetry and Grammar" and *How To Write*).

"All Alone with English": Teaching Stein in a Multilingual Context

Jane Malcolm

For the past five years, I have been teaching Gertrude Stein to nonnative English speakers at the Université de Montréal in Quebec, where most of the students are culturally francophone and functionally bi- or trilingual. I have come to consider this context—where English is not a language of mastery—an ideal pedagogical environment for reading and thinking about Stein and recontextualizing (even politicizing) her relation to the English language.[1]

Montreal is one of the few places in the world where francophone, anglophone, and allophone cultures truly intermix. Its language demographics are the direct outcome of the Quiet Revolution, when in the 1960s political, economic, and social institutions previously controlled by an English-speaking minority were reclaimed by a French-speaking majority. Since 1977, French has been the official language in the province, and, though French-English bilingualism thrives, English literary traditions do not constitute a de facto master canon for Quebecers. English literature is thus a minor literature, particularly at the francophone Université de Montréal, where we talk about English in contact with other languages and cultures and where students might be reading Stein in my course on modernism while also learning English grammar in another—which is to say that many of my students are learning to read English texts grammatically, closely, and analytically by reading Stein. Though Steinian language may be doubly foreign (English and experimental) to them, my experience suggests that it can be less alienating than for native English speakers. In fact, I have found that students who are new to and ambivalent about close reading practices often are open to experimentation with English and consider Steinian language *abordable* ("accessible") or, as the origins of the word suggest, welcomed onboard. In this essay, I propose a pedagogical approach to Stein's writing that emphasizes the students' experience of experimental modernism in contact and presents Stein as a writer whose work values a nonnative reader and invites nonfluency as a reading strategy, in the Quebec context and elsewhere. In this way we might understand what F. W. Dupee once called "Steinese"—a "[g]nomic, repetitive, illogical, sparsely punctuated" dialect (ix)—as a foreign language that resists even (or especially) its anglophone readers, so that nonfluency becomes not something for nonnative speakers to overcome but something for all readers of Stein to embrace.

Stein characterized her relation to English in terms of foreignness and defamiliarization, and I have found it pedagogically useful, in the multilingual classroom, to frame her work in these terms. I emphasize to students from the outset that her writing requires the reader to reconceptualize grammar and fixed meaning and that these exigencies relate to (and perhaps derive from)

Stein's expatriate experience as an Anglophone in France, as outlined in *The Autobiography of Alice B. Toklas* (1933):

> One of the things that I have liked all these years is to be surrounded by people who know no english. It has left me more intensely alone with my eyes and my english. I do not know if it would have been possible to have english be so all in all to me otherwise. And they none of them could read a word I wrote, most of them did not even know that I did write. No, I like living with so very many people and being all alone with english and myself. (70)

Her living "all alone with english" allowed the language to become "my english," a private, evolving Steinian idiom whose idiosyncrasies emerged from a background of nonnative interlocutors. Being at a distance from spoken English and "intensely alone with my eyes" brought her close to English especially in its written form. Being "alone with english" can produce both excitement and anxiety in my francophone students, but the process of Stein's defamiliarization resonates with them, and their interactions with the English language are similarly plastic. Stein expresses her desire to be "surrounded by people who know no english" and describes being misperceived as an "imperfect" or nonnative speaker (of both French and English) herself (68).[2] As Juliana Spahr has suggested, Stein "aligns her work with . . . non-standard Englishes" (*Everybody's Autonomy* 22), and her sense of her foreignness in a French environment makes her immediately relatable to my francophone students in an English one.

To add nuance to what it means to relate to a disruptive Steinian grammar, I contextualize Stein in her historical moment, noting that modernism on the whole welcomed experiments and transgressions but that her writing was seen by many of her contemporaries as having gone too far. I often begin by assigning the "Objects" section from *Tender Buttons* (1914) so that students arrive feeling curious, baffled, or even aggravated by Stein's language. Together we read closely "A Carafe, That Is a Blind Glass," paying attention to its disorienting grammar as we attempt to diagram the sentences:

> A kind in glass and a cousin, a spectacle and nothing strange a single hurt color and an arrangement in a system to pointing. All this and not ordinary, not unordered in not resembling. The difference is spreading. (11)

Students are often confused or shocked by Stein's incorrect or farcical grammar—missing conjugations, series of dependent clauses, lack of punctuation. At the same time, they describe feeling a sense of relief: the mistakes in Stein's work give them permission to make their own and to see in them an empowerment that derives from open experimentation with the language.

We contrast Stein with T. S. Eliot, her jazz-like rhythms a counterpoint to his mythic allusions. In his review of her *Composition as Explanation* pamphlet

(1926), Eliot reveals that he finds Stein's English, its unsophisticated diction and disordered syntax, "barbaric," arguing that its "peculiar hypnotic power" is "not good for one's mind" ("Charleston").[3] In this review at least, he rejects the open text, which, as Lyn Hejinian explains, "invites participation, rejects the authority of the writer over the reader and thus, by analogy, the authority implicit in other (social, economic, cultural) hierarchies" (43). We discuss how Stein's text is open: it disrupts the connection between sign and signifier, evacuates sense from the sentence, and values repetition and sound play. Attempting to deconstruct even a single Steinian sentence with my students provokes various responses about the role of grammar in the vexed relation among author, text, and reader. I suggest to students that, though the inclination to read Stein as nonsense is understandable (especially when English texts can seem inherently nonsensical to nonnative speakers), we would do better to interact with her texts as indeterminate language fields, in which sense is given or created by readers. Sense cannot be mined; and it does not emerge sui generis. The empowered reader interacting with the words on the page becomes the source of meaning or affect in the moment of reading, and Stein's language can be understood as an "arrangement in a system to pointing" (1), that is, as a system of open, radiating signifiers.

To better understand how my students apprehend Stein's English, I have asked them to answer this question informally in their writing journals: What effect does your relation to English have on how you appreciate or understand Stein? I see uncanny similarities in how they describe the process of knowing (or coming to know) in the moment of reading. One writes, "I hate not understanding. I love not understanding." Another explains, "[W]ords are words, and in her case, they simply happen to be English ones and I just happen to get them." I am interested in how Stein's words are got, especially by the nonnative or nonspecialist reader, and how "not understanding" can incite or enhance a dynamic critical reading practice. As Spahr has suggested, second-language speakers see in Stein "a reflection and validation of their sense that English is unusually structured, almost as if her works had been written for the cross-lingual skills of second-language speakers" (*Everybody's Autonomy* 43). The tone of acceptance in my students' responses likewise lends support for Sarah Wilson's perspective on Stein, that she helped make "the melting pot new . . . just as the melting pot helped to make [Stein's] work new" (12). If we understand the multilingual classroom as a version of Wilson's melting pot, our collective and individual understandings and misunderstandings of a Steinian modernism thus reflect Stein's own sense of American literature as a series of what Priscilla Wald terms "group stories" and "cultural plots" that enfold multiple subjectivities (294).

When time allows, I examine more thoroughly the argument, articulated by Spahr (see especially the first chapter in her *Everybody's Autonomy*), that the defamiliarizing reading practice required for Steinese emboldens rather than alienates its audience and should be taught in ways that make other kinds of experimental writing accessible rather than rebarbative to all nonspecialist readers. I discuss with students the phenomenon of Stein's celebrity status in the 1930s. The massive success of the *Autobiography* invited a wide American readership to try her Steinese,[4] and her post-*Autobiography* lectures and interviews emphasize its democratic attributes, articulating an everybody's modernism and everybody's English. In a 1935 interview with John Hyde Preston, for instance, Stein insists that her writing is neither rarefied nor exclusionary, that it simply purports to "become aware of the ways things can be felt and known in words." As a popular literary figure she demystified modernist language for the everyday reader and broadened the reach of experimentalism, asserting to Preston that "perhaps if I feel them [words] and know them myself in the new ways it is enough, and I know fully enough there will be a note of sureness and confidence that will make others know too" ("Conversation" 194).

To illustrate further the extent of her celebrity and to demonstrate how the experience of reading Stein is to encounter a destabilizing language, I often screen a scene from the 1935 film *Top Hat*, a screwball comedy starring Fred Astaire and Ginger Rogers. The scene depicts Dale Tremont, Rogers's androgynously named model turned socialite, arguing with Alberto Beddini, a dandified Italian fashion designer, when a telegram is abruptly delivered and read aloud by Beddini in an exaggerated Italian accent:

> ALBERTO: COME AHEAD STOP STOP BEING A SAP STOP YOU CAN EVEN BRING ALBERTO STOP MY HUSBAND IS STOPPING AT YOUR HOTEL STOP WHEN DO YOU START STOP . . . I cannot understand who wrote this!
>
> DALE: Sounds like Gertrude Stein.

This joke inevitably draws a laugh from my students, who both identify with the confused Beddini and understand Dale's flippant retort: the hyperliteral reading of a series of unpunctuated, repetitive words in an unfamiliar (telegraphic) code does indeed sound like Stein. We discuss why the words in themselves are not Steinian but become so when performed by a nonnative English speaker, which is to say that reader and text (telegram) interact to produce Steinese. Though Beddini's reading may be bad or exaggerated, any performance of Steinian language that relies on syntactic and grammatical contortions can spur classroom discussions of how to understand her process of linguistic defamiliarization, which is parodied and embodied by Beddini in the scene.

As a complement to the telegram scene, I ask students to comment on the following passage from *How to Write* (1931), in which Stein explains how and why her sentences produce meaning without grammatical cues, without being "sewn":

> What is the difference between a sentence and a sewn. Pictures are important if they have been followed. Thank you for following. What is the difference between a sentence and a picture. A sentence sends it

> about most. Most is more than most. Most and best. A sentence is very mainly leave known.
>
> How can a sentence have their hope. This makes it turn around. Leave a sentence in mainly. (119)

What does it mean *to follow*? Does the parody of Stein (in *Top Hat*) work because we follow by not following? What is a Steinian sentence, and how is it sewn and unsewn? Stein's language convinces its audience (or perhaps confirms for them) that her sentences are a decipherable code only for readers who can defamiliarize themselves or readers who, like nonnative speakers, are already distanced from English grammatical expectations and must sew together words in a made-by-being-made fashion. In the 1935 interview, Preston faithfully describes the effect of following Stein's sentences: "I think that in some of her prose pieces you get that [recognition]—you do not have to follow; you suddenly know. (Of course you have followed, but it has not been by following that you have it)" ("Conversation" 188). Listening to the Steinian telegram or reading *How To Write* asks that we follow on the tail of recognition, immersed in Stein's attainable modernist dialect, in which "START STOP" and "Most and best" are not mere grammatical or graphical juxtapositions but also performative statements in a continually new and delectable idiom.

As Dorothea Lasky suggests, part of our responsibility as teachers of poetry is to offer a space in which every student can "express new ideas . . . in a novel language he or she has just created." Stein's disruptive use of English allows students to use English experimentally, both in and out of the classroom. Teaching Stein in a multilingual context gives new meaning to the ways in which her untethered, nonreferential language empowers the reader and promotes a more self-aware critical reading process. She claimed to have been "all alone with english," and in that space she radically deconstructed its conventions. I have argued here that an effective Steinian pedagogy involves approaching Steinese as a foreign language and English as a minor one. In so doing, we can explore how each of us apprehends language and constructs and reconstructs poetic meaning in idiosyncratic ways. My own experience reading and teaching Stein in contact with French speakers has transformed my approach to the Steinian edifice: when my students and I keep ourselves at a speculative distance from English, her language manipulations can be both transgressive and *abordable*. My francophone students, instead of feeling destabilized by Stein's English (as native English-speaking students often do), read her without the burden of insisting that it make sense. Teaching Stein in Quebec has changed how I think about fluency, about the politics of language ownership, and about the democratization of English. For students reading Stein for the first (or tenth) time, the critical practice should be one that encourages disorientation and discomfort and loves not understanding.

NOTES

[1] Much has been written about the politics of English-language writing in Quebec. See, for example, Moyes.

[2] See Stein's story in the *Autobiography* about a visit from a representative of Grafton Press—the publisher of *Three Lives* in 1909—who had misgivings about her fluency: "One day some one knocked at the door and a very nice very american young man asked if he might speak to Miss Stein. . . . You see, he said slightly hesitant, the director of the Grafton Press is under the impression that perhaps your knowledge of english. But I am an american said Gertrude Stein indignantly" (68).

[3] Her work, he wrote, has "a kinship with the saxophone," and "[i]f this is of the future, then the future is, as it very likely is, of the barbarians" (595). Stein's "barbarism" was then reclaimed as a positive designation by Laura Riding (51) in *Contemporaries and Snobs* (1928). Besides the "Composition as Explanation" lecture, Stein's *Composition* pamphlet included three portraits, "Preciosilla," "Sitwell Edith Sitwell," "Jean Cocteau," and a play, *A Saint in Seven*.

[4] John Malcolm Brinnin describes Stein's notoriety during her 1934–35 lecture tour as a "celebrity of such proportions that her eminence on the American scene was for a time shared only by gangsters, baseball players, and movie stars" (337).

"The Inside on the Outside": Teaching Stein's *Lectures in America*

Stacy Carson Hubbard

In 1933, when *The Autobiography of Alice B. Toklas* became a best seller in the United States, Stein, whose readership during the previous thirty years had never been large, suddenly became a literary celebrity of huge proportions. Shortly thereafter, she was persuaded by her publisher, agent, and friends to embark on an American lecture tour. However, as she took on this newly public role, she began to worry about the intrusion into her writing of the presence of an audience with specific expectations of a literary lion. She wrote, "It is all a question of the outside being outside and the inside being inside. As long as the outside does not put a value on you it remains outside but when it does put a value on you then it gets inside or rather if the outside puts a value on you then all your inside gets to be outside" (*Everybody's Autobiography* 48). The challenges of lecturing for Stein were to remain true to her writing self while simultaneously winning over an audience through the demonstration of her principles, to stay in the present moment of her unfolding utterance even as she listened to both herself and her audience, and to shed light on her earlier creations without simply repeating their ideas—that is, without explaining them, which she believed would be an uncreative use of language (*Lectures* 179–80).

For the lectures she would deliver at colleges across the United States in 1934–35, collected in *Lectures in America* (1935), Stein developed a style of folksy, commonsensical address with a charm and immediacy belonging to the tradition of American humorous performance and public oratory. Nonetheless, the lectures take up serious theoretical problems concerning identity, language, and audience, problems that would continue to preoccupy her. *Lectures in America* is often introduced into undergraduate classes as a guide to her better-known creative works—*Three Lives*, *Tender Buttons*, and the early portraits. Yet despite her frequent reassurances that "oh yes you all do understand" (177), her lectures enact the impossibility of our escaping from composition into explanation in order to save ourselves from the frustrations of reading. Though students may long for some clarity when first encountering Stein's more difficult texts, we should encourage them to trust Stein when she says that we already understand more than we know when we allow ourselves to enjoy her writing (Stein, "Gertrude Stein" 89). By approaching the lectures not as explanatory supplements but as creative enactments of the relations among identity, writing, and audience, we can lead students to a deeper understanding of the lectures as innovative contributions to her literary oeuvre. They are one part of a complex of discursive practices that work to create the author Gertrude Stein as a figure more continuous than discontinuous with American traditions of literary performance and invention.

The approach to teaching Stein's lectures that I describe in this essay belongs to a two-week unit in an upper-level undergraduate course, American Literature in the Public Sphere, that includes readings from Ralph Waldo Emerson ("Self-Reliance" and "The American Scholar"), Walt Whitman ("Song of Myself"), Harriet Beecher Stowe (*Uncle Tom's Cabin*), Sojourner Truth (newspaper accounts of speeches), Louisa May Alcott (*Little Women*), Mark Twain (stories and speeches), Henry James ("The Question of Our Speech" and selections from *The American Scene*), Theodore Dreiser (*Sister Carrie*), and poems by Stein, Robert Frost, Edna St. Vincent Millay, Langston Hughes, and Vachel Lindsay. Class lectures provide background about American oratory, the abolitionist and lyceum movements, minstrel shows, and the rise of celebrity culture. This unit, which begins with selections from *Tender Buttons* and *The Autobiography of Alice B. Toklas*, focuses on three of the six lectures: "What Is English Literature," "Portraits and Repetition," and "Poetry and Grammar." These pieces introduce students to many of Stein's major concerns, such as repetition, non-resemblance, the difference between English and American literature, the importance of grammar and punctuation to the creation of lively language, and the uses and subversions of genre. I invite students to consider the lectures in two ways: first, by closely analyzing tone, diction, repetition, direct address, and deixis in order to understand how Stein conveys complex ideas in a common-sensical and intimate style; second, by placing the lectures in their historical and cultural context and considering them as events in the history of the American public sphere (a valuable resource in this regard is William Rice's appendix to *The Letters of Gertrude Stein and Thornton Wilder* [Burns and Dydo], which provides an overview and chronology of the lecture tour). Students are thus enabled to recognize the structural and rhetorical complexity of Stein's compositions and their imbrications of obscurity with common sense, to investigate the history of literary performance and the relation of her lecture tour to earlier author tours and styles of American oratory, and to explore ways of researching and analyzing reception as an aspect of literary history.

On first encountering Stein's lectures, students may complain that her sparsely punctuated and repetitive prose is ungrammatical or disorganized. They may get tangled up in her long sentences or feel uncertain about how seriously to take her seemingly casual remarks or her generalizations. It can be helpful to address these difficulties through discussion of "Poetry and Grammar," where Stein argues for a writing unfettered from arbitrary restraints, such as commas and question marks, a writing that lives fully through the force of its verbs and the potential of its adverbs, prepositions, and pronouns to be "mistaken"—that is, to embody "the whole of the active life of writing" (220). Here she invites readers to experience language as "varied and alive" and to take an active role in listening or reading (213). To get students to actively engage with the rhetorical and compositional strategies of her lectures, I ask them to inventory her techniques: her repeated phrases, words, questions, and sentence structures; her manner of addressing her audience; her use of aphorisms; her digressions;

and her manipulations of tone. Then I ask them to make a list of the most distinctive elements of her style and, using these elements, to compose and perform their own short talks on subjects of their choosing. This exercise yields real rewards in terms of their ability to recognize the constructedness of Stein's compositions as well as the rhythmic and idiomatic qualities of her prose. Moreover, students come to recognize the frequency with which Stein claims to be asserting mere common sense ("There you completely see what I mean" [*Lectures* 45]), uses words such as "this" and "here" to focus listeners on the "continuous present" of her language as it unfolds ("I said in the beginning of saying this thing" [170]), and involves her listeners through direct address ("How do you like what you have. This is a question that anybody can ask anybody. Ask it" [171]). These techniques—common sense, the continuous present of language, and the active involvement of the audience—are key to understanding how she used her lectures to involve popular audiences in her avant-garde project.

Moving from textual analysis to an examination of historical precedents, I ask students to locate possible sources of Stein's style in texts by authors we have read previously, comparing her repetitiveness with Emerson's recursiveness in "Self-Reliance," for example, or her direct address to her audience and her self-promoting claims with Whitman's alternately intimate and bombastic modes of address in "Song of Myself," or her aphorisms and digressions with those in Twain's talks (such as his "Advice to Youth"). Idiosyncratic as her lectures may be, they are closely tied to the works of these earlier authors, each of whom was, in his own way, working to overturn formal precedents and established literary modes. Seeing these connections can help students place Stein in a long tradition of democratic performance, vernacular language, and claims to American originality. In addition to her style, her ideas about American language engage with those of earlier author-lecturers: Emerson's examination of the relation of names to things in "Nature" resonates intriguingly with her account of nouns in "Poetry and Grammar," while his claims for the renovation of language in "The American Scholar" anticipate her account of the fruitful disconnectedness of American language in "What Is English Literature." James, in his final American lecture, "The Question of Our Speech," expressed his exasperation with the corruption of British English by American speakers (25–32), whereas in *Wars I Have Seen*, Stein defends the American practice of "shoving the [English] language around" (259) to make it appropriate to a new continent and a new age. Unlike James's lectures, which often went over the heads of his listeners (see O'Donnell), Stein's lectures embody the principles of American democracy in their very language—their simplified vocabulary, homely metaphors, and conversational repetitions.[1]

"Song of Myself," a very oratorical poem, offers some intriguing comparisons with Stein's lectures. I direct students to its emphasis on common knowledge ("Only what proves itself to every man and woman is so" [54]); intimate address ("This hour I tell things in confidence, / I might not tell everybody but I will tell you" [43]); receptivity ("to me the converging objects of the universe perpetually flow" [43]); rhythmic repetition ("This is the grass that grows wherever the land is and the water is / This is the common air that bathes the globe" [41]); hubris ("I know I am august" [44]); and presentism ("there was never any more inception than there is now" [26]). With these elements of Whitman's rhetoric in mind, students examine the following passage from "Portraits and Repetition":

> I say I never repeat while I am writing because while I am writing I am most completely, and that is if you like being a genius, I am most entirely and completely listening and talking, the two in one and the one in two and that is having completely its own time and it has in it no element of remembering. Therefore there is in it no element of confusion, therefore there is in it no element of repetition. Do you do you do you really understand.
>
> And does it make any difference to you if you do understand. It makes an awful lot of difference to me. (180–81)

I encourage students to notice that Stein, like Whitman, locates herself firmly in the unfolding present of writing ("having completely its own time") and reminds us that even now she is composing ("I say"). The incantatory repetitions of her prose, which may remind students of Whitman's, are not, according to her, repetitions but rather insistences that register shifts of meaning as the sentences unfold: "no element of remembering . . . no element of confusion . . . no element of repetition." Like Whitman's, her genius consists in being at once receptive and creative, able to hear other voices while producing her own, and communicating complex meaning in the simplest language: "the two in one and the one in two." We are there with the lecturer as her thought plays out, invited into agreement—"that is if you like being a genius." Like Whitman, she urgently wants to be understood: only if we "really understand," if what she says is self-evident and ordinary, will her composition succeed. Why is this shared sense of truth so important to both writers? How do they simultaneously promote themselves as literary lions and work to democratize genius? These questions generally lead to lively discussion.

Stein's attempt to bridge the gap between difficult texts and general readers (or listeners) is part of a long tradition of democratic education, and entertainment, in America, one that students can survey by reading Thomas Wentworth Higginson's "The American Lecture System" from 1868. To give students insight into the importance of appearance and style of delivery to the public reception of lecturing authors, I have them research and write about newspaper reports of Stein's lectures (with headlines such as "Gertrude Stein Arrives and Baffles Reporters by Making Herself Clear," "Princeton Dazed by Gertrude Stein," "Miss Stein Speaks to Bewildered 500," and "Miss Stein Puzzle to Psychiatrists") together with accounts of earlier public appearances by either Emerson, Frederick Douglass, Truth, Charles Dickens, Twain, Oscar Wilde, James, or Millay. I ask students to trace how clothing, gestures, demeanor, gender, race, and tone of voice figure in the commentaries on these various figures; to what extent speakers are taken as representative of certain ideas, movements, or identities; and whether speakers are perceived as either common or elite and what values attach to these categories. Stein's concern with controlling her self-presentation—her insistence on being seated, not being introduced, and having an audience of no more than five hundred—might be compared with Dickens's practice of bringing along his own light for the lectern so as to frame himself flatteringly, a habit for which the author was criticized by the press. Or one might compare Twain's refusal to be introduced with Stein's. Twain enjoyed the confusion of spectators when they mistook him for the introducer only to discover that he was the author, a bit of humor that perhaps anticipates Stein's willingness to be mistaken for Alice in the wake of the *Autobiography*. (Many Americans did not believe Alice really existed until they saw her at Stein's lectures.)

Or students might read Sharon Kirsch's "Gertrude Stein Delivers" and Heather O'Donnell's "'My Own Funny Little Lecture Boom': Henry James's American Performance" in order to compare the motives and practices of Stein and James with regard to their respective tours. Both were seeking new readers for their difficult and largely unread works, but James charged top dollar for his lectures, whereas Stein insisted that admission to hers should be free. The newspapers' focus on her unfeminine and unfashionable appearance, her close-cropped hair, her "thick woolly stockings, and round-toed, flat-heeled oxfords," her "tweed suit" and "mannish shirt" ("Gertrude Stein Arrives") offers a contrast to descriptions of Millay's frail form wrapped in flowing, feminine gowns and scarves. In tracing these reception histories, students consider these questions: To what extent do the public personas of authors inflect the evaluation and interpretation of their writings? What cultural importance attaches to celebrity authors who are more read about than read? What is it that American audiences want from literature and authors? What has gender got to do with it?

I then turn to excerpts from Stein's postlecture writings so that students can see how her ideas about writing and authorship evolved. I select some of her comments on American popular culture—films, detective novels, newspapers—from *Everybody's Autobiography* (1937), and we discuss how they relate to her role as a popular writer. I distribute a few pages (12–18) from *Ida: A Novel* (1941) that describe its protagonist's increasing public visibility, her discovery of her twin, Winnie, and the ensuing split of these two into four (Ida, Winnie, Ida-Ida, and Winnie-Winnie), and we discuss how this fictional account of identity compares with Stein's account of her celebrity and the complexities about public and private identity that it entails. Looking at a few passages from *The Geographical History of America* (1936), we take up this issue of the inside and outside in a different way, by pondering the distinction between human nature, which is linked to identity, relations, and speaking, and human mind, which is the arena of genius, abstraction, and writing. *Geographical History* discusses audience, geography, and reception in ways that clearly reference Stein's American tour: "remember how the country looked as we passed over it [in an airplane], it made designs" (373); "an audience never does prove to you that you are you"

(405); "The human mind is the mind that writes what any human mind years after or years before can read, thousands of years or no years it makes no difference" (406–07). These examples give students a glimpse of the profound and various ways that Stein's lecturing reverberated through her later writings.

Stein's lectures belong in the tradition of American public speech and oratory; they are tours de force of vernacular wit and common sense. Though Stein feared the incursions of an imagined audience on her writing (the pressures of "human nature" on the "human mind" or the placing of the "inside" on the "outside" such that there would no longer be an inside), in the act of lecturing she realized the dynamic qualities of speech directed at and responsive to the presence of strangers. She had long said that she wrote "for myself and for strangers" (*Making* 289), and during her lecture tour strangers showed up in droves to listen. For a seen and heard you discovered through the lecture format, she created an emboldened authorial persona, combining the experiential with the experimental, and affirmed her commitment to the value of the commonplace. The texts that she produced in the decade after her tour plumbed the complexities of identity and celebrity, privacy and publicity, inside and outside for the writer who has a reading public—or who does not. They remain among the twentieth century's most profound engagements with the problems of personal identity, artistic freedom, and innovation in the face of mass communication and celebrity culture. By examining the performative or demonstrative qualities of Stein's lectures and pondering their claims about identity and language, students will be able to wrestle more productively with the themes and strategies of her experimental works. Further, they will come to understand that her status as both literary iconoclast and popular performer place her squarely in American democratic and antitraditionalist traditions. Reading Stein's lectures in relation to earlier examples of American oratory invites students to think deeply about literature as a cultural institution that participates in the broader histories of American communication and commerce.

NOTE

[1] Along with Shakespeare, James is the most often mentioned writer in *Lectures*. Stein also refers to Emerson (see 51) and Whitman (see 237 and 241), among many others.

Pictures, Portraits, and Resemblance

Loretta Stec

Gertrude Stein asserts in her essay "Pictures," "[A]lmost everybody likes a resemblance even when there is none. . . . That is a naturally pleasant human thing, to like a resemblance. And does this naturally pleasant human thing the liking a resemblance make everything difficult very difficult. Yes it certainly does" (85). The tendency of students to "like a resemblance" is one of the many factors that makes teaching Stein's works "very difficult." A two-week unit on the visual arts and Stein has been productive in classes as diverse as a survey of twentieth-century literature, a year-long exploration titled Expatriate Writers in Paris, and an MA seminar on Stein. The unit begins with her short volume *Picasso* (1938),[1] a retrospective biographical portrait of the painter, and then we move to "Pictures" and "Portraits and Repetition," from *Lectures in America* (1935). We view slides of paintings throughout the unit and end with a few of Stein's literary portraits in different styles and selections from *Tender Buttons* (1914). By moving between reading and seeing, students apprehend her thoroughgoing break with conventional modes of representation, reflect on shifting notions of identity in the modernist era, and ideally find the freedom to play with her experimental work.

In *Picasso*, we begin with Stein's emphasis on the importance of Picasso's "first cubist landscapes" (13) from Horta de Ebro, Spain, painted in 1909; three of them hung in her studio (Giroud 38). I help students develop a vocabulary to talk about the spatial relations of these canvases. For example, *The Reservoir, Horta de Ebro*, which Stein owned, refuses traditional single-point perspective (see www.moma.org/collection/works/78718). There is more than one light source, and the angular representation of the village and reservoir creates a disorienting sense that the same corners jut out or point in depending on one's angle of vision. Although Picasso applies some green paint to the interior of the reservoir, the water is a solid mass, without softness, and there appear to be boxlike structures inside. The geometric representation of a village has no trees, human beings or other animals, or other elements that are typically in landscape paintings. About these paintings Stein says, "Spaniards know that there is no agreement, neither the landscape with the houses, neither the round with the cube, neither the great number with the small number, it was natural that a Spaniard should express this in the painting of the twentieth century, the century where nothing is in agreement" (*Picasso* 24).[2]

I ask students to work in pairs to consider what Stein might mean by "agreement." When they share their thoughts with the class, eventually someone offers the suggestion that she sees these landscapes as refusing to provide the mimesis of landscape paintings of the past. As she says in "Pictures," "[T]he relation between the oil painting and the thing painted was really nobody's business" (79). We interrogate the notion of biography or literary portraiture as realistic. Stein's portrait of Picasso is too simple, too idiosyncratic to be a likeness in a conventional sense. Her looping method suggests that his oeuvre and identity have been constantly in process. By the end of our first class we have discussed the key concepts for this unit: perspective, notions of resemblance or likeness ("agreement"), identity in process, and angle of vision on the part of the visual or literary artist as well as the viewer or reader.

We look at slides of some of the paintings Stein cites in "Pictures" and consider her comments about them. When we reach the section of the essay in which she objects to Gustave Courbet's landscapes, we look at several examples.[3] Stein writes:

> But Courbet bothered me. . . . The paintings of Courbet were very real as oil paintings, they existed very really as oil painting, but did the colors that were the colors anybody could see trees and water-falls naturally were, did these colors add or did they detract from the reality of the oil painting as oil painting. . . . [T]he Courbets were really oil paintings with the real life of oil paintings as oil paintings should have. Only the Courbets being nearly something else always keeps them from being really all they are. (74–75)

Using colors too close to nature's falsified the paintings; Courbet took the traditional mimetic representational pact too seriously for a modernist's taste. Students, understanding the correspondence to nature that Courbet's paintings manifest, struggle a bit with Stein's objections to his aesthetic.

Paul Cézanne achieved for Stein the representational aims of resemblance while fully realizing the oil painting as oil painting. She acknowledges that even she had to adjust herself to his new methods (e.g., see his *Mont Sainte-Victoire*, 1902–04 [www.philamuseum.org/collections/permanent/102997.html]):

> I came to Cezanne and there you were, at least there I was, not all at once but as soon as I got used to it. . . . The landscape looked like a landscape that is to say what is yellow in the landscape looked yellow in the oil painting, and what was blue in the landscape looked blue in the oil painting and if it did not there was still the oil painting. . . . The same thing was true of the people there was no reason why it should be but it was, the same thing was true of the chairs, the same thing was true of the apples. . . . They were so entirely these things that they were not an oil painting and yet that is just what the Cezannes were they were an oil painting. (76–77)

Because the students have developed a visual vocabulary for the Picasso landscapes, they are usually adept at describing how the Cézanne landscapes differ from those of Courbet. We focus on what one critic has called Cézanne's "spatial conundrums" (Cox 100): in *Mont Sainte-Victoire*, the flattened planes of color, the obvious brushstrokes, the illusion of depth compromised by the eye's being continually drawn back to the two-dimensional surface of the canvas, the impossibility of forgetting that this is a painting even as it is clearly a representation of a mountain scene. We discuss Stein's claim that one of the reasons cubism came to exist was that in the twentieth century "each thing was as important as any other thing" ("Transatlantic Interview" 15). I explain to students that Stein attributes this innovation to Cézanne, whose "spatial conundrums" break through or even dissolve the viewer's desire for mimesis.[4]

The students are ready to turn to the concept of portrait. I ask them to brainstorm, either with me at the board or in small groups, definitions and goals of visual portraits. Our list of genre traits includes likeness; class status; symbolic methods to indicate psychological, characterological, and perhaps essential selfhood; the tradition of idealizing sitters; and the influence of modern media such as photography (and now digital venues such as *Instagram*) on how the form has changed over time, has become more democratic and instantaneously malleable. I intersperse in this discussion some facts about the history of portraiture, both visual and literary.[5] Then we look at Diego Velázquez portraits, which Stein says "bother" her because the subjects "almost looked really like people" ("Pictures" 67), which now does not surprise the students.[6]

We pursue Stein's claim in *Picasso* that the "head the face the human body these are all that exist for Picasso" (13). By comparing Jean-Auguste-Dominique Ingres's *Louis-François Bertin* (1832; www.louvre.fr/en/oeuvre-notices/louis-francois-bertin), which the Louvre's Web site calls "the most realistic portrait [Ingres] ever painted," with Picasso's 1906 portrait of Stein (www.metmuseum.org/collection/the-collection-online/search/488221), we can articulate how Picasso works in the traditional genre of portraiture while also forging a modernist representation of selfhood that complicates resemblance and knowability.[7] With its dissimilar eyes, peculiar shadows, and masklike flatness, the face in the portrait and the painted subject overall is without a center; the various parts do not fully cohere. Picasso moves his technique toward a cubist representation of multiple time frames and perspectives on the same canvas.[8] Our discussion of this painting along with Picasso's portraits of *Daniel-Henry Kahnweiler* (1910; www.artic.edu/aic/collections/artwork/111060) and *Ambroise Vollard* (1910; www.arts-museum.ru) demonstrates that modernist visual portraiture was moving farther and farther away from traditional resemblance.

Stein, meanwhile, was pursuing her own experiments in portraiture. For our third class in this unit, students read "Portraits and Repetition" and return to class with the essay "Pictures." I play the recording (on *PennSound*) of Stein reading a section of her "Matisse" (1909 or 1910), excerpted in "Pictures." Students laugh, expressing incredulity that it is a portrait, and want to discuss her use of repetition, in particular the words "certain" and "certainly," "expressing," and "clearly." They notice and often complain that these repeated words turn into sounds that they cannot readily attach to meanings; the sounds "empty themselves out" they say; they have learned nothing new about Matisse from Stein. Yet the portrait does provide statements that align with expectations of the genre, because we are able to read parts as a summation of Matisse's career and identity to that time: "This one was certainly a great man, this one was certainly clearly expressing something," even as he was "one being suffering," "expressing something being struggling" (140–41). There are contradictory assessments, however: "Some were certain that this one was clearly expressing something being struggling, some were certain that this one was not greatly expressing something being struggling" (141). Modernist multiperspectivalism is written into the portrait. Stein's use of progressive verb tenses here, as elsewhere in her work, emphasizes change and movement and so challenges the static summation of an identity associated with portraiture in favor of flux, contradiction, permutation.

Describing in "Portraits and Repetition" her process of creating portraits, Stein uses language that echoes "Pictures." She writes:

> Any one does of course by any little thing by any little way by any little expression, any one does of course resemble some one, and any one can notice this thing notice this resemblance and in so doing they have to remember some one and this is a different thing from listening and talking. In other words the making of a portrait of any one is as they are existing and as they are existing has nothing to do with remembering any one or anything. (175)

Her portraits evade, undermine, and contest resemblance and remembering, remembering as resemblance, and focus on "what was in them [other human beings] that was intrinsically exciting," a tantalizingly imprecise phrase. In order to create a portrait, she explains, "I had to find out not by what they said not by what they did not by how much or how little they resembled any other one but I had to find it out by the intensity of movement that there was in any one of them" (183). She refuses to provide the expected biographical facts, typological symbols, comparisons to others, and so on; rather, she uses a language that suggests what is "intrinsically exciting," however impermanently, about her subjects.

I reference Wendy Steiner's scholarship on the multiple phases of Stein's experiments with literary portraiture. The Matisse portrait we have considered is an example of Stein's early phase. Steiner has analyzed another early-phase portrait, "A Portrait of One: Harry Phelan Gibb" (1913), noticing its reduced vocabulary and "lack of nouns, adjectives, and adverbs" (85). In a later phase of portrait writing, Stein offers dense, vocabulary-rich works, such as "Erik Satie" (1922):

> Erick Satie benignly.
> Come to Sylvia do.
> Sylvia Sybil and Sarah
> A bird is for more cookcoo.
> And then what spreads thinner, and a letter. It is early for all.

While its musicality—its emphasis on sound over conventional sense—might be linked to the composer and musician Satie, Stein offers in this portrait what is perhaps better understood as an equivalent to the subject or person rather than a resemblance.[9] She says of another portrait from this period, "George Hugnet" (1928), "[T]here was something completely contained within itself and being contained within itself was moving, not moving in relation to anything not moving in relation to itself but just moving, I think I almost at that time did this thing" ("Portraits" 202). "Erik Satie" likewise gives us "something completely contained within itself," something "moving" that we can experience each time we read the portrait aloud. It resists the notion of resemblance, the notion of remembering, the notion that a portrait can or should sum up an individual even at a moment in time.

In the last class in the Stein unit we turn to *Tender Buttons* and experience portraits such as "Custard," "A Handkerchief," or "A Piano" without demanding resemblance. We look together at "A Waist" as a multivalent piece of medium length (24–25). After one student reads it out loud, I ask class members to spend a few minutes working on the text individually—considering what relation there might be between the title and the language of the poem, noticing repetitions and diction and images, and making notes about anything that strikes them. Students observe how the repetition of "hold" can be connected to the way a belt holds (in) a waist; how a waist "make[s] the bottom" on a person; and how the words "wood," "pine," and "country climb" bring to mind a skirt around the waist of a woman on a country walk. Then the class turns to looser interpretive play. Students remark on the repetition of the *s* sound in "A star glide, a single frantic sullenness, a single financial grass greediness," and they point out a difference in tone between the affirmative "a star glide" and the more sinister "Hold the pine, hold the dark, hold in the rush." Sexual meanings emerge from "Object that is in wood" or "bottom" or "disgrace" or the emphasis on the command to "hold." The repetition of the word "change" allows self-reflexive comments on how each interpretation of this poem will change with each reader and reading.

Not all students will have overcome their resistance to Stein's experimental works, but many comment that they now see that Stein was a serious practitioner of her literary art. Some say that her work not only reveals identities constantly in process but also gives them unprecedented freedom as readers to see interpretation as a radically evolving process. Working in groups of three or four, students choose their own sections of *Tender Buttons* to discuss, and when we reconvene as a whole class, each group reads aloud its section, and each group member makes at least one interpretive comment about it. As the unit comes to a close, students are ready for an assignment that asks them to do online postings that pair visual, plastic, or musical arts with literary works in order to develop our understanding of Paris as a site of experimentation in multiple art forms.

NOTES

[1] For a history of this book, first published in French, see Giroud 42.

[2] Students are often skeptical about Stein's generalizations, such as "Spaniards know. . . ." Here is another, from the first page of *Picasso*: "Painting in the nineteenth century was only done in France and by Frenchmen." Students note the elliptical nature of Stein's chronology and her repetition of facts about Picasso's life, both of which frustrate some and strike others as elegant and effective.

[3] One example is *Landscape in the Jura* (art.famsf.org/gustave-courbet/landscape-jura-196110); another is *Le ruisseau noir*, one of many Courbets at the *Musée d'Orsay* (www.musee-orsay.fr).

[4] For a recent consideration of Stein's indebtedness to Cézanne for her ideas on composition, see Voris, "Interpreting" and "'Shutters.'"

[5] On visual portraiture, see Brilliant. On literary portraiture, see Haselstein; Steiner.

[6] We view *Juan de Pareja* (1650; www.metmuseum.org/collection/the-collection-online/search/437869). We also view *Francisco Pacheco* (1620) and others from the extensive collection at Museo Nacional del Prado (www.museodelprado.es).

[7] For the claim that Picasso "based his portrait" of Stein on Cézanne's *The Artist's Wife with a Fan* (1878–88), purchased by Stein and her brother Leo in 1900, see www.buehrle.ch/works_detail.php?lang=en&id_pic=54.

[8] The well-known influence on Picasso of African masks and Iberian masklike statues (Corn and Latimer 29; Klein 26) helped him challenge Western notions of selfhood in the tradition of portraiture (Warner 18).

[9] In 1912 Roger Fry suggested that Cézanne's followers (Stein was one) "do not seek to give what can after all, be but a pale reflex of actual appearance, but to arouse the conviction of a new and definite reality. They do not seek to imitate form, but to create form; not to imitate life, but to find an equivalent for life. By that I mean that they wish to make images by which the clearness of their logical structure, and by their closely-knit unity of texture, shall appeal to our disinterested and contemplative imagination with something of the same vividness as the things of actual life appeal to our practical activities. In fact, they aim not at illusion but at reality" (qtd. in Bullen xvii).

Someone Puts a Stein Apple Together: Ways to Widen a Workshop

Laura Mullen

> Supposing a sentence is clear whose is it.
>
> —Gertrude Stein, *How to Write*

Supposing Gertrude Stein's works still constitute "An uncivil shape like a gigantic haw," as Wallace Stevens said about his pineapple ("Three Academic Pieces" 86)—why not approach the author from various angles, with differing foci, investigating an array of her discoveries and challenges? Supposing the creative writing workshop to be the site of an inquiry into the possibilities of writing and a chance to expand awareness, my essay opens vistas for further exploration, attempting to make a home for academic inquiry without reducing the author's uncanniness. Stein's work, however it might be useful,[1] challenges a presupposition being wielded with some force in classrooms all over America: that writing should be clear. This challenge exposes an emphasis on transparency as a focus on reception. Making vivid the socially shaped conditions of accepted truth or an accepted truth, Stein's unmarked question highlights the subjective aspect of apprehension, raising issues of ownership and marketability. The clear, she reminds us, is the result of shared culture, repeated encounters, and similar sorts of instruction in approved modes of communicating, among other agreements. A clear sentence belongs to everyone to whom it is clear and to those who make possible that clarity. Those to whom things are clear are comforted by the sense of (as they read) being at home or belonging, and to recognize meaning is to feel, in turn, recognized. When readers say that Stein's work means nothing, what they are pointing to, it often turns out, is the feeling that they have not been considered by the author or not in the way they imagine they should be. Yet readers (plural and indefinite) are frequently addressed in Stein's work, and there is no shortage of thinking about audience. "I am writing for myself and strangers" (*Making* 289), Stein famously noted, and the honesty and intelligence of her admission are worth remarking. Here "strangers" has replaced that definite article abstraction imported from provincial journalism or genre fiction, *the reader* (so often invoked in the workshop formula "What the reader wants . . ."). There is, of course, no such person in the world, and this invented spook, whose dim but menacing presence can turn young writers into unhappy guests in the house of their own talent and times, is dispelled by the recognition that readers are strange or at least different and that the action of reading changes over time. Those who claim that Stein is interested only in the writer or a writer are ignoring her focus on reception: in fact, as her question reveals, she is interested in the negotiations around transient, various, and insecure belongings in the evolving space between author and audience.

An unclear sentence is a space of contested readings—that is to say, a space for mistakes as well as ongoing discussion. How comfortable students feel with an open-ended question in a text can tell us much about their previous training: in classes devoted to reading and writing poetry, extensive exposure to a limited hermeneutics and timid, controlling pedagogies can leave them feeling that polysemous sentences and complex messages always belong to some distant, mocking author and his or her ally, the supercilious teacher. But a steady and unhurried engagement with Stein's puns, sound play, and deliberately unpredictable and uneasy sentences, an engagement focused on observable facts rather than opinions, provides a salutary challenge to previous modes of reading and discussing the literary object. It makes a space for the strange and difficult to thrive. Supposing a refusal to provide answers opened space to ask questions? Supposing the point of the creative writing workshop is to generate inquiries that, insofar as they change our relation to the world, enable us to change our reality? Learning to be with what happens rather than imposing expectations makes room for students to attend to their own experience and ideas about that experience. This pedagogy involves an interest in process and a focus on the many inarguable realities of a text (those aspects that may lead to interpretation but do not require it). As Stein noticed, "the everlasting feeling of sentences as they diagram themselves" is a "way [of] completely possessing something and incidentally one's self" ("Poetry" 211). Oddly enough, going back to basics might be the first step toward a wider freedom.

Career: The Ecstasy of Influence

Creative writing students have much to gain from a consideration of the steep learning curve revealed by Stein's oeuvre, where—over the course of her career—experiments in syntax, grammar, and narrative emerge as the recognized and welcome result of seeing, reading, thinking, and conversing. This artist is not isolated or unbalanced but part of a collectivity: "the essence of genius," Stein announced, "is being one who is at the same time talking and listening" ("Portraits" 170). There's a healthy model here, in the hostess who preferred to be "exact and concentrated and sober" (198), and important knowledge to be gained first about learning itself (and the many contexts in which it can take place) and then about what writing can do with understandings gained from exposure to other disciplines (psychology, for instance, and visual art). Stein's first work, *Q. E. D.* (1903), although ahead of its time in terms of its subject matter (a lesbian love triangle), is written in the stiffish prose of its moment. But the influence of Gustave Flaubert's *Trois contes* (1877) on *Three Lives* (1905–06) as well as the questions about representation raised by the postimpressionist art Stein was collecting are examples that show the salutary result of wide exposure and engagement. An introduction to the work of William James, with whom she studied, allows students to recognize her art's overlap with contemporary scientific inquiry. Her rejection, in *Tender Buttons* (1912), of received descriptive modes for something closer to her friend Pablo Picasso's analytic cubism is an effective model for the use of contemporary art as a goad for creative writing. Teachers interested in following up on this idea of wide exposure and engagement might ask students to respond to challenging art today, to map innovative research in another field onto their projects, or to consider the effects of a particular technological innovation on their approach to writing. Stein insisted that writing can be, must be, contemporary, a statement that sounds obvious but actually takes a while to get to, hindered as we are by the idea that good writing is timeless if not in fact restricted to the past. Discoveries made in the context of contemporary practices form important contributions to the way we live our lives, and noticing how (to put it in Stein's words) "what is seen depends on how everybody is doing everything" ("Composition" 495) is foundational for those who wish to do more than successfully imitate a previous way of proceeding.[2]

Energy

"When I first began writing, I felt that writing should go on" ("Poetry" 217). Stein's emphasis on keeping writing going and alive—for both writer and reader—can help students appreciate the process and resist the homogenizing effect of an emphasis on craft. Teaching students to reproduce effects they admire has its place, but writers need the freedom as well as the tools to take an experimental approach. Asking students to consider what *they* feel about punctuation, for instance, and assigning Stein's "Poetry and Grammar" (1935) alongside Anne Carson's lyric sequence "The Life of Towns" in *Plainwater* (1995) or Alice Notley's *The Descent of Alette* (1996), provides evidence that there's more at stake than the mastery of particular rules. Recognizably good writing—writing, that is, that resembles previous work accepted as good, all too often soaking in unacknowledged ideology and inextricably entangled in barely recognized prejudices (class, gender, race)—is no longer the only goal where the possibility of enjoying the process emerges. Permission is key, as Toni Morrison notes, speaking of the difficulty of coming to think of herself as a writer, and making a place for pleasure expands the range of results while improving the workshop atmosphere. Stein's assertion in a 1934 radio interview that enjoyment *is* understanding has radical implications for writers and readers inside the classroom and out ("Gertrude Stein" 89). Attention to how things sound (for example, loud in "Susie Asado") is part of Stein's modeling of pleasure in the materiality of the word, and her use of the sentence as a "tuning fork"[3] offers a way of proceeding that allows students to develop sensitivity to their own rhythms and to treat the sentence as less a delivery system for information and more an event. Bringing a Stein poem into the workshop and thinking about the challenges it poses to specific expectations can restore flexibility to a too-brittle set of criteria, and setting assignments based on her work or her methods is an extremely effective means of helping students find ways to make language more pleasurable and more their own.

Errors As Exemplary

Whereas doing it right is revealed as fitting neatly into the structure of previous ideas and approved expectations, doing it wrong can be a productive part of an exploratory process. Mistakes illuminate prejudices that might otherwise take years to become obvious, in all their limiting, restrictive power, and disappointment and chagrin function as X-rays, illuminating other possibilities and offering an opportunity to enlarge our ideas of what should be to include what is. Stein embraced the verb over the noun because the verb "can be so mistaken. It is wonderful the number of mistakes a verb can make" ("Poetry" 211). Her celebration of mistakes as a means of discovery can form the basis for successful writing prompts, supplying an inexhaustible source of material for every author interested in pushing the boundaries of what we can say and how we can say it.[4] One of the her most frequently used strategies is what philosophers (as far back as Aristotle) call category mistakes, "arguably the only [kind] of sentences that might be considered syntactically well-formed but [are] meaningless" (Magidor 6). Examples of category mistakes, which are more commonly known in linguistics as selectional violations, include Noam Chomsky's famous "colorless green ideas sleep furiously" (15). They make up most of *Tender Buttons*, from "a single hurt color" on. This freedom to choose the wrong word, displacing or revising preconceptions, enlivening consciousness, and critiquing "an arrangement in a [language] system" (11), has as yet been only sporadically explored in contemporary literature, though the work of the Language poets provides exemplary instances. Young writers can learn a great deal about their medium and the otherwise unseen restrictions and pressures on their production by consciously rupturing the smooth surface of communication.

The Play with Genres

Unusual[5] and edifying.[6]

Images

When the production of pictures, before the advent of photography, required trained experts, expensive materials, and time, the verbal image was important in ways it may never be again. Though reportage of what one sees will always be of interest as a form of translation, Stein swiftly grasped the possibilities for the verbal image in the wake of the invention of the photography—that is, in a world in which images as records were bound to be ever more available and cheap. Cameras for pictures both still and moving free the verbal image (and painting) to become an inquiry into experience, a phenomenology, a kinesthesia, an examination of the medium and the work of representation itself. Instead of insisting that we describe an object to make it recognizable to another—the labor of the journalist or writer of instruction manuals—Stein provides a corrective to the illusion that one can speak without displaying subjectivity; she charges writers to locate their perspective and be ready for others to come and stand where they are. Her exemplary work with "Objects," "Food," and "Rooms" in *Tender Buttons* provides an opportunity, as yet unmatched, to enjoy a looking that is "not confusing itself with remembering" ("Portraits" 188), where description remains, at each instant, original, particular, earned, and new. Students in the workshop are inspired by the example of her work and respond energetically to the pressure to use language in innovative ways, often surprising themselves while accessing new modes of reflecting on and expressing their lives.

Pronouns

One of Stein's major innovations is the turn from the *I* and *thou* to an *I* and *others*. When John Ashbery calls *Stanzas in Meditation* "a poem about the world, about 'them,'" he is pointing to Stein's unusual use of pronouns: the many *shes*, *hes*, and *theys* that, encountered in her work, seem both momentary and murky ("Impossible" 51). Students who have been taught to make sure the reader knows whom they are talking about find overwhelming the encounter with these slippery, vague, important, but uncertainly assigned presences. This looseness of human connection is already recognized by the language that allows us to substitute pronouns for nouns and draw attention, through further substitutions, to relationships changed by time. "She will be me when this you see," Stein writes (*Stanzas* 154), pointing to the instability of identity, to the work we do to anchor reference across the line and the text as a whole, and to the transience of meaning: "me" is turned to "she" when death confines the subject to the third person.

To read Stein is not only to let go of a too-anxious desire to be sure of the subject but also to find oneself slipping in and out of her rooms or stanzas, located sometimes in her *I* and also numbered among *them*, to be one of her anticipated readers or guests. Her exploration of the potential of pronouns to be mistaken is part of her inquiry into the medium's possibilities, but this enlarged sense of the world, bigger than the dyad and a lot less stable, might also be chalked up to her situation as a (queer) lover whose affections were denied legal recognition. It certainly displays her extraordinary apprehension of fame. To have one's words or image in the possession of millions of unknown others in one's own lifetime is a relatively new human experience, and Stein's repeated references to a *they* who may refuse to "open" her work but cannot "close" it (*Stanzas* 249) reveal how alive Stein was to the unprecedented effects of the increased speed and reach of information. Students who have seen the breathtaking expansion of possibilities for knowing and being known by people they will never meet have much to gain from a consideration of her pronouns as part of their own thinking about how ever faster and more pervasive media affect senses of solitude, company, and crowds, about—in brief—what it means to be human now.[7]

Ways to Wander

Parataxis—to which Stein was devoted and which she (arguably) got Ernest Hemingway to appreciate—is by now an obvious and attractive example of one of her innovative ways of proceeding. Quick juxtapositions of sentences, clauses, and phrases bring her writing and our reading up to the speed of modern life. Anacoluthon—an abrupt change or disruption in syntax—is a less discussed but equally constant Steinian strategy for keeping sentence energy high and ensuring that readers also, responding to unexpected turns, stay lively. The sentence that starts this essay is one example. "What is the custom, the custom is in the center," from *Tender Buttons* (43), is another: here the question about what something is is met by an assertion of where it is, an answer that is at once brilliant and askew. Such abrupt shifts give access to other perspectives, providing a chance for us to critique and revise shared assumptions. Often perceived as being inconsequential, Stein is actually intervening in and revising received understandings of consequences. Among the lessons a contemporary poet like Harryette Mullen learned from her, anacoluthon stands out: in works such as *S*PeRM**K*T* and titles like "Wipe that Simile off Your Aphasia" (*Sleeping* 80), students can easily see how wonderfully this rhetorical effect works for those who want to question preconceptions, resist clichés, or laugh off the seductive blandishments of advertisements.

Stein's digressions and displacements, her refusal of custom, and her resistance to making sense are all meant to put readers into that state of heightened, almost hallucinatory attention, loose but sharp, that Stein enjoyed: a state that, in the "Melanctha" section of *Three Lives*, she calls "wandering" (130) and that appears to be a necessary prelude to both wisdom and love. It is nonhierarchical: the structure of value is not received but is there to be found. The greatest benefit to bringing Stein into the creative writing classroom is the way her writing can put into question the usual workshop mode. The many uncertainties students and teachers face together when discussing her work can expose the confining walls of a particular aesthetic and make room for a consideration of the other things we might want writing to do. Difficult writing, confronted, challenges received ideas about what is successful and forces workshop participants to seek new strategies for reading and discussing what their peers are producing. All of which is a way of saying that perhaps the first lesson Stein has to teach us is also the simplest: How to read. We think we know that already, yet no one who has sat in on a workshop is unaware of how reading, in that location, is attested to most often not by an accurate description of what is on the page but by a perfect tornado of opinions about what should or could be on the page instead. If Gertrude Stein can teach us to account for, respond to, encourage, and intelligently consider the actual productions of our contemporaries, we will have been given the greatest gift of all: an open understanding, which is our only real chance of happiness, "completely possessing something and incidentally one's self."

NOTES

[1] As notoriously difficult as she is surprisingly didactic, Stein frequently invokes an idea of the text as a site for understanding and improvement. In her syntax and language (as in the endless "this shows" or "this makes" phrasing in *Tender Buttons*, for instance) as well as in titles such as *Q. E. D.*, "Composition as Explanation," *Useful Knowledge*, and *How to Write*, we see her gesture toward expectations about literature's social function in order to stage writing as a series of philosophical propositions or an ongoing experiment.

[2] It is productive to look at Stein's "Susie Asado" (composed in 1913 and published in 1922) and Robert Frost's "The Road Not Taken" (published in 1916) together with students and then ask, after careful discussion of the poems, which poet is exploring a path less well traveled.

[3] "She also liked then to set a sentence for herself as a sort of tuning fork and metronome and then write to that time and tune" (*Autobiography* 206).

[4] John Ashbery's asking his students to "write a bad poem" is a good example, as is Jorie Graham's assigning interviews with the painter Francis Bacon to help students, in their writing process, value and incorporate the accidental.

[5] What price is paid for insisting (beginning at the undergraduate level) that students identify as poets, fiction writers, or writers of creative nonfiction? What's the long-term cost of this immediate professionalization of creativity? What have we lost in the way of talent—meaning, what has the world lost—by requiring that students decide what they are going to write (what it will look like, how it can be categorized) long before they enter a graduate program? What do we gain by forcing students whose interests include more than one genre to narrow their horizons? What do we gain by penalizing writers who do not wish to meet expectations but to expand them? Stein's work, and this is no doubt part of why it is so often left off the syllabus, challenges our ways of proceeding on the level of program structure: to open the door to her work is to say yes to hybrid genres, the multimodal, and the interdisciplinary.

[6] Teju Cole: "I made a sideways move from art history into writing, and I think this, in part, is why I also find the stern distinction between fiction and nonfiction odd. It's not at all a natural way of splitting up narrated experience, just as we don't go around the museum looking for fictional or nonfictional paintings. Painters know that everything is a combination of what's observed, what's imagined, what's overheard, and what's been done before. Is Monet a nonfiction painter and Ingres a fiction painter? It's the least illuminating thing we could ask about their works. Some lean more heavily on what's seen, some more on what's imagined, but all draw on various sources."

[7] Pronouns matter to writers attempting to respond to shifting gender identities and complex political realities. Examples of poets today putting a Steinian pressure on this part of speech would include Juliana Spahr and Myung Mi Kim. Writing exercises will suggest themselves by the score once we start thinking of Stein as canny rather than careless. Asking students, for instance, to think about how the bromide about sexually transmitted diseases ("You are sleeping with everyone your partner slept with") might affect a description of a love scene on the level of pronouns and proper nouns.

The Bothersome Pleasures of Teaching Stein

Sharon J. Kirsch

Going into the classroom to teach Gertrude Stein, how can we take seriously as a pedagogical precept her sly solicitation, "Oh how can you bother with me" ("History" 256)? To bother is to take the trouble to do something or to trouble or annoy someone by interrupting or causing inconvenience. Stein's writing is not convenient as a matter of literary form and rhetorical principle, does not offer easy access, and often pesters readers with repetition, opacity, and ostensible nonsense. Stein on the page or Stein in the classroom is bothersome, even frustrating, but also, in my experience of teaching her, amusing and pleasurable. Reading her confronts students with their own habituated reading practices. Teaching her, like reading her, requires me to work and play with her writing and take the trouble to do something with her words. Stein's writing will never save us the bother.

Too often my students, in the face of what they perceive to be overwhelming complexity or utter absurdity, quickly become frustrated, even dismissive. Literally or metaphorically, they slam their books closed and claim they cannot do it. They cannot make sense of the words, let alone offer an interpretation. There's no "there there" (*Everybody's Autobiography* 298). My goals, when I teach Stein, are to move students beyond this initial resistance, to help them find ways to experience and talk about her writing, and to challenge them to gain a self-reflexive understanding of reading as a practice of recognizing and making meaning. In courses as wide-ranging as Introduction to Literary Studies, Literature in the United States after 1860, History of Literary Criticism, Studies in Critical Theory, Rhetorical Studies, and Studies in Women and Literature, I try to entice my students to recognize and experience the pleasure of working with Stein's writing.

Regardless of the course or text I teach, I begin by calling attention to the tacit expectation of students that what they read must make sense in certain prepackaged ways. During her lecture tour across the United States, Stein addressed the challenges posed by her writing by expanding what constitutes understanding: "You mean by understanding that you can talk about it in the way that you have the habit of talking . . . but I mean by understanding enjoyment. . . . If you enjoy it you understand it, and lots of people have enjoyed it so lots of people have understood it" ("Gertrude Stein" 89). Following Stein's lead, I offer students the example of toddlers who go to a playground for the first time. They rarely ask for a detailed explanation for how to use the monkey bars or what to do with the sand. They do not need objectives and learning outcomes. They experiment and try things without concern about messing up or getting it right. They play and enjoy the process. Stein's concept of "intellectual recreation" ("Poetry" 238) defines an approach to reading, writing, and thinking that uses the intellect not only as a faculty of reasoning or objective understanding but also as a way to work and play creatively and inventively with words. The point is not to avoid trying in any way to make meaning of Stein's writing but to avoid too quick an expectation of reading mastery. If we take Stein at her word, reading can be recreation, an activity done for enjoyment, but also re-creation, to create again.

Even when I am not teaching from *How to Write* (1931), I like to take snippets from it as directives for rethinking how to read: "Happy is to find what it does" (33); "Successions of words are so agreeable. / It is about this" (39); "It is impossible to avoid meaning" (71). How might we focus less on what something means and more on what it does? How might we proceed in such a way that we can find successions of words agreeable—another way of saying enjoyable and pleasant? If it is impossible to avoid meaning, then how can we discover meaning in Stein's writing? Her repeated imperatives tell readers exactly what they need to do: "Try again" (26); "Think of a use for a paragraph" (27); "Think if you can" (28); "Think of how do you do" (28); "Now listen" (29); "Think that a sentence has been made" (30); "Think of a sentence" (30); and "Now think of a sentence" (31). Imperative sentences by definition have the same missing subject: *you*. Stein's imperatives both address and make note of the absence of *you*. Thus you are invited, even commanded, to be present in the reading and are tasked with a recursive reading project: to think, to try again, to think some more, to listen if you can. Her demands are not dictatorial; they beckon, cajole, and offer strategies for reading, experiencing, and enjoying her writing. Furthermore, this change of habits, if it takes place, invigorates students as readers of literature across the board. As I see them bring lessons from reading Stein to other texts in radically different contexts, I am struck by the general importance for literary studies of attending to bothersome texts.

Helping students learn to bother with Stein's writing requires teaching them to read and respond playfully and creatively, to embrace what Charles Bernstein calls "reading as creative performance" (*Attack* 44). I share his reshuffling of pedagogical priorities when he says, "I am less concerned with analysis or explanation of individual poems than with finding ways to intensify the experience of poetry, of the poetic, through a consideration of how the different styles and structures and forms of contemporary poetry can affect the way we see and understand the world" (18).[1] This emphasis on intensifying experience and moving away from analysis, at least initially, enables students to bracket their sense of not getting it, which opens up opportunities for inventing new habits for engaging with texts.

Ladies' Voices (1916) has been particularly fun and effective for students new to Stein and, more generally, to challenging texts. I have students address this two-page play collaboratively. First they brainstorm reading strategies; then in a large-group discussion, we compare responses; then individually again, students choose several options they are willing to try.[2] For the next class meeting, they write a one-page response detailing their creative reading efforts and commenting on which approaches were generative and how. I begin the next class with a brief discussion, asking for examples of helpful approaches. I want students to compare the relative successes and failures of different ways of reading and, beyond that, to assess what does and does not constitute successful reading. I want them to model for one another that they are game to give new approaches to reading a try.

We move on to an in-class performance of *Ladies' Voices*, which provides an opportunity for students to work with the text performatively, playfully, and repeatedly. In groups of three to five, they have fifteen minutes to prepare a dramatic reading. Each group begins by reading the piece aloud. Group members then decide on the number of speakers, how to deliver the lines, and how to approach different acts and scenes. After several groups perform their interpretations for the class, we compare how the different voices were portrayed and what was suggested about gossip, identity, and ladies. Some groups notice the voice of a narrator or lines that sound like stage direction: "Ladies voices give pleasure" and "Ladies voices together and then she came in" (555). Others notice that Stein provides only fragments of conversations, as if chatting people are walking by. After this discussion, I stage another performance, pulling strong readers from different groups and drawing on our observations about stage directions. Here is one example: the person performing the role of the narrator sits in the middle of the room, orchestrating and commenting on the scenes and characters. Act 1 readers stand by the classroom door. Act 2 readers repeat their lines walking back and forth in the front of the room. For act 3, a small group of readers gather in a circle bantering and reading the lines. The reader for act 4, who could be the narrator, reads from the center of the room. Act 5 readers are in a corner whispering. Nonperforming students, the audience, are scattered around the room listening in, taking notes, and preparing to comment.

I follow Bernstein's sense that reading creatively and performatively is also "ground for subsequent critical interpretation, based on the aesthetic principle that *you can't interpret what you don't experience*" (*Attack* 44). Moving away from analysis and exposition, at least initially, and asking students to read and respond playfully and creatively offer them different ways to bother with Stein's writing. In the space of just over an hour they will have read, discussed, listened to, and performed *Ladies' Voices* many times. I send them off to reflect in writing on how reading, performing, and watching changed and shaped their understanding of the play. Citing specifics from the text, they consider issues of genre, the structure of a play, the function of the acts, the shifts in voices, and the representations of identity, gender specifically. One student noted, "[T]he difference between reading it silently to myself and listening to the performances of the play in class. I think you can hear more clearly than you can see. I loved the way the voices all blended together like being in a roomful of chatting people. But we *were* a roomful of chatting people conversing with Stein's *Ladies*." Another student connected it to the bar scene (lines 139–72) in T. S. Eliot's *The*

Waste Land and decided that Stein's play "gives voice to the kind of voices we often dismiss, gossiping ladies." Referencing a passage from Stein's *Lectures in America* that we had discussed in class, another student cited Stein's comment about *Ladies' Voices,* "I wanted still more to tell what could be told if one did not tell anything" ("Plays" 119), and concluded that "[m]ore than telling us a full story or complete portrait of a person, Stein wants us to listen and hear that 'There is always a story going on' [119] around us."

I often begin the semester by calling into question traditional generic distinctions and asking my students to define a poem (or novel, play, essay, sentence) or explain how they know it when they see it. I also ask them how Stein's writing provides answers to or examples of its own contradictory assertions. Part of her challenge or invitation, which we can highlight and engage in our classrooms, is to be open, take risks, play on syntactic and semantic levels, and bother with the elements of writing that we tend to take for granted because they are most basic. For example, readers of *How To Write* are confronted with questions that appear so elementary their answers are assumed: "What is a sentence?" (33), "What is a question" (35), "What is an answer" (74), "What is a noun" (122), "What is sense" (131), "What is a difficult thing" (174). To respond to these questions, students must delve deeply into the details of the text by looking at specific words, noticing the structures of sentences, and observing patterns of sound and repetition.

In my course Studies in Women and Literature and my course Rhetorical Studies, we read Lyn Hejinian's "The Rejection of Closure" (1983) along with several of Stein's portraits. Stein's writing makes tangible for students what Hejinian calls an "open text," which foregrounds "process, either the process of the original composition or of subsequent compositions by readers, and thus resists the cultural tendencies that seek to identify and fix material and turn it into a product" (43). Reading an open text, says Hejinian, is "an improvisation; one moves through the work not in straight lines but in curves, swirls, and across intersections, to words that catch the eye or attract attention repeatedly" (44). Students use weekly responses or in-class writings to track the challenges they face as readers of the portraits, and Hejinian's essay gives them a critical vocabulary as they try for an open-minded approach. One of my students developed her own three-part process: look, listen, feel.

> First, I flipped through the pages, got an understanding of the lines to come and how Stein presents her poem. I noticed the repetition and let words stand out from the page. Second, I began again at the beginning and read aloud, listening to the sound of the words, the similarities, the way they felt when repeated. . . . Finally, I approached Stein [by asking] how did this poem make me feel, beyond confusion?

In this way reading can become a productive, inquisitive, playful engagement with the text.

I ask the students to compose a Steinian selfie, a self-portrait in words: they are to turn language on themselves to investigate how words make and reflect our senses of self. Stein's image, painted by Picasso, photographed by Man Ray and by Cecil Beaton, sculpted by Jacques Lipchitz and by Jo Davidson, was one of the most famous in the early twentieth century. In addition, Stein wrote many portraits of her famous friends that reframe the issue of identity as an ongoing exploration of how we know or create anything, including our selves across time and in language.[3] Contextualizing her participation in a long history of portraiture, I offer my students a brief overview, including sculptures of Egyptian gods, heads of ancient Greek orators, a self-portrait by Jan Van Eyck, Leonardo da Vinci's drawings, a series of Rembrandt's self-portraits, photographs of Walt Whitman, Van Gogh's famous self-portrait with a bandaged head, Mary Cassatt's portraits of women, Frida Kahlo's self-portraits, and Warhol's photo-booth style self-portraits. The selfie, well known to our students, reworks an old genre.[4] Staged with an arm's-length angle, it plays with self-representation and captures, again and again, a moment, a continuous present reinventing itself in snapshots that impart instant visual communication. This assignment asks students to participate in the portrait genre by examining and then mimicking Stein's style in composing a word portrait from a moment in their lives.

To give students a sense of Stein's portraits, I assign "Matisse" (1911), "Susie Asado" (1913), "Cezanne" (1923), and "If I Told Him A Completed Portrait of Picasso" (1923). When students come to class, we listen to her reading of "If I Told Him" (available on *PennSound*) and analyze how her language portrays its subject. We brainstorm how to explain to someone who never heard of Stein how she wrote her portrait of Picasso and how they might adopt a similar style. Students have come up with many possibilities: use a descriptive title with the person's name; open with a sentence questioning whether or not the recipient will like this portrait; repeat a sentence but alter its syntax; add a historical figure who offers a point of reference or comparison (e.g., Napoleon); add a reference to royalty; add something that opens and closes and gives a peek (shutters); call attention to how well the portrait resembles the person; include sections with long lines to give the look of a paragraph and others with short lines to give the look of a poem; include many pronouns without clear referents; use simple diction; use very few grammatically intact and properly punctuated sentences; call attention to time; and reference famous phrases (such as Paul Revere's "One if by land, and two if by sea").

Students then generate and write a list of facts and phrases about themselves in a chronological encyclopedic entry that includes details about birth, childhood, teenage years, best friends, hobbies, college years, performed roles (daughter or son, sibling, neighbor, friend, etc.). Next they craft their selfie by selecting from and modifying the steps we saw in "If I Told Him." For example, a student who "played soccer from ages 6–14" might revise her description to read, "I ran and ran and ran and ran and kicked and ran and ran and scored and ran and ran and ran and practiced and ran. I ran." Working in pairs, students exchange early drafts and make recommendations to revise phrasing and play with syntax to make the selfie look and sound like Stein. One student who self-identified as a bad writer reworked the idea of writer's block to read, "A desk and idea, idea and never moving." Another student conveyed the relentless demands of his high school football coach this way: "The best way. The best. Is this the best. The best this is. The best. The best. Wants he wants he more. Best. Who's best. Wants and wants and wants he more. The best. Best. Best. Best. Only the best. More. More. Best." When the first drafts are done, students pair off again, read each other's selfies, make comparisons with "If I Told Him," and offer suggestions for revision. They revise and hand in a final version with a five-hundred-word explanation of how their selfie's exploration of identity mirrors and differs from Stein's.

The goal here goes beyond teaching a method of literary portraiture; it is to provide a lesson in reading self-assertion or in the assertion of self. Bothering with Stein's writing requires finding a place for polysemy, chaos, intuition, and appreciation before or in tandem with understanding. This way of teaching reading cuts against the grain of students' received notions about literary interpretation as decoding. It is my hope that these kinds of bothersome lessons, which draw on their creative abilities, will engage them in a pleasurable, open-ended process of interacting with language to play with, explore, and create meaning.

NOTES

[1] Bernstein offers more details on his pedagogy in "Wreading, Writing, Wresponding" (*Attack* 49–64).

[2] Over the years, suggested reading strategies have included: read without thinking; read in different physical spaces; read nonstop with laser focus for a set amount of time (from two minutes to fifteen minutes); reread; read backward; sing the words aloud; read random pages or sections; record yourself reading and listen to the recording; transcribe a page, then read the transcription; read aloud using the voice of an elderly person, a child, a reprimanding parent, a disappointed friend; read aloud as if the text were a prayer or mantra; read while walking; and read with a friend.

[3] For a detailed discussion of Stein's exploration of identity, particularly through variations of her phrase "I am I because my little dog knows me" (*Identity* 588) in a number of her works in the 1930s, see my *Gertrude Stein and the Reinvention of Rhetoric* (33–35).

[4] Hall makes clear that selfies are not a new phenomenon but a have a rich cultural history (7–10).

NOTES ON CONTRIBUTORS

Meg Albrinck is provost and vice president for academic affairs at Lakeland University, where she also serves as professor of literature and writing. Her teaching interests include gender studies, cultural studies, twentieth-century literature, and visual culture. She has published articles and reviews on Gertrude Stein, Virginia Woolf, First World War narratives, and popular film and television.

Corinne E. Blackmer is associate professor of English and Judaic studies at Southern Connecticut State University. She is the editor of *En Travesti: Women, Gender Subversion, Opera* (1995) and the author of *Remembrance and Forgetting in Contemporary Israeli Literature* (2016) and *Queering Anti-Zionism: LGBT Intellectual Boycott, Divestment, and Sanctions Activism* (2018).

Laurel Bollinger is professor of English and director of English Graduate Studies at the University of Alabama, Huntsville. She has published on James, Faulkner, Porter, Twain, and Frost as well as on science fiction writers, including Jack London, Richard Matheson, Greg Bear, and Octavia Butler. Her current research focuses on the intersections between science and literature, with particular attention to microbes, cognition, and embodiment.

Michelle J. Brazier is assistant professor of English at Raritan Valley Community College, a professional violinist, and an opera lover. She is the editor of *Points of Departure: A Collection of Contemporary Essays* (2004, 2011) and a contributor to *Teaching Literature in Community College Classrooms* (2013). She is the coauthor of *Writing from the Inside Out* (forthcoming), a freshman composition textbook-reader that highlights the practice and pedagogies of critical reading.

Jody Cardinal is director of the Writing Center at the State University of New York, Old Westbury, where she teaches in the MAT program. Her work on Stein has appeared in *Primary Stein: Returning to the Writing of Gertrude Stein*. She is currently coediting an essay collection on modernist women writers and American social engagement.

Leonard Diepeveen is George Munro Professor of Literature and Rhetoric at Dalhousie University. He is the author of *The Difficulties of Modernism* (2003) and *Mock Modernism: An Anthology of Parodies, Travesties, Frauds, 1910–1935* (2014) and coauthor, with Timothy van Laar, of *Artworld Prestige: Arguing Cultural Value* (2013). His edition of *Tender Buttons* (with a host of contextual materials) was published in 2017.

Logan Esdale is a lecturer in English at Chapman University and at California State University, Long Beach. He is the editor of Gertrude Stein's *Ida A Novel* (2012) and has published articles on Walt Whitman, Emily Dickinson, Marianne Moore, and Stein that address the epistolary genre and the inseparability of private and public. His current project is "Gertrude Stein in Letters," a monograph.

J. Ashley Foster is assistant professor of twentieth- and twenty-first-century British literature with emphasis in digital humanities at California State University, Fresno. She received her PhD from The Graduate Center, City University of New York. Her work traces the relations among literary, artistic, and activist networks of the long twentieth entury and facilitates intertextual readings between literature and archives.

Adam Frank is professor in the Department of English and cochair of the Graduate Program in Science and Technology Studies at the University of British Columbia. He is the author of *Transferential Poetics, from Poe to Warhol* (2015); the coeditor, with Eve Kosofsky Sedgwick, of *Shame and Its Sisters: A Silvan Tomkins Reader* (1995); and the producer of the *Radio Free Stein* project.

Roger Gilbert is professor of English at Cornell University. He is the author of *Walks in the World: Representation and Experience in Modern American Poetry* (1991). He is currently writing a critical biography of A. R. Ammons.

Jonathan Goldberg is Arts and Sciences Distinguished Professor Emeritus at Emory University. He is the author of *Melodrama: An Aesthetics of Impossibility* and the editor, with Marcie Frank and Karen Newman, of *This Distracted Globe: Worldmaking in Early Modern Literature*. He is currently writing about modernist aesthetics and early modern literature and about Sappho.

Julie Goodspeed-Chadwick is professor of English, affiliate faculty in women's studies, and director of the Office of Student Research at Indiana University–Purdue University, Columbus. She is the author of *Modernist Women Writers and War: Trauma and the Female Body in Djuna Barnes, H.D., and Gertrude Stein* (2011). She is working on a book about gender, women's bodies, identity, and power in the lives and work of Assia Wevill, Ted Hughes, and Sylvia Plath.

Wenwen Guo is a PhD candidate in the English department at Emory University. Her dissertation interrogates the fictions of Henry James, Nella Larsen, Ernest Hemingway, and Toni Morrison with an affective lens—particularly the affect of shame.

Elisabeth Hedrick-Moser is an independent scholar based in San Antonio. She is the author of "Mary Astell: Some Reflections upon Trauma" (in *Feminist Interpretations of Mary Astell*). She is currently writing essays on experiences of motherhood mediated through the paradigm of pilgrimage. One such essay, "Speed and Space of Mind," was recently published in *Lucia Journal*.

Susannah Hollister is the coeditor, with Emily Setina, of Gertrude Stein's *Stanzas in Meditation: The Corrected Edition* (2012). Her current work considers uses of literature in the growing civil-military divide after 9/11. Her recent publications include "Counting Cards: A Poetics for Deployment" (in *Rumba under Fire: The Arts of Survival from West Point to Delhi* [2016]).

Stacy Carson Hubbard is associate professor of English at the University of Buffalo, State University of New York. She is a coeditor, with Elizabeth Gregory, of *Twenty-First Century Marianne Moore: Essays from a Critical Renaissance* (2017) and is currently at work on a book manuscript entitled "'The Past Is the Present': Marianne Moore's Histories." She recieved the Florence Howe Award for Feminist Scholarship from the Women's Caucus of the MLA.

Erica J. Kaufman is the director of the Bard College Institute for Writing and Thinking and visiting assistant professor of literacy education in the program Master of Arts in Teaching. She is the author of the poetry collections *INSTANT CLASSIC*

(2013) and *censory impulse* (2009) and coeditor of *No Gender: Reflections on the Life and Work of kari edwards* and of *Adrienne Rich Teaching at CUNY, 1968–1974* (2014).

Sharon J. Kirsch is associate professor of English and rhetorical studies in the New College at Arizona State University. She is the author of *Gertrude Stein and the Reinvention of Rhetoric* (2014), the coeditor of *Primary Stein: Returning to the Writing of Gertrude Stein* (2014), and the series coeditor of Innovation and Activism in American Women's Writing.

Kimberly Lamm is associate professor of gender, sexuality, and feminist studies at Duke University. She is the author of *Addressing the Other Woman: Textual Correspondences in Feminist Art and Writing* (2017) and currently working on a manuscript that brings Gayatri Spivak's theoretical concepts to bear on the artwork of Theresa Hak Kyung Cha, Mona Hatoum, and Lorna Simpson.

Jane Malcolm is assistant professor of English at the Université de Montréal. Her work has appeared in *Arizona Quarterly*, *Jacket2*, and *Amodern*. She is a coeditor, with Laura Heffernan, of Laura Riding's *Contemporaries and Snobs* (2014). She is currently working on a book about feminist ambivalence and modernist innovation in the work of H.D., Mina Loy, Laura Riding, and Gertrude Stein.

E. L. McCallum is associate professor of English at Michigan State University. She is the author of *Object Lessons: How to Do Things with Fetishism* (1999) and *Unmaking* The Making of Americans: *Toward an Aesthetic Ontology* (2018) and the coeditor, with Mikko Tuhkanen, of *The Cambridge History of Gay and Lesbian Literature* (2014) and *Queer Times, Queer Becomings* (2011).

Deborah M. Mix is professor of English at Ball State University. She is the author of *"A Vocabulary of Thinking": Gertrude Stein and North American Women's Experimental Writing* (2007) and essays in *The Cambridge History of Twentieth-Century American Women's Poetry*, *Producing Public Memory*, and *Modernist Star Maps*. Her current project is on representations of embodiment in contemporary African American women's writing.

Michael Moon is currently professor of women's, gender, and sexuality studies at Emory University. He previously taught in the English departments of Duke and Johns Hopkins. He is the author of, among other books, *Arabian Nights* (2016) and *Darger's Resources* (2012).

Laura Mullen is McElveen Professor at Louisiana State University and the author of eight books, most recently *Complicated Grief* (2015). Her work has been widely anthologized, and recognitions for her poetry include a National Endowment for the Arts Fellowship and a Rona Jaffe Award. She is currently at work on a book-length meditation on a logo.

James Peck is professor of theater at Muhlenberg College. He is the author of numerous scholarly articles and book chapters and served as editor of *Theatre Topics*. He has directed over sixty plays, operas, and musicals, including Gertrude Stein's *Listen to Me, Counting Her Dresses,* and *Saints and Singing*. He is currently series editor of Great North American Theatre Directors.

Lee Rumbarger is director of the Teaching Engagement Program at the University of Oregon, where she convenes faculty conversations around good teaching. She has taught courses on academic writing; gender and modernism; theories of literacy; and representations of teachers, scholars, students, and writers.

Patricia A. Schechter is professor of history at Portland State University. Her current projects are a podcast called *Fanny and Sam: A New York Love Story*, set in the 1920s, and a book-length study of a Spanish mining village in the interwar period. She is the author of *Exploring the Decolonial Imaginary: Four Transnational Lives* (2012).

Emily Setina is assistant professor of English at the University of Nevada, Las Vegas. With Susannah Hollister, she coedited Gertrude Stein's *Stanzas in Meditation: The Corrected Edition* (2012). She is writing a literary and cultural history of photography and modernist literature as told through the archives and published works of Stein, Virginia Woolf, and Marianne Moore.

Loretta Stec is professor of English at San Francisco State University. She has published on writers of the modernist era, including Virginia Woolf, Rebecca West, D. H. Lawrence, Vera Brittain, and Gertrude Stein. Her current projects focus on writers from southern Africa.

Linda Voris is associate professor of literature at American University, where she teaches twentieth-century American and British literature as well as contemporary experimental poetry. She is the author of *The Composition of Sense in Gertrude Stein's Landscape Writing* (2016). Her current book project explores the action of chance and its relation to time in the poetry of Lyn Hejinian.

Rebecca Walsh is associate professor of English at North Carolina State University. She is the author of *The Geopoetics of Modernism* (2015), which examines environmental determinist academic geography, the *National Geographic Magazine*, and globally engaged American poetry. She is the editor of *Global Diasporas*, a special issue of *Interventions*. She is currently working on African American and Indian transnational networks of resistance, 1930s–1950s.

SURVEY RESPONDENTS

Meg Albrinck, Lakeland College
Steven Axelrod, University of California, Riverside
Michele Balze, University of Rochester
Sarah Bay-Cheng, University at Buffalo
Matt Bell, Bridgewater State University
Kristin Bergen, Howard University
Charles Bernstein, University of Pennsylvania
Corinne E. Blackmer, Southern Connecticut State University
Julia Bloch, University of Pennsylvania
Laurel Bollinger, University of Alabama, Huntsville
Michelle J. Brazier, Raritan Valley Community College
Brian Caraher, Queen's University Belfast
Chris Coffman, University of Alaska, Fairbanks
Maria Damon, Pratt Institute
Jessica Datema, Bergen Community College
Leonard Diepeveen, Dalhousie University
Janice Doane, Saint Mary's College of California
Cathy Downs, Texas A&M University, Kingsville
Iris Jamahl Dunkle, Napa Valley College
Rachel Blau DuPlessis, Temple University
Jonathan S. Feinberg, University of Pittsburgh, Greensburg
Elizabeth Fifer, Lehigh University
Adam Frank, University of British Columbia
Loren Glass, University of Iowa
Julie Goodspeed-Chadwick, Indiana University–Purdue University, Columbus
Mark R. Harris, Tecnologico de Monterrey, Sinaloa
Brady Harrison, University of Montana
Lori Harrison-Kahan, Boston College
Stephanie L. Hawkins, University of North Texas
Elisabeth Hedrick-Moser, Saint Louis University
Jeffrey Hogrefe, Pratt Institute
Erica Kaufman, Bard College
Sharon Kirsch, Arizona State University
Rajiv C. Krishnan, English and Foreign Languages University
Kimberly Lamm, Duke University
Kate Levin, Barnard College
Sara Lundquist, University of Toledo
Jacqueline Lyons, California Lutheran University
Jane Malcolm, Université de Montréal
Rebecca Mark, Tulane University
E. L. McCallum, Michigan State University
Sean McCann, Wesleyan University
Michelle Mitchell-Foust, Phoenix Talent Unified School District

Mena Mitrano, Loyola University Chicago, John Felice Rome Center
Laura Mullen, Louisiana State University
Georgina Nugent-Folan, Trinity College Dublin
Maria O'Malley, University of Nebraska, Kearney
Jan Osborn, Chapman University
Justin Parks, University of Turku
James Peck, Muhlenberg College
Sarah Posman, Ghent University
Ioanna Ragkousi, National and Kapodistrian University of Athens
David Rando, Trinity University
Robert Reginio, Alfred University
Eric Rettberg, University of Virginia
Kevin Riordan, Nanyang Technological University
Marilyn Gaddis Rose, Binghamton University
Forrest Roth, Niagara University
Vivian Ruiz, Valencia College
Lee Rumbarger, University of Oregon
Craig Saper, University of Maryland, Baltimore County
Judith Saunders, Marist College
Patricia A. Schechter, Portland State University
Dana Seitler, University of Toronto
Juliana Spahr, Mills College
William Spurlin, Brunel University London
Loretta Stec, San Francisco State University
Heather Stewart, University of Alaska, Fairbanks
Rita Costabile Tobin, Hunter College, City University of New York
Andrew Vogel, Kutztown University
Marci Vogel, University of Southern California
Linda Voris, American University
Shira Wohlberg, independent artist
Krzysztof Ziarek, University at Buffalo

WORKS CITED

Readers will note that certain Stein titles appear one way in parts 1 and 2 and in some of the essays of this volume and another way in the works-cited list. In the text of the volume, the styling—capitalization and punctuation—follows that used by Stein scholars and that appears in the archival record (e.g., *Ida A Novel*); in the works-cited list, the styling follows the *MLA Handbook* (e.g., *Ida: A Novel*).

Adato, Perry Miller. *Chapter 3: When This You See Remember Me. YouTube*, 2 Sept. 2013, www.youtube.com/watch?v=wMn5bxk7d4U.

Adorno, Theodor. *Current of Music: Elements of a Radio Theory*. Edited and introduced by Robert Hullot-Kentor, Polity Press, 2009.

Alarcó, Paloma, and Malcolm Warner, editors. *The Mirror and the Mask: Portraiture in the Age of Picasso*. Yale UP, 2007.

Aldington, Richard. "The Disciples of Gertrude Stein." *Poetry*, vol. 17, no. 1, Oct. 1920, pp. 35–40.

Altieri, Charles. *Painterly Abstraction in Modernist American Poetry*. Cambridge UP, 1989.

Anderson, Sherwood. "The Work of Gertrude Stein." Stein, *Geography*, pp. 5–8.

Andrews, Bruce, and Charles Bernstein, eds. *The L=A=N=G=U=A=G=E Book*. Southern Illinois UP, 1984.

Andrews, William L., editor. *Classic American Autobiographies*. Signet, 1992.

Anthony, Susan B. "First Appeal of 1854." *History of Woman Suffrage: Vol. 1, 1848–1861*, edited by Elizabeth Cady Stanton et al., Fowler and Wells, 1881, pp. 856–58.

Antliff, Mark, and Patricia Leighten. *Cubism and Culture*. Thames and Hudson, 2001.

Aronson, Arnold. *American Avant-Garde Theatre: A History*. Routledge, 2000.

Arvidson, Heather. "A Landscape Called Not and Now." 2005. U of British Columbia, MA thesis.

Ashbery, John. "Being in Her." *PEN America: A Journal for Writers and Readers*, vol. 3, no. 5, 2004, pp. 83–86.

———. "The Impossible: Gertrude Stein." 1957. Stein, *Stanzas*, pp. 50–55.

Ashton, Jennifer. *From Modernism to Postmodernism: American Poetry and Theory in the Twentieth Century*. Cambridge UP, 2005.

Axelrod, Steven Gould. "*Mrs. Reynolds*: Stein's Anti-Nazi Novel." Boyd and Kirsch, pp. 259–76.

Baldassari, Anne, et al., editors. *Matisse Picasso*. Museum of Modern Art, 2002.

Barlow, Judith E., editor. *Plays by American Women, 1930–1960*. Applause Theater, 1994.

Barthes, Roland. *S/Z*. 1970. Translated by Richard Miller, Hill and Wang, 1974.

Bartholomae, David. *Writing on the Margins: Essays on Composition and Teaching.* Bedford–St. Martins, 2005.

Barton, John Cyril, et al. "Reading Detectives: Teaching Analysis and Argument in First-Year Writing." *Integrating Literature and Writing Instruction: First-Year English, Humanities Core Courses, Seminars*, edited by Judith Anderson and Christine Farris, Modern Language Association, 2007, pp. 174–92.

Bay-Cheng, Sarah. *Mama Dada: Gertrude Stein's Avant-Garde Theater.* Routledge, 2004.

Bechdel, Alison. *Are You My Mother? A Comic Drama.* Houghton Mifflin Harcourt, 2012.

Beegel, Susan F., editor. *Hemingway's Neglected Short Fiction: New Perspectives.* U of Alabama P, 1989.

Beeton, Isabella. *Mrs. Beeton's Book of Household Management.* Edited by Nicola Humble, Oxford UP, 2000.

Bell, Julian, editor. *We Did Not Fight: 1914–18 Experiences of War Resisters.* Cobden-Sanderson, 1935.

Benjamin, Walter. "Thesis on the Philosophy of History." *Illuminations*, translated by Harry Zohn, Harcourt Brace Jovanovich, 1968, pp. 253–64.

Bennett, Warren. " 'That's Not Very Polite': Sexual Identity in Hemingway's 'The Sea Change.' " Beegel, pp. 225–45.

Bergen, Kristin. "Modernist and Future Ex-modernist." Boyd and Kirsch, pp. 215–34.

Berman, Jessica. *Modernist Commitments: Ethics, Politics, and Transnational Modernism.* Columbia UP, 2012.

———. *Modernist Fiction, Cosmopolitanism, and the Politics of Community.* Cambridge UP, 2001.

Bernstein, Charles. *Attack of the Difficult Poems.* U of Chicago P, 2011.

———, editor. *Close Listening: Poetry and the Performed Word.* Oxford UP, 1998.

———, editor. *Gertrude Stein's War Years: Setting the Record Straight: A Dossier.* Special edition of *Jacket2*, 9 May 2012, jacket2.org/feature/gertrude-steins-war-years-setting-record-straight.

———. Preface. Bernstein, *Gertrude Stein's War Years.*

Berry, Ellen E. *Curved Thought and Textual Wandering: Gertrude Stein's Postmodernism.* U of Michigan P, 1992.

Berthoff, Ann E. "Recognition, Representation, and Revision." *The Sense of Learning*, Boynton/Cook Publishers, 1990, pp. 28–41.

Bishop, Janet, et al., editors. *The Steins Collect: Matisse, Picasso, and the Parisian Avant-Garde.* San Francisco Museum of Modern Art / Yale UP, 2011.

Blackmer, Corinne. "African Masks and Passing in Stein and Larsen." 1993. Stein, *Three Lives*, pp. 407–28.

Bowers, Jane Palatini. *"They Watch Me As They Watch This": Gertrude Stein's Metadrama.* U of Pennsylvania P, 1991.

Boyd, Janet. "Gertrude Stein's Geographical History of Literature." Boyd and Kirsch, pp. 199–214.

Boyd, Janet, and Sharon J. Kirsch, editors. *Primary Stein: Returning to the Writing of Gertrude Stein*. Lexington, 2014.

Braddock, Jeremy. *Collecting as Modernist Practice*. Johns Hopkins UP, 2012.

Braun, Emily. "Saturday Evenings at the Steins.'" Bishop et al., pp. 49–67.

Brenner, Gerry. "A Semiotic Inquiry into Hemingway's 'A Simple Enquiry.'" Beegel, pp. 195–207.

Bridgman, Richard. *Gertrude Stein in Pieces*. Oxford UP, 1970.

Brilliant, Richard. *Portraiture*. Harvard UP, 1991.

Brinnin, John Malcolm. *The Third Rose: Gertrude Stein and Her World*. Little, Brown, 1959.

Bruffee, Kenneth A. "Collaborative Learning and the 'Conversation of Mankind.'" *College English*, vol. 46, no. 7, Nov. 1984, pp. 635–52.

Bruss, Elizabeth W. "Eye for I: Making and Unmaking Autobiography in Film." Olney, pp. 296–320.

Bullen, J. B. Introduction. *Vision and Design*, by Roger Fry. 1920. Dover, 1998, pp. xi–xxv.

Burke, Carolyn. "Gertrude Stein, the Cone Sisters, and the Puzzle of Female Friendship." *Critical Inquiry*, vol. 8, no. 3, Spring 1982, pp. 543–64.

Burns, Edward. "Gertrude Stein: A Complex Itinerary, 1940–1944." Bernstein, *Gertrude Stein's War Years*.

———, editor. *Staying On Alone: Letters of Alice B. Toklas*. Liveright, 1973.

Burns, Edward, and Ulla E. Dydo. "Gertrude Stein: September 1942 to September 1944." Burns and Dydo, *Letters*, pp. 401–21.

———, editors. *The Letters of Gertrude Stein and Thornton Wilder*. With William Rice, Yale UP, 1996.

Cage, John. *Empty Words: Writings, '73–'78*. Wesleyan UP, 1979.

Campbell, JoAnn. "Controlling Voices: The Legacy of English A at Radcliffe College, 1883–1917." *College Composition and Communication*, vol. 43, no. 4, Dec. 1992, pp. 472–85.

Cardinal, Jody. "'Come Too': 1920s Erotic Rights Discourse and Gertrude Stein's 'Patriarchal Poetry.'" Boyd and Kirsch, pp. 57–75.

Carr, Nicholas. "Is Google Making Us Stupid? What the Internet Is Doing to Our Brains." *The Atlantic*, July-Aug. 2008, www.theatlantic.com/magazine/archive/2008/07/is-google-making-us-stupid/306868/.

Carroll, Lewis. *Through the Looking-Glass*. *Project Gutenberg*, 6 Oct. 2016, www.gutenberg.org/files/12/12-h/12-h.htm.

Cecire, Natalia. "Ways of Not Reading Gertrude Stein." *ELH*, vol. 82, no. 1, Spring 2015, pp. 281–312.

Chauncey, George, Jr. "From Sexual Inversion to Homosexuality: Medicine and the Changing Conceptualization of Female Deviance." *Salmagundi*, no. 58–59, Fall-Winter 1982–83, pp. 114–46.

Chomsky, Noam. *Syntactic Structures*. Mouton, 1957.

Cixous, Hélène. "Castration or Decapitation?" Translated by Annette Kuhn, *Signs*, vol. 7, no. 1, Autumn 1981, pp. 41–55.

Claire Marie's New Books for Exotic Tastes. 1914. Gertrude Stein and Alice B. Toklas Papers, Yale Collection of American Literature, Beinecke Rare Book and Manuscript Library, Yale U. Box 75, folder 1370.

Clark, T. J. "Cubism and Collectivity." *Farewell to an Idea: Episodes from a History of Modernism*, Yale UP, 1999, pp. 169–223.

Cole, Teju. "Teju Cole." Interview by Aleksandar Hemon. *Bomb: Artists in Conversation*, vol. 127, Spring 2014, bombmagazine.org/article/10023/teju-cole.

Comley, Nancy R., and Robert Scholes. *Hemingway's Genders: Rereading the Hemingway Text*. Yale UP, 1994.

Corn, Wanda M., and Tirza True Latimer. *Seeing Gertrude Stein: Five Stories*. U of California P, 2011.

Cott, Nancy F. *The Grounding of Modern Feminism*. Yale UP, 1987.

Cox, Neil. *Cubism*. Phaidon, 2000.

Curnutt, Kirk, editor. *The Critical Response to Gertrude Stein*. Greenwood Press, 2000.

———. "Parody and Pedagogy: Teaching Style, Voice, and Authorial Intent in the Works of Gertrude Stein." *College Literature*, vol. 23, no. 2, June 1996, pp. 1–24.

Damon, Maria. "Gertrude Stein's Jewishness, Jewish Social Scientists, and the 'Jewish Question.'" *Modern Fiction Studies*, vol. 42, no. 3, Fall 1996, pp. 489–506.

Davis, Phoebe Stein. "'Even Cake Gets to Have Another Meaning': History, Narrative, and 'Daily Living' in Gertrude Stein's World War II Writings." *Modern Fiction Studies*, vol. 44, no. 3, Fall 1998, pp. 568–607.

———. "Subjectivity and the Aesthetics of National Identity in Gertrude Stein's *The Autobiography of Alice B. Toklas*." *Twentieth Century Literature*, vol. 45, no. 1, 1999, pp. 18–45.

Dean, Gabrielle. "Make It Plain: Stein and Toklas Publish the Plain Edition." Boyd and Kirsch, pp. 13–35.

DeKoven, Marianne. *A Different Language: Gertrude Stein's Experimental Writing*. U of Wisconsin P, 1983.

———. "Second Reappreciation of Gertrude Stein." *(HOW)ever*, www.asu.edu/pipercwcenter/how2journal/archive/print_archive/alerts0186.html.

D'Emilio, John, and Estelle B. Freedman. *Intimate Matters: A History of Sexuality in America*. 2nd ed., U of Chicago P, 1997.

Dickinson, Emily. *The Poems of Emily Dickinson: Reading Edition*. Edited by R. W. Franklin, Harvard UP, 1999.

Diepeveen, Leonard. *Mock Modernism: An Anthology of Parodies, Travesties, Frauds, 1910–1935*. U of Toronto P, 2014.

Doane, Janice L. *Silence and Narrative: The Early Novels of Gertrude Stein*. Greenwood, 1986.

Dodge, Mabel. "Speculations; or, Post-impressionism in Prose." *Arts and Decoration*, Mar. 1913, pp. 172, 174.

Doolittle, Hilda. *Collected Poems, 1912–1944*. Edited by Louis Martz, New Directions, 1983.

Douglass, Frederick. *Narrative of the Life of Frederick Douglass*. Andrews, pp. 229–327.

DuBois, Ellen Carol. *Feminism and Suffrage: The Emergence of an Independent Women's Movement in America, 1848–1869*. 2nd ed., Cornell UP, 1999.

Dupee, F. W. "General Introduction." Stein, *Selected Writings*, pp. ix–xvii.

DuPlessis, Rachel Blau. *Genders, Races, and Religious Cultures in Modern American Poetry, 1908–1934*. Cambridge UP, 2001.

———. "Woolfenstein, the Sequel." Boyd and Kirsch, pp. 37–55.

Dydo, Ulla E. *Gertrude Stein: The Language That Rises, 1923–1934*. With William Rice, Northwestern UP, 2003.

———. Introduction to "Ada." Dydo, *Stein Reader*, pp. 100–01.

———, editor. *A Stein Reader*. Northwestern UP, 1993.

Elbow, Peter. *Everyone Can Write: Essays toward a Hopeful Theory of Writing and Teaching Writing*. Oxford UP, 2000.

———. *Writing with Power: Techniques for Mastering the Writing Process*. Oxford UP, 1981.

Eliot, T. S. "Charleston, Hey! Hey!" *The Nation and Athenaeum*, 29 Jan. 1927, p. 595.

———. *The Waste Land*. *Bartleby.com*, Aug. 2011, www.bartleby.com/201/1.html.

Ellis, Havelock. *Analysis of the Sexual Impulse, Love and Pain, The Sexual Impulse in Women*. 1903. 2nd ed., F. A. Davis, 1913. Vol. 3 of *Studies in the Psychology of Sex*. 7 vols., 1897–1928.

———. *Sex in Relation to Society*. 1910. F. A. Davis, 1913. Vol. 6 of *Studies in the Psychology of Sex*.

———. *Sexual Inversion*. 1901. 3rd ed. F. A. Davis, 1915. Vol. 2 of *Studies in the Psychology of Sex*.

Emerson, Ralph Waldo. *Selected Essays*. Penguin, 1982.

———. "Self-Reliance." *Ralph Waldo Emerson Texts*, www.emersoncentral.com/texts/essays-first-series/self-reliance/.

Emig, Janet. *The Web of Meaning: Essays on Writing, Teaching, Learning, and Thinking*. Edited by Dixie Goswami and Maureen Butler, Boynton/Cook, 1983.

English, Hugh. "Learning and Unlearning Historical Sexual Identities." *Radical Teacher*, vol. 66, Spring 2003, pp. 5–10.

Esdale, Logan. "Gertrude Stein's Twin." *Textual Practice*, vol. 25, no. 6, Dec. 2011, pp. 989–1014.

———. "Unoriginal Genius: Student Poems Made from *Tender Buttons*." *Modernism/modernity*, 2 Mar. 2016, modernismmodernity.org/forums/posts/unoriginal-genius-student-poems-made-tender-buttons. Print Plus.

Faderman, Lillian. *Odd Girls and Twilight Lovers: A History of Lesbian Life in Twentieth-Century America*. Penguin, 1991.

Farland, Maria. "Gertrude Stein's Brain Work." *American Literature*, vol. 76, no. 1, Mar. 2004, pp. 117–48.

Felski, Rita. "Modernist Studies and Cultural Studies: Reflections on Method." *Modernism/modernity*, vol. 10, no. 3, Sept. 2003, pp. 501–17.

Fifer, Elizabeth. *Rescued Readings: A Reconstruction of Gertrude Stein's Difficult Texts*. Wayne State UP, 1992.

Foucault, Michel. "Friendship as a Way of Life." *Ethics*, edited by Paul Rabinow, New Press, 1997, pp. 135–40. Vol. 1 of *The Essential Works of Foucault, 1954–1984.*

Four Americans in Paris: The Collections of Gertrude Stein and Her Family. Musuem of Modern Art, 1970.

Four Saints in Three Acts. 1934. *YouTube*, 23 Feb. 2012, www.youtube.com/watch?v=sXINp5iuUyw.

Frank, Adam. *Transferential Poetics, from Poe to Warhol.* Fordham UP, 2015.

Franklin, Benjamin. *The Autobiography of Benjamin Franklin.* Andrews, pp. 70–228.

Friedman, Susan Stanford. "Women's Autobiographical Selves: Theory and Practice." *The Private Self: Theory and Practice of Women's Autobiographical Writings*, U of North Carolina P, 1988, pp. 34–62.

Frost, Elisabeth. *The Feminist Avant-Garde in American Poetry.* U of Iowa P, 2003.

Frost, Robert. *North of Boston. Internet Archive*, 18 Sept. 2006, archive.org/details/northofboston00frosrish.

Fussell, Paul. *The Boys' Crusade: The American Infantry in Northwestern Europe, 1944–1945.* Modern Library, 2003.

———. *Wartime: Understanding and Behavior in the Second World War.* Oxford UP, 1989.

Gallagher, Jean. "Occupation and Observer: Gertrude Stein in Vichy France." *The World Wars through the Female Gaze*, Southern Illinois UP, 1998, pp. 116–50.

Gallup, Donald. "Always Gtrde Stein." *Southwest Review*, vol. 34, no. 4, Summer 1949, pp. 254–58.

———. "Du Côté de Chez Stein." *The Book Collector*, 19 Sept. 1970, pp. 169–84.

———. "The Gertrude Stein Collection." *The Yale University Library Gazette*, vol. 22, no. 2, Oct. 1947, pp. 21–32.

Galvin, Rachel. "Gertrude Stein, Pétain, and the Politics of Translation." *ELH*, vol. 83, no. 1, Spring 2016, pp. 259–92.

Gass, William H. Introduction. *The Geographical History of America; or, The Relation of Human Nature to the Human Mind*, Johns Hopkins UP, 1995, pp. 3–42.

"Gay, 4d." *Oxford English Dictionary*, 3rd ed. *OED Online*, dictionary.oed.com.

"Gertrude Stein Arrives and Baffles Reporters by Making Herself Clear." *The New York Times*, 25 Oct. 1934, p. 25.

Gilbert, Sandra M., and Susan Gubar. *Sexchanges.* Yale UP, 1989. Vol. 2 of *No Man's Land: The Place of the Woman Writer in the Twentieth Century.*

Gilman, Charlotte Perkins. *Women and Economics: A Study of the Economic Relation between Men and Women as a Factor in Social Evolution.* 1898. *Digital Library*, Penn Libraries, U of Pennsylvania, digital.library.upenn.edu/women/gilman/economics/economics.html.

Gilman, Sander L. *Difference and Pathology: Stereotypes of Sexuality, Race, and Madness.* Cornell UP, 1985.

Giroud, Vincent. *Picasso and Gertrude Stein.* Metropolitan Museum of Art, 2006.

Goodspeed-Chadwick, Julie. *Trauma and the Female Body in Djuna Barnes, H.D., and Gertrude Stein: Modernist Women Writers and War.* Louisiana State UP, 2011.

Gordon, Michael. "From an Unfortunate Necessity to a Cult of Mutual Orgasm: Sex in American Marital Education Literature, 1830–1940." *Studies in the Sociology of Sex*, edited by James M. Henslin, Appleton-Century-Crofts, 1971, pp. 53–77.

Graff, Gerald. *Beyond the Culture Wars: How Teaching the Conflicts Can Revitalize American Education.* Norton, 1992.

Graff, Gerald, and Cathy Birkenstein. *They Say / I Say: The Moves That Matter in Academic Writing.* 3rd ed., W. W. Norton, 2014.

Grosser, Maurice. "Scenario." Stein and Thomson, pp. iii–v.

———. "Visiting Gertrude and Alice." *The New York Review of Books*, 6 Nov. 1986, www.nybooks.com/articles/1986/11/06/visiting-gertrude-and-alice/.

Gusdorf, Georges. "Conditions and Limits of Autobiography." Olney, pp. 28–48.

Guy, Alfred E., Jr. "Process Writing: Reflection and the Arts of Writing and Teaching." *Writing-Based Teaching: Essential Practices and Enduring Questions*, edited by Teresa Vilardi and Mary Chang, State U of New York P, 2009, pp. 53–70.

Haas, Robert Bartlett, and Donald Clifford Gallup. *A Catalogue of the Published and Unpublished Writings of Gertrude Stein.* Yale U Library, 1941.

Hacker, Diana, and Nancy Sommers. *Rules for Writers.* 7th ed., Bedford–St. Martin's, 2011.

Hadas, Pamela. "Spreading the Difference: One Way to Read Gertrude Stein's *Tender Buttons*." *Twentieth Century Literature*, vol. 24, no. 1, Spring 1978, pp. 57–75.

Hall, John. *The Self-Portrait: A Cultural History.* Thames and Hudson, 2014.

Haselstein, Ulla. "Gertrude Stein's Portraits of Matisse and Picasso." *New Literary History*, vol. 34, no. 4, Autumn 2003, pp. 723–43.

Hejinian, Lyn. *The Language of Inquiry.* U of California P, 2000.

Hemingway, Ernest. *The Complete Short Stories of Ernest Hemingway.* Scribner, 2003.

———. *Garden of Eden.* Scribner, 1986.

———. *Green Hills of Africa.* Scribner, 1987.

———. *A Moveable Feast.* Scribner, 2003.

———. *The Sun Also Rises.* Scribner, 2006.

———. *The Torrents of Spring.* Scribner, 1998.

Higginson, Thomas Wentworth. "The American Lecture System." *Littell's Living Age*, 6 June 1868, pp. 630–37.

Hinkle, James. "What's Funny in *The Sun Also Rises*." *The Hemingway Review*, vol. 4, no. 2, Spring 1985, pp. 31–41.

Hinnov, Emily M., et al., editors. *Communal Modernisms: Teaching Twentieth-Century Literature and Culture in the Twenty-First-Century Classroom.* Palgrave Macmillan, 2013.

———. "Communal Modernisms: Teaching Twentieth-Century Literature and Culture in the Twenty-First-Century Classroom." Hinnov et al., *Communal Modernisms*, pp. 1–17.

Hitchcock, H. Wiley, and Charles Fussell, editors. *Four Saints in Three Acts*. By Virgil Thomson and Gertrude Stein, A-R Editions, 2008.

Hobhouse, Janet. *Everybody Who Was Anybody: A Biography of Gertrude Stein*. Putnam, 1975.

Hoffman, Michael, editor. *Critical Essays on Gertrude Stein*. G. K. Hall, 1986.

Holbrook, Susan, and Thomas Dilworth, editors. *The Letters of Gertrude Stein and Virgil Thomson: Composition as Collaboration*. Oxford UP, 2010.

Hovey, Jaime. "Gertrude Stein: *Three Lives*." *A Companion to Modernist Literature and Culture*, edited by David Bradshaw and Kevin J. H. Dettmar, Blackwell, 2005, pp. 450–58.

Howarth, William L. "Some Principles of Autobiography." Olney, pp. 84–114.

Howe, Susan. *My Emily Dickinson*. North Atlantic Books, 1985.

Inness, Sherrie A. "Who's Afraid of Stephen Gordon?: The Lesbian in the United States Popular Imagination of the 1920s." *NWSA Journal*, vol. 4, no. 3, Autumn 1992, pp. 303–20.

Jackson, Julian. *France: The Dark Years, 1940–1944*. Oxford UP, 2001.

James, Henry. Preface to *Roderick Hudson*. *The Art of the Novel*, edited by R. P. Blackmur, Charles Scribner's Sons, 1934, pp. 3–19.

———. *"The Question of Our Speech" [and] "The Lesson of Balzac": Two Lectures*. Riverside, 1905.

———. *The Wings of the Dove*. Edited by J. Donald Crowley and Richard A. Hocks, Norton, 2003.

James, William. "The Place of Affectional Facts in a World of Pure Experience." *The Journal of Philosophy, Psychology, and Scientific Methods*, vol. 2, no. 11, 1905, pp. 281–87.

———. *Principles of Psychology*. *Internet Archive*, 5 Sept. 2006, archive.org/details/theprinciplesofp01jameuoft.

———. "What Is an Emotion?" *Mind*, vol. 9, 1884, pp. 188–205.

Jelinek, Estelle C. *The Tradition of Women's Autobiography: From Antiquity to the Present*. Twayne, 1986.

Johnston, Georgia. *The Formation of Twentieth-Century Queer Autobiography: Reading Vita Sackville-West, Virginia Woolf, Hilda Doolittle, and Gertrude Stein*. Palgrave Macmillan, 2007.

Jones, Susan. "'Savage and Superb': Primitivism in Text and Dance." *Literature, Modernism, and Dance*, Oxford UP, 2013, pp. 151–78.

Justice, Hilary K. "'Well, Well, Well': Cross-Gendered Autobiography and the Manuscript of 'Hills like White Elephants.'" *The Hemingway Review*, vol. 18, no. 1, Fall 1998, pp. 17–32.

Kane, Daniel. "Book Was There: Teaching Gertrude Stein's *Tender Buttons* to Young and Old." *The Teachers and Writers Guide to Classic American Literature*, edited by Christopher Edgar and Gary Lenhart, Teachers and Writers Collaborative, 2001, pp. 153–62.

Kaplan, Amy. *The Anarchy of Empire in the Making of U.S. Culture*. Harvard UP, 2002.

Karmel, Pepe. *Picasso and the Invention of Cubism*. Yale UP, 2003.

Katz, Leon. "The First Making of *The Making of Americans*: A Study Based on Gertrude Stein's Notebooks and Early Versions of Her Novel, 1902–1908." 1963. Columbia U, PhD dissertation.

———. Introduction. *Fernhurst,* Q.E.D.*, and Other Early Writings*, by Gertrude Stein, Liveright, 1971, pp. ix–xlii.

———. "A Year with Alice B. Toklas." *The Yale Review*, vol. 100, no. 3, July 2012, pp. 1–22.

Keighren, Innes. *Bringing Geography to Book: Ellen Semple and the Reception of Geographical Knowledge.* I. B. Tauris, 2010.

Keith, Philip M. "How to Write like Gertrude Stein." *Audits of Meaning*, edited by Louise Z. Smith, Boynton/Cook–Heinemann, 1988, pp. 229–37.

Kellner, Bruce. *A Gertrude Stein Companion: Content with the Example.* Greenwood, 1988.

Kirsch, Sharon J. *Gertrude Stein and the Reinvention of Rhetoric.* U of Alabama P, 2014.

———. "Gertrude Stein Delivers." *Rhetoric Review*, vol. 31, no. 3, July 2012, pp. 254–70.

———. "How to Read *How To Write*: Bothering with Gertrude Stein." Boyd and Kirsch, pp. 109–24.

Klein, John. "The Mask as Image and Strategy." Alarcó and Warner, pp. 25–35.

Kostelanetz, Richard. Introduction. Kostelanetz, *Yale Gertrude Stein*, pp. xiii–xxxi.

———, editor. *The Yale Gertrude Stein.* Yale UP, 1980.

LaCapra, Dominick. *Writing History, Writing Trauma.* Johns Hopkins UP, 2001.

Laird, Holly. *Women Coauthors.* U of Illinois P, 2000.

Lamb, Robert Paul. *Art Matters: Hemingway, Craft, and the Creation of the Modern Short Story.* Louisiana State UP, 2010.

———. *The Hemingway Short Story: A Study in Craft for Writers and Readers.* Louisiana State UP, 2013.

Larsen, Lyle. *Stein and Hemingway: The Story of a Turbulent Friendship.* McFarland, 2011.

Lasky, Dorothea. "What Poetry Teaches Us about the Power of Persuasion." *The Atlantic*, 13 Oct. 2012, www.theatlantic.com/national/archive/2012/10/what-poetry-teaches-us-about-the-power-of-persuasion/263551/.

Leick, Karen. *Gertrude Stein and the Making of an American Celebrity.* Routledge, 2009.

Lejeune, Philippe. *On Autobiography.* Edited by Paul John Eakin, translated by Katherine Leary, U of Minnesota P, 1989.

Lénárt-Cheng, Helga. "Autobiography as Advertisement: Why Do Gertrude Stein's Sentences Get under Our Skin?" *New Literary History*, vol. 34, no. 1, Winter 2003, pp. 117–31.

Lewis, Wyndham. *Time and Western Man.* Chatto and Windus, 1927.

Loeffelholz, Mary. "History as Conjugation: Stein's *Stanzas in Meditation* and the Literary History of the Modernist Long Poem." *Gendered Modernisms: American Women Poets and Their Readers*, edited by Margaret Dickie and Thomas Travisano, U of Pennsylvania P, 1996, pp. 26–42.

Lorange, Astrid. *How Reading Is Written: A Brief Index to Gertrude Stein*. Wesleyan UP, 2014.

Luckhurst, Roger. *The Trauma Question*. Routledge, 2008.

MacKinnon, Catharine A. "Engaged Scholarship as Method and Vocation." *Yale Journal of Law and Feminism*, vol. 22, no. 2, 2010, pp. 193–205.

Magidor, Ofra. *Category Mistakes*. Oxford UP, 2013.

Malcolm, Janet. *Two Lives: Gertrude and Alice*. Yale UP, 2007.

Marcus, Jane. "Afterword: Some Notes on Radical Teaching." Hinnov et al., *Communal Modernisms*, pp. 189–98.

———. *Art and Anger: Reading like a Woman*. Ohio State UP, 1998.

Marranca, Bonnie. Introduction. Stein, *Last Operas*, pp. vii–xxvii.

Matisse, Henri. *La femme au chapeau*. 1905, oil on canvas, San Francisco Museum of Modern Art.

McCallum, E. L. "Stein und Zeit." *Queer Times, Queer Becomings*, edited by McCallum and Mikko Tuhkanen, State U of New York P, 2011, pp. 233–56.

———. *Unmaking* The Making of Americans*: Toward an Aesthetic Ontology*, State U of New York P, 2018.

McElwee, Ross. *Time Indefinite*. McElwee Productions, 1993.

McLeod, Susan. "The Pedagogy of Writing across the Curriculum." *A Guide to Composition Pedagogies*, edited by Gary Tate et al., Oxford UP, 2001, pp. 149–64.

Mellow, James. *Charmed Circle: Gertrude Stein and Company*. Praeger, 1974.

Meyer, Steven. *Irresistible Dictation: Gertrude Stein and the Correlations of Writing and Science*. Stanford UP, 2001.

Miller, Eugene E. "Richard Wright and Gertrude Stein." *Black American Literature Forum*, vol. 16, no. 3, Fall 1982, pp. 107–12.

Miller, Rosalind S. *Gertrude Stein: Form and Intelligibility*. Exposition Press, 1949.

Mills, Jean. "Gertrude on the Block: Writing, Love, and Fame in *Stanzas in Meditation*." *Philological Quarterly*, vol. 83, no. 2, Spring 2004, pp. 197–210.

"Miss Stein Puzzle to Psychiatrists." *The New York Times*, 29 Nov. 1934, p. 29.

"Miss Stein Speaks to Bewildered 500." *The New York Times*, 2 Nov. 1934, p. 23.

Mix, Deborah M. "Gertrude Stein's Currency." *Modernist Star Maps: Celebrity, Modernity, Culture*, edited by Aaron Jaffe and Jonathan Goldman, Ashgate, 2010, pp. 93–104.

———. *A Vocabulary of Thinking: Gertrude Stein and Contemporary North American Women's Innovative Writing*. U of Iowa P, 2007.

Moad, Rosalind. "1914–16: Years of Innovation in Gertrude Stein's Writing." 1993. U of York, PhD dissertation.

Monroe, Jonathan. *A Poverty of Objects: The Prose Poem and the Politics of Genre*. Cornell UP, 1987.

Moore, George. *Gertrude Stein's* The Making of Americans*: Repetition and the Emergence of Modernism*. Peter Lang, 1998.

Moretti, Franco. *Signs Taken for Wonders: On the Sociology of Literary Forms*. Verso, 1983.

Morrison, Toni. "Toni Morrison: The Art of Fiction." Interview by Elissa Schappell. *The Paris Review*, vol. 128, Fall 1993, www.theparisreview.org/interviews/1888/the-art-of-fiction-no-134-toni-morrison.

Moyes, Lianne, editor. *Gail Scott: Essays on Her Works.* Guernica Editions, 2002.

Mullen, Harryette. "If Lilies are Lily White: From the Stain of Miscegenation in Stein's 'Melanctha' to the 'Clean Mixture' of White and Color in *Tender Buttons*." *The Cracks between What We Are and What We Are Supposed to Be*, U of Alabama P, 2012, pp. 20–28.

———. Interview by Cynthia Hogue. *Postmodern Culture*, vol. 9, no. 2, Jan. 1999. *Project MUSE*, muse.jhu.edu/article/27693.

———. *Sleeping with the Dictionary.* U of California P, 2002.

———. *S*PeRM**K*T.* Singing Horse Press, 1992.

Nelson, Cary. "The Fate of Gender in Modern American Poetry." *Marketing Modernisms: Self-Promotion, Canonization, Rereading*, edited by Kevin J. H. Dettmar and Stephen Watt, U of Michigan P, 1996, pp. 321–60.

Neuman, Shirley, and Ira Nadel. *Gertrude Stein and the Making of Literature.* Macmillan, 1988.

News bulletin. Records of the university librarian, 1938–1950, Yale U Archives. Series 2, box 102, folder 1406.

Newton, Esther. "The Mythic Mannish Lesbian: Radclyffe Hall and the New Woman." *Signs*, vol. 9, no. 4, Summer 1984, pp. 557–75.

North, Michael. *The Dialect of Modernism: Race, Language, and Twentieth-Century Literature.* Oxford UP, 1994.

Nussbaum, Martha. *Cultivating Humanity: A Classical Defense of Reform in Liberal Education.* Harvard UP, 1997.

O'Brien, Tim. *In the Lake of the Woods.* Houghton Mifflin Harcourt, 2006.

Odita, E. Okechukwu. "African Art: The Concept in European Literature." *Journal of Black Studies*, vol. 8, no. 2, Dec. 1977, pp. 189–204.

O'Donnell, Heather. "'My Own Funny Little Lecture Boom': Henry James's American Performance." *Henry James Review*, vol. 24, no. 2, Spring 2003, pp. 133–45.

Olney, James, editor. *Autobiography: Essays Theoretical and Critical.* Princeton UP, 1980.

Olson, Liesl. "'An Invincible Force Meets an Immovable Object': Gertrude Stein Comes to Chicago." *Modernism/modernity*, vol. 17, no. 2, Apr. 2010, pp. 331–61.

Paxton, Robert. *Vichy France: Old Guard, New Order, 1940–1944.* Knopf, 1972.

Pearson, Norman Holmes. "The Gertrude Stein Collection." *The Yale University Library Gazette*, vol. 16, no. 3, Jan. 1942, pp. 45–47.

Peck, James, and Kelly Howe. "Learning with Gertrude Stein: Playgrounds of Aggression and Grace." *Theatre Topics*, vol. 14, no. 2, Sept. 2004, pp. 379–96.

Perl, Sondra. "The Composing Processes of Unskilled Writers." *Research in the Teaching of English*, vol. 13, no. 4, 1979, pp. 317–36. *ERIC*, eric.ed.gov/?id=ED147819.

Perloff, Marjorie. "'A Cessation of Resemblances': Stein/Picasso/Duchamp." *Moving Modernisms: Motion, Technology, and Modernity*, edited by David Bradshaw et al., Oxford UP, 2016, pp. 127–42.

———. "Poetry as Word-System: The Art of Gertrude Stein." *The Poetics of Indeterminacy: Rimbaud to Cage*, Northwestern UP, 1999, pp. 67–109.

Peters, Carl. *Studies in Description: Reading Gertrude Stein's* Tender Buttons. Talonbooks, 2016.

Picasso, Pablo. *Gertrude Stein.* 1905–06, oil on canvas, Metropolitan Museum of Art, New York.

Pitchford, Nicola. "Unlikely Modernism, Unlikely Postmodernism: Stein's *Tender Buttons.*" *American Literary History*, vol. 11, no. 4, Winter 1999, pp. 642–67.

Pollack-Pelzner, Daniel. "Swiping Stein: The Ambivalence of Hemingway Parodies." *The Hemingway Review*, vol. 30, no. 1, Fall 2010, pp. 69–82.

Pondrom, Cyrena N. "An Introduction to the Achievement of Gertrude Stein." *Geography and Plays*, by Gertrude Stein, U of Wisconsin P, 1993, pp. vii–lv.

Porte, Rebecca Ariel. "Long Dull Poems: Stein's *Stanzas in Meditation* and Wordsworth's *The Prelude.*" Boyd and Kirsch, pp. 77–95.

Porter, Katherine Anne. "Gertrude Stein: Three Views." *The Collected Essays and Occasional Writings*, Delacorte, 1970, pp. 251–70.

Posman, Sarah, and Laura Luise Schultz, editors. *Gertrude Stein in Europe: Reconfigurations across Media, Disciplines and Traditions.* Bloomsbury Academic, 2015.

Pound, Scott. "The Difference Sound Makes: Gertrude Stein and the Poetics of Intonation." *English Studies in Canada*, vol. 33, no. 4, Winter 2007, pp. 25–35.

Poznanski, Renée. *Jews in France during World War II.* Translated by Nathan Bracher, Brandeis UP / UP of New England, 2001.

"Princeton Dazed by Gertrude Stein." *The New York Times*, 6 Nov. 1934, p. 23.

Puchner, Martin. *Stage Fright: Modernism, Anti-theatricality, and Drama.* Johns Hopkins UP, 2002.

Rabinow, Rebecca. "Discovering Modern Art: The Steins' Early Years in Paris, 1903–1907." Bishop et al., pp. 21–47.

Ramazani, Jahan, editor. *The Norton Anthology of Modern and Contemporary Poetry.* Vol. 1, 3rd ed., Norton, 2003.

Renner, Stanley. "Moving to the Girl's Side of 'Hills like White Elephants.'" *The Hemingway Review*, vol. 15, no. 1, Fall 1995, pp. 27–41.

Retallack, Joan, editor. *Gertrude Stein: Selections.* U of California P, 2008.

———. "On Not Not Reading *Stanzas in Meditation*: Pressure and Pleasures of the Text." Stein, *Stanzas*, pp. 1–27.

———. *The Poethical Wager.* U of California P, 2003.

Richardson, John. *A Life of Picasso: Volume 1, 1881–1906.* Random House, 1991.

Riding, Laura. *Contemporaries and Snobs.* 1928. Edited by Laura Heffernan and Jane Malcolm, U of Alabama P, 2014.

Rieke, Alison. "Gertrude Stein: Mastering Pieces." *The Senses of Nonsense*, U of Iowa P, 1992, pp. 60–92.

Robbins, Amy Moorman. *American Hybrid Poetics: Gender, Mass Culture, and Form.* Rutgers UP, 2014.

Roberts, Mary Louise. *What Soldiers Do: Sex and the American GI in World War II France*. U of Chicago P, 2013.

Robinson, Marc. *The American Play, 1787–2000*. Yale UP, 2009.

———. *The Other American Drama*. Johns Hopkins UP, 1997.

Rogers, William Garland. *When This You See Remember Me: Gertrude Stein in Person*. Rinehart, 1948.

Rosario, Vernon A., editor. *Science and Homosexualities*. Routledge, 1997.

Rosenblatt, Roger. "Black Autobiography: Life as the Death Weapon." Olney, pp. 169–80.

Ruddick, Lisa. *Reading Gertrude Stein: Body, Text, Gnosis*. Cornell UP, 1990.

Rumbarger, Lee. "We Moderns: Women Modernists Writing on War and Home." *ProQuest*, gradworks.umi.com/32/45/3245341.html. 2006, U of Texas, Austin, dissertation.

Ryan, Betsy Alayne. *Gertrude Stein's Theatre of the Absolute*. UMI Research Press, 1984.

Sanger, Margaret. *Happiness in Marriage*. 1926. Maxwell Reprint, 1969.

Sayre, Robert F. "Autobiography and the Making of America." Olney, pp. 146–68.

Schmitz, Neil. "The Difference of Her Likeness: Gertrude Stein's *Stanzas in Meditation*." Neuman and Nadel, pp. 124–49.

Schultz, Susan. "Gertrude Stein's Self-Advertisement." *Raritan*, vol. 12, no. 1, Fall 1992, pp. 71–88.

Schuster, Joshua. "The Making of *Tender Buttons*: Gertrude Stein's Subjects, Objects, and the Illegible." *Jacket2*, 21 Apr. 2011, jacket2.org/article/making-tender-buttons.

Sedgwick, Eve Kosofsky. *Epistemology of the Closet*. U of California P, 2008.

———. "Is the Rectum Straight? Identification and Identity in *The Wings of the Dove*." *Tendencies*, Duke UP, 1993, pp. 73–103.

Semple, Ellen Churchill. *American History and Its Geographic Conditions*. 1903. Rev. ed., Houghton Mifflin, 1933.

Setina, Emily. "From 'Impossible' Writing to a Poetics of Intimacy: John Ashbery's Reading of Gertrude Stein." *Genre*, vol. 45, no. 1, Spring 2012, pp. 143–66.

Shiff, Richard. *Cézanne and the End of Impressionism: A Study of the Theory, Technique, and Critical Evaluation of Modern Art*. U of Chicago P, 1984.

Simmons, Christina. "Modern Sexuality and the Myth of Victorian Repression." *Passion and Power: Sexuality in History*, edited by Kathy Peiss et al., Temple UP, 1989, pp. 157–77.

Simon, Linda. *The Biography of Alice B. Toklas*. Doubleday, 1977.

Smedman, Lorna. "'Cousin to Cooning': Relation, Difference, and Racialized Language in Stein's Nonrepresentational Texts." *Modern Fiction Studies*, vol. 42, no. 3, Fall 1996, pp. 569–88.

Smith, Sidonie, and Julia Watson. *Reading Autobiography: A Guide for Interpreting Life Narratives*. U of Minneapolis P, 2010.

Smith-Rosenberg, Carroll. "The Female World of Love and Ritual: Relations between Women in Nineteenth-Century America." *Signs*, vol. 1, no. 1, Autumn 1975, pp. 1–29.

Sollors, Werner. "Gertrude Stein and 'Negro Sunshine.'" *Ethnic Modernism*, Harvard UP, 2008, pp. 17–34.

Solomons, Leon M., and Gertrude Stein. "Normal Motor Automatism." *Psychological Review*, vol. 3, no. 5, Sept. 1896, pp. 492–512.

Souhami, Diana. *Gertrude and Alice*. Pandora Press, 1991.

Spahr, Juliana. Afterword. Stein, *Tender Buttons*, pp. 109–25.

———. *Everybody's Autonomy: Connective Reading and Collective Identity*. U of Alabama P, 2001.

Sprigge, Elizabeth. *Gertrude Stein: Her Life and Work*. Harper, 1957.

Stein, Gertrude. "Ada." 1910. Dydo, *Stein Reader*, pp. 101–03.

———. "An American and France." 1935. *What Are Masterpieces*, Pitman, 1970, pp. 61–70.

———. "As Fine as Melanctha." 1922. *As Fine as Melanctha, 1914–1930*, Yale UP, 1954, pp. 255–69.

———. *The Autobiography of Alice B. Toklas*. 1933. Vintage, 1990.

———. *Blood on the Dining-Room Floor*. 1948. Dover, 2008.

———. "A Book Concluding with 'As a Wife Has a Cow: A Love Story.'" 1923. Stein, *Gertrude Stein*, vol. 1, pp. 495–503.

———. *Brewsie and Willie*. 1946. Stein, *Gertrude Stein*, vol. 2, pp. 715–78.

———. "Composition as Explanation." 1926. Dydo, *Stein Reader*, pp. 495–503.

———. "A Conversation." Interview by John Hyde Preston, *The Atlantic Monthly*, Aug. 1935, pp. 187–94.

———. "Cultivated Motor Automatism: A Study of the Character in Its Relation to Attention." *Psychological Review*, vol. 5, no. 3, May 1898, pp. 295–306.

———. "Erik Satie." 1922. Stein, *Gertrude Stein*, vol. 1, p. 493.

———. *Everybody's Autobiography*. 1937. Exact Change, 1993.

———. *Four Saints in Three Acts*. 1934. Stein, *Selected Writings*, pp. 577–612.

———. *The Geographical History of America; or, The Relation of Human Nature to the Human Mind*. 1936. Stein, *Gertrude Stein*, vol. 2, pp. 367–488.

———. *Geography and Plays*. 1922. Dover, 1999.

———. "Gertrude Stein: A Radio Interview." By William Lundell. *Paris Review*, vol. 32, no. 116, Fall 1990, pp. 85–97.

———. *Gertrude Stein: Writings, 1903–1946*. 2 vols., edited by Catharine R. Stimpson and Harriet Chessman, Library of America, 1998.

———. "The Gradual Making of *The Making of Americans*." Stein, *Lectures*, pp. 135–61.

———. "History; or, Messages from History." Retallack, *Gertrude Stein*, pp. 254–74.

———. "How She Bowed to Her Brother." *PennSound*, media.sas.upenn.edu /pennsound/authors/Stein/Speech-Lab-Recordings/Stein-Gertrude_17_384B

_How-She-Bowed-To-Her-Brother_Speech-Lab-Recordings_New-York_1935.mp3. Read by Gertrude Stein and recorded 30 Jan. 1935.

———. *How to Write*. 1931. Edited by Patricia Meyerowitz, Dover, 1975.

———. "How Writing Is Written." Stein, *Ida*, pp. 262–75.

———. *How Writing Is Written*. Edited by Robert Bartlett Haas, Black Sparrow Press, 1974.

———. *Ida: A Novel*. 1941. Edited by Logan Esdale, Yale UP, 2012.

———. *Identity: A Poem*. 1935. Dydo, *Stein Reader*, pp. 588–94.

———. "If I Told Him: A Completed Portrait of Picasso." 1924. Dydo, *Stein Reader*, pp. 464–66.

———. "Introduction to Pétain's *Paroles aux français*." 1942. Burns and Dydo, *Letters*, pp. 406–08.

———. "Introduction to the Speeches of Maréchal Pétain." *Modernism/modernity*, vol. 3, no. 3, Sept. 1996, pp. 93–95.

———. *Ladies' Voices*. 1922. Stein, *Selected Writings*, pp. 555–56.

———. *Last Operas and Plays*. 1949. Johns Hopkins UP, 1995.

———. *Lectures in America*. 1935. Beacon Press, 1985.

———. Literary notes. Gertrude Stein and Alice B. Toklas Papers, Yale Collection of American Literature, Beinecke Rare Book and Manuscript Library, Yale U. Box 33, folder 699.

———. "A Long Gay Book." 1911–12. Dydo, *Stein Reader*, pp. 152–253.

———. *The Making of Americans: Being a History of a Family's Progress*. 1925. Dalkey Archive, 1995.

———. "Matisse." 1909–10. Dydo, *Stein Reader*, pp. 139–41.

———. *The Mother of Us All*. 1946. Stein, *Gertrude Stein*, vol. 2, pp. 781–819.

———. *A Novel of Thank You*. 1925–26. Dalkey Archive Press, 1994.

———. "Off We All Went to See Germany." *Life*, 6 Aug. 1945, pp. 54+.

———. *Paris France*. 1940. Liveright, 1970.

———. "Patriarchal Poetry." 1927. Stein, *Gertrude Stein*, vol. 1, pp. 567–607.

———. "Picasso." 1909–10. Dydo, *A Stein Reader*, pp. 142–43.

———. *Picasso*. 1938. Dover, 1984.

———. "Pictures." Stein, *Lectures*, pp. 59–90.

———. "Plays." Stein, *Lectures*, pp. 93–131.

———. "Poetry and Grammar." Stein, *Lectures*, pp. 209–46.

———. "Portraits and Repetition." Stein, *Lectures*, pp. 165–206.

———. *A Primer for the Gradual Understanding of Gertrude Stein*. Edited by Robert Bartlett Haas, Black Sparrow Press, 1971.

———. *Selected Writings of Gertrude Stein*. 1946. Edited by Carl Van Vechten, Vintage, 1990.

———. "A Sonatina Followed by Another." 1921. Kostelanetz, *Yale Gertrude Stein*, pp. 287–315.

———. *Stanzas in Meditation: The Corrected Edition*. Edited by Susannah Hollister and Emily Setina, Yale UP, 2012.

———. *Tender Buttons: The Corrected Centennial Edition*. Edited by Seth Perlow, City Lights, 2014.

———. Three Lives *and* Q. E. D. Edited by Marianne DeKoven, W. W. Norton, 2006.

———. "A Transatlantic Interview." By Robert Bartlett Haas, with William S. Sutton. Stein, *Primer*, pp. 15–35.

———. *Wars I Have Seen*. Random House, 1945.

———. "What Are Master-pieces and Why Are There So Few of Them." 1935. Stein, *Gertrude Stein*, vol. 2, pp. 355–63.

Stein, Gertrude, and Virgil Thomson. *Four Saints in Three Acts: An Opera*. Scenario by Maurice Grosser, Schirmer, 1948.

Steiner, Wendy. *Exact Resemblance to Exact Resemblance: The Literary Portraiture of Gertrude Stein*. Yale UP, 1978.

Stendahl, Renate. *Gertrude Stein: In Words and Pictures: A Photobiography*. Algonquin, 1994.

Stevens, Wallace. "Three Academic Pieces." *The Necessary Angel*, Vintage, 1951, pp. 71–89.

———. *Wallace Stevens: Collected Poetry and Prose*. Edited by Frank Kermode and Joan Richardson, Library of America, 1997.

Steward, Samuel M. "The Memoir." *Dear Sammy: Letters from Gertrude Stein and Alice B. Toklas*, Houghton Mifflin, 1977, pp. 3–117.

Stimpson, Catharine R. "Gertrude Stein and the Transposition of Gender." *The Poetics of Gender*, edited by Nancy K. Miller, Columbia UP, 1986, pp. 1–18.

Strychacz, Thomas. *Hemingway's Theaters of Masculinity*. Louisiana State UP, 2003.

Sutherland, Donald. *Gertrude Stein: A Biography of Her Work*. Yale UP, 1951.

———. "The Turning Point." 1956. Stein, *Stanzas*, pp. 28–49.

Terborg-Penn, Rosalyn. *African American Women in the Struggle for the Vote, 1850–1920*. Indiana UP, 1998.

Terry, Jennifer, and Jacqueline Urla, editors. *Deviant Bodies: Critical Perspectives on Difference in Science and Popular Culture*. Indiana UP, 1995.

Testimony against Gertrude Stein. By Georges Braque et al. Servire Press, Feb. 1935. *UbuWeb*, ubutext.memoryoftheworld.org/Stein-Gertrude_Testimony_Against_1935.pdf. Originally in *Transition*, no. 23, Feb. 1935.

Thomson, Virgil. *Four Saints in Three Acts (Abridged by the Composer)*. Libretto by Gertrude Stein, chorus and orchestra conducted by Thomson, 1947. BMG / RCA Studios, 1996. CD.

———. "Gertrude Stein's France in War: Realistic Picture of Life Closed to Us More Than Four Years." *New York Herald Tribune Weekly Book Review*, 11 Mar. 1945. Holbrook and Dilworth, pp. 270–71.

———. *Music with Words: A Composer's View*. Yale UP, 1989.

———. Preface. *"Bee Time Vine" and Other Pieces, 1913–1927*, by Gertrude Stein, Yale UP, 1953, pp. v–vii.

———. *Virgil Thomson*. Knopf, 1966.

Tischler, Alyson. "A Rose Is a Pose: Steinian Modernism and Mass Culture." *Journal of Modern Literature*, vol. 26. nos. 3–4, Summer 2003, pp. 12–27.

Toklas, Alice B. *The Alice B. Toklas Cook Book*. 1954. Harper Perennial, 2010.

———. *What Is Remembered*. Holt, Rinehart and Winston, 1963.

Top Hat. Directed by Erik Sandrich, written by Allan Scott and Dwight Taylor, performed by Fred Astaire et al., 1935. DVD.

"Trauma- and Stressor-Related Disorders." *Diagnostic and Statistical Manual of Mental Disorders*, 5th ed., *PsychiatryOnline*, dx.doi.org/10.1176/appi.books.9780890425596.dsm07.

Turner, Frederick Jackson. *History, Frontier, and Section: Three Essays*. U of New Mexico P, 1993.

Turner, Kay, editor. *Baby Precious Always Shines: Selected Love Notes between Gertrude Stein and Alice B. Toklas*. St. Martin's Press, 1999.

Twain, Mark. "Advice to Youth." *Mark Twain: Collected Tales, Sketches, Speeches, and Essays, 1852–1890*, edited by Louis J. Budd, Library of America, 1992, pp. 801–03.

Van Dusen, Wanda. "Portrait of a National Fetish: Gertrude Stein's 'Introduction to the Speeches of Maréchal Pétain' (1942)." *Modernism/modernity*, vol. 3, no. 3, Sept. 1996, pp. 69–92.

Van Vechten, Carl. "How to Read Gertrude Stein." *The Trend*, vol. 7, no. 5, Aug. 1914, pp. 553–57.

———. Program notes for the New York production of *Four Saints in Three Acts*, 13 Feb. 1934. Gertrude Stein and Alice B. Toklas Papers, Yale Collection of American Literature, Beinecke Rare Book and Manuscript Library, Yale U. Box 21, folder 402.

———. "A Stein Song." Stein, *Selected Writings*, pp. xviii–xxv.

Voris, Linda. *The Composition of Sense in Gertrude Stein's Landscape Writing*. Palgrave Macmillan, 2016.

———. "Interpreting Cézanne: Immanence in Gertrude Stein's First Landscape Play, *Lend a Hand; or, Four Religions*." *Modernism/modernity*, vol. 19, no. 1, Jan. 2012, pp. 73–93.

———. "'Shutters Shut and Open': Making Sense of Gertrude Stein's Second Portrait of Picasso." *Studies in American Fiction*, vol. 39, no. 2, Fall 2012, pp. 175–205.

Wagner-Martin, Linda. *"Favored Strangers": Gertrude Stein and Her Family*. Rutgers UP, 1995.

Wahl, Jean. "Miss Stein's Battle." *The New Republic*, 19 Mar. 1945, pp. 396–98. Reprinted in Hoffman, pp. 83–85.

Wald, Priscilla. *Constituting Americans: Cultural Anxiety and Narrative Form*. Duke UP, 1995.

Walker, Jayne. *The Making of a Modernist: Gertrude Stein from* Three Lives *to* Tender Buttons. U of Massachusetts P, 1984.

Walsh, Rebecca. *The Geopoetics of Modernism*. UP of Florida, 2015.

Warner, Malcolm. "Portraits about Portraiture." Alarcó and Warner, pp. 11–23.

Watson, Dana Cairns. *Gertrude Stein and the Essence of What Happens*. Vanderbilt UP, 2005.

Watson, Steven. *Prepare for Saints: Gertrude Stein, Virgil Thomson, and the Mainstreaming of American Modernism*. U of California P, 2000.

Weiss, M. Lynn. *Gertrude Stein and Richard Wright: The Poetics and Politics of Modernism*. UP of Mississippi, 1998.

White, Heather Cass. "How to Have a Conversation with Gertrude Stein: An Essay in Four Steps." *Connotations*, vol. 10, nos. 2–3, 2000–01, pp. 124–46.

White, Ray Lewis. *Gertrude Stein and Alice B. Toklas: A Reference Guide*. G. K. Hall, 1984.

Whitman, Walt. *Leaves of Grass: The Original 1855 Edition*. Dover, 2007.

Whittier-Ferguson, John. "'Once out of Nature': Gertrude Stein and the Fashioning of War." *Mortality and Form in Late Modernist Literature*, Cambridge UP, 2014, pp. 80–139.

Wilcox, Wendell. "A Note on Stein and Abstraction." *Poetry*, vol. 55, no. 5, Feb. 1940, pp. 254–57.

Wilder, Thornton. Introduction. *Four in America*, by Gertrude Stein, Yale UP, 1947, pp. v–xxvii.

Will, Barbara. *Unlikely Collaboration: Gertrude Stein, Bernard Faÿ, and the Vichy Dilemma*. Columbia UP, 2011.

Wilson, Edmund. *Axel's Castle: A Study in the Imaginative Literature of 1870–1930*. C. Scribner's Sons, 1931.

Wilson, Robert A. *Gertrude Stein: A Bibliography*. Phoenix Bookshop, 1974.

Wilson, Sarah. *Melting-Pot Modernism*. Cornell UP, 2010.

Wilson, Sondra Kathryn, editor. The Crisis *Reader: Stories, Poetry, and Essays from the N.A.A.C.P.'s* Crisis *Magazine*. Modern Library, 1999.

Wineapple, Brenda. *Sister Brother: Gertrude and Leo Stein*. Putnam, 1996.

Winston, Elizabeth. "Gertrude Stein's Mediating Stanzas." *Biography*, vol. 9, no. 3, Summer 1986, pp. 229–46.

Winthrop, John. "A Model of Christian Charity." *The Harper American Literature, Volume 1*, edited by Donald McQuade et al., Harper and Row, 1987, pp. 146–50.

Wright, Richard. "Why I Chose 'Melanctha.'" *I Wish I'd Written That*, edited by Eugene J. Woods, McGraw Hill, 1946, p. 234.

Young, Caroline. "This Is Not a No-Since: Multisensory Approaches to Teaching Gertrude Stein's *Tender Buttons*." *Teaching American Literature: A Journal of Theory and Practice*, vol. 8, no. 3, Fall 2016. PDF file.

Zox-Weaver, Annalisa. "Stein's Secret Sharers." *Women Modernists and Fascism*, Cambridge UP, 2011, pp. 59–107.

Zuccotti, Susan. *The Holcaust, the French, and the Jews*. U of Nebraska P, 1999.

INDEX OF WORKS BY GERTRUDE STEIN

INDEX OF NAMES